FÚTBOL, JEWS, AND THE
MAKING OF ARGENTINA

FÚTBOL, JEWS, AND THE MAKING OF ARGENTINA

RAANAN REIN

Translated by Martha Grenzeback

Stanford University Press
Stanford, California

Stanford University Press
Stanford, California

Printed in the United States of America on acid-free, archival-quality paper.

Library of Congress Cataloging-in-Publication Data

Rein, Raanan, 1960– author.
  [Bohemios de Villa Crespo. English]
  Fútbol, Jews, and the making of Argentina / Raanan Rein ; translated by Martha Grenzeback.
    pages cm
  "A shorter, popularized version of this work was published in Spanish . . . under the title Los bohemios de Villa Crespo: judíos y fútbol en la Argentina (Buenos Aires: Sudamericana, 2012)."
  Includes bibliographical references and index.
  ISBN 978-0-8047-9200-4 (cloth : alk. paper)—ISBN 978-0-8047-9341-4 (pbk. : alk. paper)
  1. Club Atlético Atlanta (Soccer team)—History. 2. Soccer teams—Argentina—Buenos Aires—History. 3. Jews—Sports—Argentina—Buenos Aires—History. 4. Jews—Argentina—Buenos Aires—Identity—History. 5. Soccer—Social aspects—Argentina—Buenos Aires—History. 6. Villa Crespo (Buenos Aires, Argentina)—Social life and customs. 7. Buenos Aires (Argentina)—Ethnic relations. I. Title.
  GV943.6.C486R4513 2014
  796.3340982'11—dc23

2014031078

ISBN 978-0-8047-9304-9 (electronic)

Typeset by Classic Typography in 10/14 Minion Pro

To my father, Shlomo, and my son, Omer,
who taught me what it means to love *fútbol*

CONTENTS

ILLUSTRATIONS

Figures

Maps

Tables

ACKNOWLEDGMENTS

First of all, I would like to thank Jorge Gelman, who encouraged me to write this book after hearing a presentation I gave on Club Atlanta in New York several years ago. A shorter, popularized version of this work was published in Spanish in his series "Nudos de la Historia Argentina," under the title *Los bohemios de Villa Crespo: judíos y fútbol en la Argentina* (Buenos Aires: Sudamericana, 2012). My thanks also go to Martha Grenzeback. This is the fifth book that she has translated for me, and it has been a privilege working with her.

During the three years I spent collecting material for this work I benefited from the assistance and good advice of librarians, archivists, colleagues, and many friends in different countries. I owe a particular debt of gratitude to Jeffrey Lesser of Emory University, David Sheinin of Trent University, and José Moya of Barnard College, for inspiring and continuing intellectual dialogue on topics of immigration, ethnicity, transnationalism, and sports. In the early stages of this project, I had interesting conversations with the late Jorge Kolbowski and Ariel Korob. Adriana Brodsky, Rodrigo Daskal, Alejandro Dujovne, Julio Frydenberg, Emmanuel Kahan, Edgardo Imas, Alejandro Mellincovsky, Néstor Straimel, and Nerina Visacovsky, and all helped me obtain important material for my research. I would also like to acknowledge Rosalie Sitman of Tel Aviv University and Eliezer Nowodworski, who are always partners in my studies of twentieth-century Argentina. Thanks also go to the dozens of Atlanta fans and club officials, past and present, whom I have interviewed, as well as to several of my current and former students, Ilan Diner, Ariel Noyjovich, Uri Rosenheck, and Ariel Svarch, for their help in locating some of the sources I used in this research. My research assistant, Maayan Pasamanik, contributed much to the preparation of the manuscript.

Last but not least, I would like to thank my wife, Mónica, who was born in Villa Crespo; my son, Omer, who shares my passion for football (although we often find ourselves rooting for rival teams); my daughter, Noa; and the

Walovnik, Fryd, and Bichman families (the last two are fervent fans of Club Atlético Atlanta), who always open their doors (and hearts) to me during my research trips to Buenos Aires.

I began writing this book during my stay as Distinguished Visiting Professor at the Fox Center for Humanistic Inquiry at Emory University. At Tel Aviv University I have enjoyed the support of the S. Daniel Abraham Center for International and Regional Studies and the Elías Sourasky Chair of Iberian and Latin American Studies. I thank them all for having made this book possible. Parts of the Introduction appear in my essay "People of the Book or People of the (Foot) Ball? On the Pitch with the Fans of Atlanta in Buenos Aires," in *Narratives of Body and Space in Latin America*, ed. David Sheinin (Pittsburgh, PA: University of Pittsburgh Press, 2014). Parts of Chapter 7 are included in "'My Bobeh was Praying and Suffering for Atlanta': Family, Food, and Language Among the Jewish-Argentine Fans of the Club Atlético Atlanta," in *Muscling in on New Worlds: Jews, Sport, and the Making of the Americas*, ed. David Sheinin and Raanan Rein (Boston: Brill, 2014).

FÚTBOL, JEWS, AND THE MAKING OF ARGENTINA

INTRODUCTION

While most historians would agree on the importance of sports in general and of *fútbol* in particular in Latin American societies, very little has been written about ethnicity and sports in immigrant societies such as Argentina and Brazil.[1] This is noteworthy since the role that *fútbol* ("soccer" in the United States) plays in society, as well as in the construction and reshaping of national, ethnic, class, and gender identities, has already been firmly established. At the same time, just as sports historians of Latin America do not pay enough attention to the ethnic aspect of sports, unless it has to do with players of African descent, social histories of Jews in Latin America, produced primarily for internal community consumption, tend to neglect many aspects of the rich culture of everyday life in Buenos Aires created by Jewish immigrants and their descendants, especially by Jews unaffiliated with community institutions. Too much of the historiography of Jews in Latin America has concentrated on anti-Semitism. There is an urgent need to recreate something of the world and the active part played by Jewish Latin Americans in shaping the local culture for their own purposes. Accordingly, recent years have seen the blossoming of a different historiography of Jewish Argentines, one that explores the thoughts and achievements of Jews more than the hate expressed against them. In this new perspective, Jews are not passive participants or victims, but take an active role in determining their relations with the non-Jewish Argentine majority.[2]

This book focuses on the history of the Club Atlético Atlanta (CAA), a football club located in the Buenos Aires neighborhood of Villa Crespo, and on soccer as a privileged avenue in Argentina for negotiating ethnic and national identities. Although populated by many ethnic groups, Villa Crespo, together with Once, has long been considered, by Jews and non-Jews alike, as a Jewish neighborhood, to the point that one of its nicknames is "Villa Kreplaj" (*kreplach*, an Ashkenazi dumpling similar to Italian ravioli or Chinese won-ton). During the second half of the twentieth century and the beginning of the twenty-first, Jews have constituted a substantial proportion of the fans, administrators, and presidents of Atlanta, so much so that the fans of rival teams often chant anti-Semitic slogans during matches. Other football clubs in Buenos Aires, such as River Plate, might have a greater number of Jewish fans—especially the more affluent clubs in recent decades—but Atlanta has always been the main attraction for football-mad Jews in Buenos Aires and the only professional football club to be considered "Jewish."

In the absence of any previous academic monographs devoted to this soc-cer club, this book will review the history of Atlanta and its fans as a means of exploring the social integration of Jewish immigrants and their Argentine-born offspring into urban life in what came to be known as "*la Gran Aldea*." I believe that for the first generation of these immigrants, belonging to the club was a way of becoming Argentines. Ultimately, sports are not just a marker of the social identity one has already established but also a means of creating a new social identity.[3]

For the second, native-born, generation, which was ready to integrate Ar-gentine national identity into its own cultural mosaic and in search of upward mobility, club membership was also a way of maintaining an ethnic Jewish identity, while for the third generation it became primarily a family tradi-tion. (See Figure I.1.) This is additional proof of the argument that "histori-cally, football has offered an arena where ethnic or other social groups can affirm identity, but where they can also integrate themselves—and not just on the elite's terms—into the nation."[4] *Fútbol, Jews, and the Making of Argentina* looks at how Jewish Argentines negotiated their national and ethnic identities inside and outside the football stadium, and traces the way these identities evolved over the years.

This study further posits that Atlanta has constituted one of the few spaces for interaction between Jews and non-Jews, affiliated Jews and unaffiliated Jews, Zionists and non-Zionists, and Ashkenazi and Sephardic Jews. In this way, like many other football clubs, Atlanta has provided its *socios* (members) with an intergenerational, subcultural marker of identity.[5]

This book is based on a wide range of primary and secondary sources, including the minutes of Atlanta's board of directors (*Actas de las Comisio-nes Directivas*), the club's annual reports (*Memorias y Balances*), and data from a questionnaire answered by more than fifty Atlanta fans. My research

FIGURE I.1   The Fryds: Third generation of Atlanta fans; relatives of the author.
Source: Photo by Beny Fryd.

contributes to a better understanding of issues related to ethnicity, social integration, hybrid identities, and generational conflict within the context of
modern Argentina. It also offers an additional perspective on competing no-
tions of *argentinidad* (Argentine collective identity) on and off the field. At the
same time, it is part of a recent effort by various researchers to analyze sports
associations, reflecting a recognition that such clubs—with their culture and
internal political activity, their relations with other community organizations,
and their histories and traditions—might be a political arena worth studying.
However, up to now researchers have focused solely on the "big five" football clubs: River Plate, Boca Juniors, Racing, Independiente, and San Lorenzo.
Even these internationally renowned clubs, however, have never been the subject of thorough historical study.

Academic scholarship on *fútbol* in Argentina has remained surprisingly
thin until recently. Notable exceptions have been the works of anthropologist
Eduardo Archetti, who pioneered the discussion of gender and national identity in football; sociologist Pablo Alabarces, who analyzed the ways journalists

elaborated myths about the uniqueness of *criollo* (native) *fútbol*, as opposed to European football; and historian Julio Frydenberg, who published the first social history of football in Buenos Aires during its amateur phase—that is, from the late nineteenth century to the early 1930s.[6]

I found the following sentence on an Internet site: "Atlanta is not Villa Crespo, but Villa Crespo would not be Villa Crespo without Atlanta. The neighborhood and the club are joined in many ways."[7] This premise, though very probably tinged with the typical hyperbole of football fans, has some basis. Football in Villa Crespo played a central role in the development of neighborhood loyalties, and the neighborhood's history has been closely tied to football. In the mid-1930s Villa Crespo boasted no fewer than fifteen clubs dedicated to this sport, more than all other neighborhoods. The names of at least three major clubs (Argentinos Juniors, Chacarita Juniors, and Atlanta) have been connected with Villa Crespo at some point in their histories. However, since the mid-1940s Atlanta has reigned alone in Villa Crespo, and accordingly it has channeled the identities and loyalties of many of the local inhabitants. It would be utterly impossible to write a history of the neighborhood—one of the neighborhoods that can be considered to represent the best of Buenos Aires, including tango and football—without taking into account the history of Club Atlético Atlanta. Cayetano Francavilla, a historian of Villa Crespo, has expressed this idea clearly: "To talk about Atlanta is to follow the progress of our barrio together with our football fan neighbor."[8]

Atlanta's centrality in the life of Villa Crespo and in the collective identity of its residents was clearly demonstrated in March 2009 by the great festivities that marked the reopening, after a three-year hiatus, of the stadium named after Atlanta's legendary president, León Kolbowski.[9] Two years later, Villa Crespo once again dressed up in blue and yellow to celebrate Atlanta's winning the championship in the third division, Primera B Metropolitana (one of the two leagues in the third level of the Argentine football league), and rising to the second division, the Primera B Nacional. Atlanta fans, who were dressed in the team jerseys and caps, flooded the main streets of the neighborhood and gathered in bars and cafés on the outskirts of the football field. That day they waved flags and yelled on the street corners, "Go champs! Go champs!"[10] (See Figure I.2.) Atlanta returned to the B Nacional and the veterans of the club reminisced about times past and the classic rivalry with Chacarita, or the time that River Plate and Atlanta had played each other in the same division. Although the football team may not have racked up any

FIGURE I.2   Atlanta fans celebrating the team's promotion
to the B Nacional Division, May 2011.

Source: Photo by Daniel Rosin. "Al gran pueblo bohemio ¡Salud!," 9 May 2011; http://
www.planetabohemio.com.ar/2011/paginas/torneo2011/danielcam.htm.

significant or momentous achievements since the 1980s, it is still a primary
focus of identity for neighborhood residents.

At the same time, as I contend in this book, it is certainly arguable that
the history of the Jewish experience in Argentina cannot be written without
paying special attention to Atlanta. Accordingly, we might venture to ask a
provocative question: If we cannot write the history of Argentine Jews without including the history of the Jews of Buenos Aires, and if we cannot write
the history of Buenos Aires Jews without including the history of the Jews of
Villa Crespo, can we write the history of Argentine Jews without mentioning
the Atlanta football club? After all, this sports club, established on October 12,
1904, has been an integral part of the daily life of this ostensibly Jewish neighborhood for more than a century.

The following anecdote may serve to illustrate some of the points I will be
making in the various chapters of this book about Atlanta's importance for

the barrio and its Jewish inhabitants. Esther Rollansky, the daughter of an intellectual and a cultural "entrepreneur" who was one of the most renowned Yiddish scholars in Argentina, worked as a teacher of the Yiddish language in the 1950s. Every Monday she confronted the problem that the children in her class wanted to talk about their Sunday experiences instead of studying. Many of those experiences related to the most recent game played by the neighborhood football team, the team of the club to which many of the boys belonged. Rollansky had an idea: they would talk about the match, but on condition that they did so in Yiddish. The trick worked well, as Esther told me with a smile years later; between free throws, penalties, and goals scored, she took the opportunity to correct their Yiddish and at the same time teach them declensions, verb conjugations, and vocabulary.[11] The neighborhood in question was Villa Crespo and the club was, of course, the Atlanta Athletic Club.

Sport as culture is a relatively new field of study in Jewish history; it has been a challenge to get past the stereotype of Jews as the People of the Book who have supposedly always emphasized intellectual enterprises over physical ones. Although physical activities of all sorts have been integral to the lives of millions of Jews in the modern era, Jewish scholars and intellectuals have tended to belittle their importance. This is true for both North and South America, as well as Europe.[12] It is even true for Palestine/Israel, although Zionism used to cultivate the myth of the "new" Jew, who, unlike his brothers in the Diaspora, was a strong, healthy person fit for the physical and intellectual challenges involved in establishing a sovereign state in the Land of Israel.[13]

Despite the stereotype of the frail, intellectual Jew and Jews' status as the People of the Book, many of the new Jewish immigrants to Argentina were not highly educated and had no deep attachment to Jewish religious orthodoxy. Sports played an important part in their lives both in the urban, modernized setting of Buenos Aires and elsewhere, as it did for other ethnic groups in Argentina. Most Jews eagerly embraced the opportunities open to them in their new homeland and did their best to become Argentines. For many, this included a love of sports in general and football in particular.

Jews in Buenos Aires participated in various sports and also joined the throngs of spectators at ball games during a time when organized sports were gradually becoming an important social institution and a major part of leisure consumer culture in Argentina. Football topped the list as the single most popular sport in the country. As a result, for immigrants, and especially for their children, sports became a critical space where majority and minority groups intersected. Jews and other minorities could eradicate their foreign-ness by embracing the national sport. At the same time, as personal testimo-nies show, it was also a meeting point for immigrant parents (the mothers as well as the fathers in some cases) and their children. The various demands of the workplace, life in the crowded *conventillos* (tenements) and later in small apartments, and the occasionally intolerant social atmosphere all tended to limit opportunities and choices for Jews. Sports, by contrast, as a leisure ac-tivity that they chose themselves, became one component of their lives over which they were able to exert control. This was especially true for Jews born in Argentina, who enjoyed life in a society far freer and more open than any-thing their immigrant parents had ever experienced in either Eastern or Cen-tral Europe or the Mediterranean basin.

Thus, for parents, young adults, and children, participating in sports in one way or another could counteract feelings of helplessness and alienation and strengthen their identities as Jews and as Argentines. Furthermore, in Argentina as in the United States, participating in a common national experi-ence helped Jews, consciously or not, to dispel all kinds of stereotypes and be-liefs about Jews being aliens who could not or would not assimilate. As Peter Levine says about Jews and sports in the United States, "The experience of participating as the majority in an American game also carried special mean-ing for participants and spectators alike, especially for second-generation youth who found in the game opportunities of freedom, mobility, and choice not always available to their fathers and mothers."[14]

Exclusion from certain athletic activities and especially elite sports led some Jewish Argentines to create their own institutions, such as the Hebrew Maccabi Organization in 1928 and the Club Náutico Hacoaj in 1935, but many more of them actively participated in non-Jewish sports clubs. They prac-ticed boxing, basketball, weightlifting, and, above all, football. Unlike Jews in the United States, however, not many Jews became sports champions in Argentina, unless, perhaps, you count chess.[15] Relatively few Jews made it into the major leagues and were able to serve as symbols of Jewish integra-tion into Argentine society. There was no Hank Greenberg, Red Auerbach, Moe Berg, or Mark Spitz in Argentina, although this does not mean that no Jews made names for themselves in Argentine sports. Prominent Jewish foot-ballers have included, among others, Leopoldo Bard, the first team captain and president of River Plate; Ezra Sued, a striker on both the Racing and na-tional teams; Aaron Werfiker, stopper on the River and national teams (his fellow players had trouble pronouncing his name, so they called him "Pérez"); Miguel Reznik, who played for Huracán; and, more recently, Juan Pablo Sorín, midfielder for River as well as a Spanish team. All these examples challenge the myth of there being no Jews in Argentine football. At any rate, simply buying a ticket to a game, learning the names of all the members of a team, following the sport in the media, or rooting for your favorite team or player was enough to make you an active participant in Argentine popular culture.

Most books about Argentine football tend to claim that religious and ethnic differences have not been issues in Argentina's national sports. This claim is not confined to sports history. The fact is that many intellectuals in Latin America reject ethnicity as a significant analytical category (unless they are discussing the indigenous population or people of African descent), even if they themselves are part of an ethnic minority. Thus, football is presented as a channel of social mobility based on talent alone and as the sport that best represents some of the most cherished Argentine values and character traits, irrespective of the players' ethnic origins. Not surprisingly, several fans I approached refused to be interviewed for this book, insisting that ethnicity had nothing to do with Argentine football and/or with the Atlanta club.

Since the 1920s the notion of a *criollo* style of football has developed and spread. This was reflected in the pages of the popular sports weekly *El Gráfico* as well as in the sports sections of the daily newspapers. The Argentine style of football was supposedly epitomized by the art of dribbling, which showcased the individual player's ability and creativity, and this style was presented as a contrast to the allegedly rigid, robotic style of British players. Matthew Karush quotes several articles from the popular daily *Crítica* that mentioned the "*picardía y astucia*" (craftiness and cunning) of Argentine players in the 1928 Olympics in Amsterdam. These articles generally referred to Argentina's football players as *criollos* (Argentine natives), regardless of their ethnicity.[16]

Nevertheless, one of my contentions in this book is that in sports, as in other social activities, Jewish Argentines struggled to strike a meaningful balance (which differed from one individual to the next) between ethnic values and tradition and the hopes they wanted to fulfill in the Promised Land of the Río de la Plata. Sports were an additional way for them both to shape their own collective and individual identities and to contribute to the shaping of Argentine national culture,[17] since in the realm of sports Jews were part of the interaction between generations of their fellow Jews as well as between ethnic minority and majority cultures. In a sense, then, they simultaneously adapted their traditional practices to new local realities and ethnicized their Argentine experiences. The Club Atlético Atlanta is an illustrative microcosm of these processes, since for many Jews participating in this club both confirmed a meaningful Jewish identity and helped them gain social integration and acceptance. Football clubs and their stadiums speak to many people across generations and give them a focus for imagining their collective past and future.[18] Like other stadiums, Atlanta's stadium, named some ten years ago in honor of the club's legendary president León Kolbowski, has provided many Villa Crespo Jews with a public space that has shaped their collective social and ethnic memories.

Abraham "Tío" (Uncle) Petacóvsky, the main character in a short story by Enrique Espinosa (the nom de plume of Samuel Glusberg) entitled "Mate Amargo" (1924), never learned to speak Spanish well. However, in the story his successful adaptation to life in Buenos Aires was reflected by his clothing, especially his rope-soled sandals, and by the quantities of *mate* that he drank.[19] In my book, Mario Fryd and José Bichman, Polish Jews who settled in Villa Crespo a few years after the establishment of the CAA and who never quite managed to get rid of their Yiddish accents, adapted to life in their new country in part by becoming fans of the local football team. Their Argentine-born children, grandchildren, and great-grandchildren have continued the family loyalty to the Atlanta team jersey—even after moving to other parts of the city. Football was the most popular sport in Argentina in the twentieth century; in their soccer dictionary, Tomás Sánz and Roberto Fontanarrosa describe the country as a place whose inhabitants, prior to 1958, were certain they had invented football.[20] The Fryds and the Bichmans adopted the sport enthusiastically as a way of becoming Argentines.

Divided into seven brief chapters, this book begins with the history of Jewish immigration to Argentina from the end of the nineteenth century until the mid-1900s. Although Central European, Middle Eastern, and Maghrebi Jews all emigrated to the Southern Cone, most of Argentina's Jewish community had traveled across the Atlantic from villages and small towns in Eastern Europe. In moving to this new land, they transformed their habits, clothing, and customs as they adapted to an unfamiliar climate, a foreign language, a political system different from their own, music and songs they had never heard before—in short, another culture. Like other non-Western minorities who settled in Argentina, such as the Japanese and the Syrio-Lebanese, the East European Jews had to overcome a greater sociocultural gap than that faced by Spaniards and Italians, the two majority groups, who came from Catholic societies and spoke Latin languages.

In Buenos Aires, two neighborhoods became the main centers of Jewish life and business: first Once, and later Villa Crespo. The second chapter focuses on the history of Villa Crespo, a neighborhood established in the 1880s, which took the name of the mayor at the time, Antonio Crespo. This neighborhood housed a substantial number of immigrants, thereby gaining a cosmopolitan character; Jews began moving in after the First World War. As early as 1919 Alberto Vaccarezza titled one of his short plays about Villa Crespo *El barrio de los judíos* (The neighborhood of the Jews).[21] That same year, during the pogroms of the Semana Trágica (Tragic Week), the so-called *niños bien* ("upper-crust boys") of the Argentine Patriotic League headed toward both Once and Villa Crespo, to hunt *"rusos"* ("Russians"—in other words, Jews). In the following decades Manuel Gleizer's bookstore, the playwright Samuel Eichelbaum, the journalist Julio Jorge Nelson (Julio Rosofsky), and the writer César Tiempo (Israel Zeitlin) were all part of the cultural and intellectual life that turned Villa Crespo into a symbol of Buenos Aires. Unsurprisingly, football had a great many followers in this *porteño* neighborhood.

Fútbol has been played in Argentina since the 1860s. It was originally introduced by British sailors, merchants, and immigrants, and in 1884 Alexander Watson Hutton used it to instill good moral character and discipline in his students at the exclusive Buenos Aires English High School.[22] By the early twentieth century, however, football was no longer restricted to the colony of English immigrants. It had gained a massive following and formed an integral part of the social life of all sectors in Buenos Aires, as well as in the provinces of the interior. The city fathers supported the foundation of clubs, considering physical exercise and playing sports to be essential to a moral upbringing and personal hygiene.[23]

From its foundation in October 1904 up to its settlement in the neighborhood of Villa Crespo, the Club Atlético Atlanta was continually in search of a playing field to call its own. This search gave the club its nickname of *"bohemio,"* or "gypsy," and at a later stage created the myth of the "wandering Jew" searching for a homeland and finally arriving at the promised land of Villa Crespo. This early period in the club's history is the focus of Chapter 3, which also covers the first years of Argentine professional football. During that time Atlanta had reached the verge of extinction when, in 1934, the Argentine Football Association (AFA) decided to merge it with the Argentinos

Juniors club. The failure of this merger led to a two-month official intervention from which Atlanta, like the phoenix, reemerged stronger than ever.

In the mid-1940s, Atlanta drove the Chacarita Juniors club out of Villa Crespo, and the rivalry between the two teams has shaped the identity of both clubs ever since. In those years both the neighborhood and the club assumed a Jewish identity even though Jews were a minority in the neighborhood and Atlanta had never formally been a Jewish institution. In this sense its "Jewish identity," imposed from outside, is comparable to that associated with the European clubs of Ajax in Amsterdam or Tottenham Hotspur in north London, both located in supposedly Jewish neighborhoods.[24] Emphasizing Atlanta's influence on Villa Crespo life in the 1940s and afterward, Chapter 4 also mentions other sports played in the club in addition to football (although football always came first), as well as social and cultural activities that it sponsored, from balls with tango orchestras (such as those of Feliciano Brunelli and Osvaldo Pugliese), to the establishment of a kindergarten and a cooperative in later years. The growing inclusion of women and children in the club's sports and sociocultural activities increased Atlanta's presence and influence in the neighborhood.

The Peronization of Argentine sports, which will be analyzed in Chapter 5, had repercussions for the country's football activities and clubs, and Atlanta was no exception. Two of its members were elected national deputies for the Peronist faction, and from that moment on served as liaisons between the club and the authorities: Manuel García (Labor Party) and Manuel Álvarez Pereyra (Unión Cívica Radical–Junta Renovadora). Álvarez Pereyra held the office of club president from December 1, 1946, until he resigned at the end of the following October. Club Atlanta's reports from those years are filled with Peronist rhetoric about justicialism (the Peronist creed) and the "New Argentina," as well as accolades for the government and its policy of aiding sports organizations in general and Atlanta in particular. The club received loans for the purpose of building a new stadium, which was to be named after Eva Perón. Juan Perón himself was designated Honorary President of the Club, and his wife was given a lifetime membership. During the first months of the Liberating Revolution, after Perón's overthrow in September 1955, Atlanta would pay a high price for its support of justicialism.

Atlanta fans and Villa Crespo residents consider the 1960s as the club's glory years, coinciding with the administration of León Kolbowski. Chapter 6 is devoted to Kolbowski, his relations with the Argentine Communist Party, the inauguration of the stadium in Humboldt Street that bears his name, and the reasons that Kolbowski left the club after presiding over it for more than a decade. During this period Atlanta's image as a progressive Jewish club became more pronounced. The installation of Kolbowski as president of the club represented the culmination of a process that had begun in 1922 with Osvaldo Simón Piackin, the first Jewish member of the Atlanta board of directors. In 1968, in what turned out to be the last year of León Kolbowski's presidency, Jewish Argentines became a majority among the board members for the first time: twelve out of twenty-two. From then on Jewishness became an integral part of the club's culture.

The last chapter centers on the fans and their habits and rituals, as well as the stadium as a space for the creation of collective identities and a social imaginary. After sketching the club's ups and downs from the 1970s on and the decline of the neighborhood clubs, the weakening of neighborhood loyalties, and the commercialization of football—all processes that contributed to Atlanta's deterioration after the military dictatorship and the reestablishment of democracy—I focus on the racism, xenophobia, and anti-Semitism that attend Argentine football. By analyzing the construction of collective identities in general and those of soccer fans in particular, we can cast some light on the processes by which the antagonistic tension between "us" and "them," the "others," was created, especially in material spaces such as football fields.

The perception of Atlanta as "the Jews' club" is to a large extent an identification imposed from outside, by rival fans. Among the anti-Semitic slogans chanted by the fans of rival teams in recent decades we might mention the infamous "Ahí viene Hitler por el callejón, matando judíos para hacer jabón" (Here comes Hitler down the street, killing Jews to make soap).[25] During the Gulf War in the early 1990s supporters of Atlanta's rival also shouted "Olé, olé, Saddam Hussein." In the mid-1990s, after the attacks on the Israeli embassy and the Asociación Mutual Israelita Argentina (AMIA, a Jewish community organization) building, the fans of All Boys sang: " . . . les volamos la embajada, les volamos la mutual, les vamos a quemar la cancha, para que no jodan más . . . " (We blew up the embassy, we blew up the community center, we're going to burn up your field so you don't screw with anyone any more . . .). Atlanta fans provide their own share of racist taunts, especially in games against their arch rival, Chacarita Juniors.

This volume is, in its way, an invitation to historians of Latin American sports to extend their research to the hitherto barely examined ethnic dimension of their subject, as exemplified by cases such as the Chilean football club of Deportivo Palestino, the Argentine Deportivo Armenio or the Sociedade Esportiva Palmeiras of São Paulo, Brazil, founded in 1914 as Palestra Italia.[26] Other examples might include Alianza Lima, representing the black community of La Victoria in Lima, and Vasco da Gama, representing the Portuguese community in Rio de Janeiro.[27] At the same time, it is also a call to the historians of the Jewish experience in South America to cover some of the less studied aspects of social and cultural history, particularly those concerning Jews unaffiliated with community institutions—in the case that concerns us in this book, those who turned the Atlanta soccer field into a temple where they expressed their Jewish Argentine identity.

1

FROM GRIN┌

They came
the vision o┐
packed tightl┐
jargon, tyrann┐
in the land of So
never see again. ┐
there in Argentina
with their pale wive┐
slaughter or pillaging.
then others. Their relat   ┌u in
Corrientes Street, in Lav   ┌ibertad. Those
who knew the trade of tai┐   ┐ and selling.[1]

Buenos Aires was a colonial city of limited importance up to the end of the eighteenth century. In 1776, as part of the Bourbon reforms, the Spanish crown founded the viceroyalty of the Río de la Plata, and Buenos Aires became the seat of the viceroy. Even a few decades after Argentina achieved independence from Spain, Buenos Aires was still a relatively minor commercial port. It was not until the late nineteenth or early twentieth century that the city began to grow at a dizzying rate, becoming the largest and most populous metropolitan area of Latin America. By 1910 the population had multiplied seven times, from a meager 180,000 inhabitants in 1870 to a total of 1,300,000. Buenos Aires became a city of European immigrants, especially Italians and Spaniards. Its architecture and urban planning, its cafes and cultural institutions earned it the nickname of "the Paris of South America."[2]

During the second half of the nineteenth century the Argentine elites and the national authorities adopted a strategic policy, inspired by positivist ideals, to encourage immigration from Europe. The main motivation for this policy was a desire to increase the relatively small population and to "improve" (a euphemism for "whiten") the local demographic makeup by attracting immigrants, preferably from northern Europe, who would import European civilization at the expense of the "barbarous" indigenous population. In this way the immigrants of "capable races" could promote the development and modernization of the Republic. "Gobernar es poblar" ("to govern is to populate") was a maxim coined in 1853 by Juan Bautista Alberdi, a prominent liberal intellectual and politician.[3]

This maxim was translated into action, and in barely three years, from 1888 to 1890, Argentine agents in Europe distributed more than 133,000 free ship tickets to Buenos Aires. It should be remembered that when Argentina began the process of freeing itself from the yoke of Spanish colonialism in 1810, the country measured some 2,780,000 square kilometers in area—the equivalent of almost the entire European continent—yet it had fewer than half a million inhabitants, which, at the time, was about a quarter of the population of the small and mountainous Swiss Confederation, or a fifth of the population of London. Argentina was destined to play an important role in the nineteenth-century world economy as a supplier of various foodstuffs, but to do so it needed tens of thousands of laborers. The demographic revolution occurring in Europe at the time fostered mass emigration to the New World, especially to the United States and the River Plate region—namely, eastern Argentina, Uruguay, and southern Brazil. Between 1880 and 1950, Argentina received more immigrants, in both absolute numbers and relative to the country's population, than any other Latin American country.[4]

The hope of making the country an attractive destination for Protestant emigrants from the more industrialized European northeast, a population that could contribute to Argentina's development and modernization, was soon dashed. Most of the new immigrants were in fact from southern and eastern Europe, primarily Italians and Spaniards, with a smaller number arriving from other countries of the Mediterranean basin or from the Balkans. A minority (including Moslems and Jews) did not profess any Christian faith at all, and many of these new immigrants did not settle even temporarily in the inland colonies, either because they did not want to or because they could not obtain land there; instead, they headed for the large urban centers, especially Buenos Aires. This city quickly became a metropolis in which, up until the 1920s, at least half the inhabitants had been born elsewhere. (See Figure 1.1.) Under these circumstances, xenophobic and nationalistic manifestations

FIGURE 1.1   Buenos Aires, 1900: A city of European immigrants.

Source: Courtesy of Archivo General de la Nación.

intensified, as did efforts to assimilate the new immigrants in the Argentine melting pot, mostly through the state education system. Sports also offered immigrants a way of winning acceptance—providing, for Jews, the added bonus of challenging anti-Semitic charges of cowardice and unmanliness.

The Jewish community in Argentina, the largest in Latin America, is basically a product of that same huge wave of transatlantic immigration from Central and Eastern Europe, and, to a smaller degree, the Middle East and the Balkans, to the Americas. With the outbreak of World War I in 1914, the Jews of Eastern Europe (Ashkenazis) became the third-largest immigrant group, and the largest of the non-Catholic minorities. At its peak, in the late 1950s and early 1960s, the Jewish population numbered some 310,000 out of a total population of 20 million (see Table 1.1).[5] In the mid-twentieth century Argentina boasted the fifth largest Jewish population in the world. Its prominence, however, easily exceeded its numbers, in large part because most Jews lived in Buenos Aires, many of them concentrated in specific neighborhoods such as Once and Villa Crespo. To this can be added the fact that many first-generation immigrants never completely mastered the Spanish language and retained an accent that was strange to many—almost as strange as the clothing of Orthodox Jews, with

TABLE 1.1 The Jewish population in Argentina, 1895–1965

Year	Census Data	Rosenswaike	Schmelz and DellaPergola
1895	6,085		
1900			14,700
1905			24,700
1910			68,100
1915			115,600
1920		120,000	126,700
1925		160,400	162,300
1930		200,200	191,400
1935		226,400	218,000
1940			254,400
1945			273,400
1947	249,326	265,000-275,000	285,800
1950			294,000
1955			305,900
1960	291,877		310,000
1965			296,600

Source: Sergio DellaPergola, "Demographic Trends of Latin American Jewry," in *The Jewish Presence in Latin America*, ed. Judith Laikin Elkin and Gilbert W. Merks (Boston: n.p., 1987), 92; and Ira Rosenswaike, "The Jewish Population of Argentina: Census and Estimate, 1887–1947," *Jewish Social Studies* XXII, no. 4 (Oct. 1960): 195–214.

their hats, suits, and distinctive sidelocks. At the same time, the accumulation of Jewish stereotypes, whether religious or racist, gave Ashkenazi Jews a visibility far greater than their demographic representation would suggest. These Jews, striving for acceptance and belonging, embraced football, among other things local, as a way to shed their Old World traits and become Argentines.

La Pampa . . . Promises

As with any other immigrant group, the factors that caused people to abandon their homes or that attracted them to other places must be analyzed in conjunction with the patterns of emigration that this particular group adopted. Toward the end of the nineteenth century, the Jews of Eastern Europe, in particular those who lived within the Pale of Settlement—an area that encompassed part of what is today Poland and Russia and was largely populated by Jews—felt an

increasing urgency to seek a better future outside Europe, impelled by a combination of physical harassment, social pressure, and economic hardship.

The year 1905 marked a milestone in Jewish immigration. The Russian
empire had lost its war against Japan and thwarted a revolution. Reactionary
groups, in collaboration with police forces loyal to the czar, embarked on a
series of pogroms in more than six hundred cities and towns in the Pale of
Settlement. The socioeconomic breakdown, the fear of violence, and the sense
of insecurity prompted mass emigration. At more or less the same time, from
the mid-nineteenth century onward, the Ottoman Empire was also undergoing a crisis, giving rise to the persecution of religious minorities, growing
Arab nationalism, and forced military service. Economic changes made life
difficult for a growing number of craftsmen and small-business owners. Thus,
Syrio-Lebanese immigration—Christian, Jewish, and Moslem alike—arose
out of a combination of political, economic, religious, and cultural factors.[6]

The Americas, both North and South, seemed to promise prosperity and a
better future for both Jews and Arabs. Argentina became home for hundreds
of thousands of them, most arriving between the late 1870s and the 1930s;
their numbers tapered off when the government began to impose the first significant barriers to immigration, largely in response to the Great Depression.

While a few Eastern European Jews sought refuge in Palestine, their real
or imagined homeland, others looked for ways to cross the Atlantic and build
lives in the New World. Jewish organizations considered various proposals for
settling these Eastern European Jews in new countries. One such proposal focused on a practically unknown land in South America. Theodor Herzl himself, in his *Judenstaat* (1896), described the choice facing the Jewish masses in
Eastern Europe as one between "Palestine or the Argentine." Of those who
took the second option, most settled in the capital, although a significant minority did become farmers, giving rise to the myth of the Jewish gauchos (a
common name for Jewish immigrants who settled in areas of inland Argentina). Those immigrants were masterfully portrayed by Alberto Gerchunoff in
his 1910 work *Jewish Gauchos of the Pampas*, the publication of which marked
the centenary of the May Revolution that had set the country on its way to
independence from Spain.[7] In later works by many Jewish-Argentine writers,
the emblematic figure of the Jewish gaucho is a recurrent theme, meant to
emphasize the Argentine Jew's authenticity, solid roots, and attachment to Argentine soil.[8] The agricultural settlements established in Argentina (and later
in Brazil) by the Jewish philanthropist Baron Maurice de Hirsch seemed to
offer a partial solution to the Jewish national question at the time.[9]

Determined to cut their ties with the former colonial power, Spain, members of the Argentine governing elite looked toward republican France as a secular, progressive model to emulate. This cultural and political orientation, together with the country's growing economic and commercial relations with Great Britain, contributed to the institution of a liberal constitution in 1853 (which guaranteed freedom of worship and reflected the welcoming attitude toward immigrants), the adoption of an equally liberal immigration law in 1876 (which did not discriminate against non-Catholic immigrants), and the enactment of state-education and civil-registration laws in 1884 (thus limiting the power and influence of the Catholic Church).

Rumors about the opportunities offered by immigration to Argentina, where anyone could live freely and prosper, spread among urban and rural Jewish communities in Central and Eastern Europe.[10] The myth of "making good in America" spread rapidly across the ocean through family and ethnic channels, as relatives, friends, and former neighbors exchanged letters containing information about opportunities and cautionary advice. For the majority of Jewish immigrants, Ashkenazi and Sephardic alike, Argentina did in fact turn out to be the "promised land," a place where they could secure a living for themselves and an education for their children, and where they could try to make a new home. Within a short time, they established community institutions and Jewish schools that satisfied their social, economic, cultural, and athletic needs. In the process they created a rich mosaic of social, cultural, political, and ideological life, which reflected a wide variety of faiths, identities, and social practices: Communists and Zionists, Orthodox and secular, those who emphasized their Jewishness and others who preferred to stress their Argentine identity.[11]

Many Jewish immigrants rose to prominent positions in Argentine social, economic, artistic, and political spheres. This does not mean that Jews, or any other ethnic immigrant group for that matter, were welcomed at all times and by everybody. Like Arabs and other ethnic groups, Jews benefited from Argentine open-door policies but also suffered, from the late nineteenth century onward, from the Argentine elites' disappointment over the outcome of the immigration project that had been intended to "Europeanize" or "whiten" their country. Jews and Arabs both encountered general anti-immigrant sentiment as a result. As nationalism, authoritarianism, and xenophobia grew, especially in the 1910s, 1920s, and 1930s, Semitic immigrants, whether Christian Arabs, Eastern European Jews, Moslem Arabs, or Jewish Arabs—basically all immigrants who were not "white" or Catholic—were targeted as undesirable. Positivist Argentine discourses often looked at the non-northern European immigrant as racially inferior, diseased, and contaminating.

An article that appeared in the *Buenos Aires Herald* in 1898 reflected this attitude: "Are we becoming a Semitic republic? The immigration of Russian Jews is now the third largest in the list, while Syrian Arabs (Turks) and Arabians are also flocking to these shores."[12] Similar articles were published by some Spanish-language newspapers. Thus *La Nación* asserted in 1910 that the deplorable trafficking in cheap trinkets by Syrio-Lebanese peddlers was a dishonor to the nation, and it called for the restriction of Levantine immigration.[13] Race, and not just economic concerns, could be used as an argument against Arab and Jewish immigration. As one provincial politician who favored the exclusion of Jews from Argentina claimed, "These people . . . can shatter the homogeneity of our race."[14]

Among the liberal elites, even the staunchest supporters of immigration embraced the concept of the melting pot. All newcomers, especially non-Catholics, were expected to abandon the customs and idiosyncrasies they had brought with them from their countries of origin in favor of the new culture that was emerging in the immigrant society of Argentina. This attitude and the pressure toward cultural homogeneity and assimilation were particularly pronounced in nationalist and xenophobic circles. Albeit a minority, these elements have always existed in Argentine society, and in certain periods they have managed to exert influence in political, military, and clerical circles, as well as on the contemporary intellectual climate. This phenomenon was a constant source of unease among Jewish Argentines, who, because of their European origins and family ties with the Old World, could not but view the evidence of growing hostility toward Jews in Argentina from a European perspective.[15]

Debate continues as to the number of Jews living in Argentina both during the twentieth century and today.[16] Part of the problem lies in the tendency of most studies to focus on those Jews affiliated with formal community institutions, even though research indicates that most Jews—in common with members of other ethnic communities—never join such institutions. Furthermore, in national population censuses many respondents have preferred not to define themselves as Jews, either because they feared identifying themselves ethnically in government databases, especially in times of authoritarian rule, or because the option of a hyphenated identity was not included and they did not wish to give Jewishness priority over their Argentine identity. Moreover, the use by many scholars of religious rather than cultural criteria to define Jews has created additional barriers to data collection in a community known until recently for its highly secular character.

According to the studies of demographer Sergio DellaPergola, the number of Jews in Argentina grew from 14,700 to 191,400 in 1930 (see Table 1.1, above). Jews from Romania, Poland, and Lithuania seeking new homes joined those who had already arrived from Russia after conditions in Eastern Europe worsened during the Great War and in the interwar period. The fact that the United States, followed by various other countries, instituted a very strict quota in 1921 that excluded most immigrants from Eastern and southern Europe increased Argentina's allure for refugees.

The number of Jews in Argentina reached 273,400 at the end of World War II and a peak of some 310,000 in the early 1960s. From then on, numbers began to decline, with Jews emigrating from Argentina to Israel, the United States, or to other countries in Latin America and Europe. At the same time, the number of exogamic marriages was increasing. Whereas in the mid-1930s the rate of marriage to non-Jews was 1 to 5 percent of all marriages involving a Jewish partner, by the early 1960s it had risen to 20 to 25 percent, reaching 35 to 40 percent in the mid-1980s. Current estimates put the number of Jews now living in Argentina at more than 200,000.[17]

Chronologically, Jewish immigrants began to arrive as early as the 1840s (in Argentina, unlike Brazil, evidence of *conversos* during the colonial period is scant), but consisted mainly in a small number of highly assimilated German and French families. The earliest synagogue was not established until 1862. The first real milestone in Jewish immigration was recorded in 1881 when, following pogroms in Russia, the Argentine government decided to send a special emissary to invite Jews from czarist Russia to settle in Argentina. The first organized group of immigrants, comprising 820 Russian Jews, arrived in August 1889 on board the ship *Wesser*. The SS *Wesser* is often referred to as the Jewish-Argentine *Mayflower*. The passengers aboard this vessel were sent to the Jewish agricultural colonies, and some of these immigrants founded the now-legendary colonies of Moises Ville (1889), Mauricio (1892), and Villa Clara (1892), among others. The Jewish Colonization Association (JCA) founded twenty-six agricultural colonies in Argentina (see Table 1.2). Although Jewish rural colonies existed in other places in the Americas, such as the United States and Brazil, their role and importance were much greater in Argentina.

However, even at their apogee, on the eve of World War I, all of them together numbered barely 20,000 Jews.[18] Many of them did not last long, and by the mid-1930s only 11 percent of Argentina's Jewish population lived in them.[19]

The government's immigration policy dramatically changed the demographic profile of the country, a fact clearly reflected in 1914 census data. In twenty years the country's population had almost doubled (to about 7.9 million). More than one-third of the inhabitants were foreign-born. In the city of Buenos Aires, this figure climbed to over 50 percent. The rate of growth for the Jewish population was even higher: from 1895 to 1919, the number of Jews increased from 6,000 to 125,000.

The original vision of an agricultural enterprise as the main focus of attraction for Jewish immigration did not last long. Although in the late nineteenth century most Argentine Jews were concentrated in the JCA colonies, by the end of World War I the majority of Jews were city dwellers, and most of them lived in Buenos Aires. In metropolitan centers, Jews tended to cluster in certain neighborhoods, which added to their urban and social visibility.[20]

TABLE 1.2 Jewish agricultural settlements established by JCA in Argentina

Colony	Province	Year
Moises Ville	Santa Fe	1889
Mauricio	Buenos Aires	1892
Clara	Entre Rios	1892
San Antonio	Entre Rios	1892
Lucienville	Entre Rios	1894
Montefiore	Entre Rios	1902
Baron Hirsch	Buenos Aires/ La Pampa	1905
Lopez y Berro	Entre Rios	1907
Santa Isabel	Entre Rios	1908
Curbelo-Moss	Entre Rios	1908
Narcisse Leven	La Pampa	1909
Dora	Santiago del Estero	1912
Palmar-Yatay	Entre Rios	1912
Louis Oungre	Entre Rios	1925
Avigdor	Entre Rios	1936
Leonard Cohen	Entre Rios	1937

Source: Author's elaboration.

With the exception of a temporary break in immigration during World War I, when the precariousness of commercial ties with Europe contributed to economic recession and unemployment, the flow of immigration to Argentina continued, including many Jews. In contrast to the immigration restrictions imposed by the United States and other countries, Argentina's liberal immigration policy remained almost unchanged, except for a few minor revisions in the mid-1920s. It was the world economic recession in the wake of the 1929 Wall Street crash that brought immigration virtually to a halt. The ensuing political upheaval provoked in September 1930 the first military coup in the country's history, which in turn reinforced the latent nationalist, Catholic, and xenophobic tendencies in Argentine society.[21]

During the 1930s the Jewish population grew to a quarter of a million. Contemporary restrictions on immigration were based on political as well as economic considerations. The social and political ferment in Europe aroused fears among the Argentine elites concerning the possible entry of "undesirable elements," people who might constitute a potential danger to the existing order. Consequently, Republican exiles and refugees fleeing from the Spanish Civil War and the new dictatorship of General Francisco Franco faced all kinds of barriers in their efforts to enter the country. National authorities feared that they might bring with them a leftist or anarchist "virus."[22] The same attitude applied to Jews, who were often assumed to be "Bolsheviks." Moreover, because of the economic recession, priority was given to those professionals who were needed by the local economy, while xenophobic attitudes put further obstacles in the way of non-Catholic immigrants or those who supposedly might have difficulties in adjusting to Argentine society and culture.[23]

Disappointment awaited those Jews who had hoped that Argentina would take a progressive position at the Evian Conference, convened in France by the League of Nations in July 1938 to discuss possible solutions to the problem of refugees from Nazi Germany and Austria. Argentina, like most other countries, was unwilling to open its gates to these refugees. This same restrictive policy was maintained throughout World War II, although between 1933 and 1945 around forty thousand Jews did enter Argentina, legally or illegally, almost a fifth of them during the years of the Holocaust.

In the mid-1940s, following the defeat of fascism and the end of hostilities in Europe, emigration to Argentina resumed, albeit not in the same magnitude as in the past. The populist president Juan Perón lifted most of the restrictions on immigration in 1947, and during the following three years some three hundred thousand immigrants entered the country, chiefly from Spain and Italy, the two main sources of Argentina's foreign-born population. Although barely fifteen hundred Jews arrived in the second half of the 1940s, the Peronist regime's decision to grant amnesty to all illegal residents enabled another ten thousand Jews to obtain legal status.[24] Unfortunately, Nazi war criminals and collaborators who had found shelter in Argentina, mostly under false identities, also benefited from this amnesty. Their presence in the country greatly contributed to the myth that Argentine society and authorities were anti-Semitic and pro-Nazi.[25]

The 1950s witnessed the last wave of Jewish immigration to Argentina (and to Brazil). These immigrants were mainly refugees from the Communist repression in Hungary in 1956, or Jews who had fled Egypt because of the hostile policy adopted by Gamal A. Nasser's regime after the joint attack by Israel, Great Britain, and France.[26] From that point onward, the number of Jews in Argentina began to decline.

Disembarking from the boats that had brought them up the Río de la Plata, many Jewish passengers spent their initial days in the country at the Hotel de Inmigrantes (the Immigrant Hotel), the first stop in the long process of becoming Argentines. The next stop for many of them was the *conventillo*, or tenement house. *Conventillos* had two or three floors, with long hallways built around one or two interior patios, giving access to a series of one- and two-room apartments. Into each badly ventilated room, one or two immigrant families were crammed, sharing the kitchen, lavatory, and washbasin. In 1887 there were already 2,885 houses of this type in Buenos Aires, lived in by some eighty thousand people. In other words, at that time more than a quarter of the population of Buenos Aires lived in tenement buildings. By 1901 this percentage had fallen to 17 percent, and by 1904 to 14 percent.

The physician and hygienist Eduardo Wilde wrote in 1877:

These omnibus houses that shelter everyone from the beggar to the small industrialist have a door out to the patio and serve for all the following: it is the bedroom of the husband, the wife, and their litter, as they say in their expressive way; that litter includes five or six duly filthy kids; it is dining room, kitchen, and pantry, a patio where the children play, a place where excrement is deposited at least temporarily, a garbage dump, a storeroom for dirty and clean—if there is any—clothing; it is the abode of the dog and the cat, the cistern, the place where fuel is stored; the place where at night an oil lamp, a candle, or a lantern burns; in short, each of these houses is a pandemonium where, against all principles of hygiene, laws of common sense and good taste, and even the requirements of the human body itself, four, five, or more people live and breathe.[27]

There are many other contemporary descriptions of the dampness, filth, and overcrowding of the *conventillos*, but as the city rapidly changed, nostalgia soon developed among those who had shared this lifestyle, highlighting the solidarity among different immigrant groups, as well as the rapid socialization of new arrivals. It was in the *conventillos* that they learned their first words of Spanish, as well as some of the cultural codes and customs of the country. Jevel Katz, the popular Yiddish singer and songwriter, enthralled Jewish Argentines throughout the 1930s by composing and singing, in a language that combined Yiddish and Buenos Aires slang (which he defined as "*casteidish*," a combination of "*castellano*," or Spanish, and "*ídish*," or Yiddish), songs that reflected with sly humor the experiences of Jewish immigrants in Argentina (some called him the "Jewish Gardel"). Katz dedicated his song "In a Conventillo" to the tenements, singing:

> Vivir vivo en caye Lavaye
> En un palacio—conventiye
> Mis muebles son la caniye
> Y sobre dos patitas una siye.

> Al *ídish* no le tengo paciensie
> Y tengo siempre *La Prensa*
> Y cuando la ubico
> frente a mis ojes
> Entiendo en ellas un kadojes.

> [I live in Lavaye Street
> In a palace—tenement
> My furniture consists of the pipes
> And a chair on two legs.

> I have no patience for Yiddish
> And I always have *La Prensa*
> And when I hold it
> in front of my eyes/ my head bursts.]

Between Once and Villa Crespo

The urban and social history of the Jews of Buenos Aires can be better understood if we examine their patterns of settlement in the various neighborhoods
of the city (see Map 1.1). Eugene Sofer noted four distinct stages in that settlement, which he linked to the development of the organized community during
the period 1890–1947. He describes the first stage as "entry and the search for
institutional and spatial stability." He calls the second stage "ghettoization and
unity," a description with which I tend to disagree; the third stage is movement
toward the west, also linked to the process of "ghettoization"; and the fourth
stage is dispersion and the fragmentation of the community.[28]

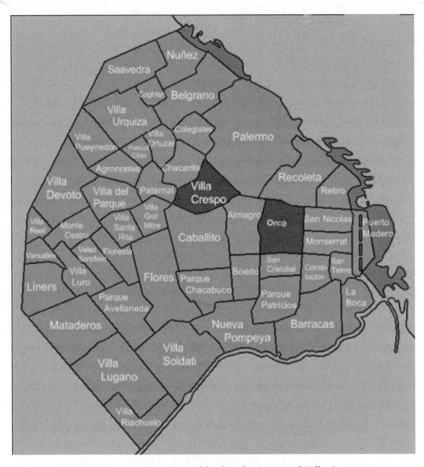

MAP 1.1 Buenos Aires neighborhoods: Once and Villa Crespo
are considered "Jewish neighborhoods."

Source: Author's elaboration.

The decision to live in one neighborhood or another was influenced by various factors that included, among other criteria, distance from the workplace, the cost of rent, available means of transportation, opportunities for starting a business, and proximity of relatives, acquaintances, and countrymen. Obviously, it is usually easier for new immigrants to integrate in an area where they can speak their mother tongue, where social and cultural institutions are available for their needs, and where the cultural codes of at least some of the inhabitants are not unfamiliar. Under these circumstances it is less of a challenge to retain aspects of one's own ethnic heritage while still developing a sense of belonging by adopting local identity elements.

In 1895, 62 percent of the city's Ashkenazi Jews lived near Plaza Lavalle, and only a minority lived in the neighborhoods to the west. Plaza Lavalle was the center of the Jewish community. Immigrants went there as soon as they had finished the immigration procedures at the port; there they found other Jews, looked for work, learned about life. It was in this area that a religious institution, Congregación Israelita, was established, followed in 1897 by the founding of the Libertad Street synagogue. For years Libertad Street was where a large part of Jewish commercial activity took place, in small shops and stands set up along its sidewalks. It was also the center of Jewish prostitution and the infamous Zwi Migdal, an organization of Jewish pimps.[29] Nevertheless, it was not a Jewish neighborhood, but rather one densely populated by immigrants from different places, with a high concentration of Jews.

Before long, Jews began to move from Plaza Lavalle to Once (a neighborhood that took its name from the local train station, "September 11 [once]." This marked the second phase of Jewish residential history, the 1907–25 period that Sofer defines as "ghettoization and unity." One consequence of the yellow fever epidemic that afflicted the city in 1871 was that the Buenos Aires elites moved to the north of the capital, which was higher in altitude and more sanitary. At the same time, population increases as a result of constant migration, together with the construction of public buildings and the development of the Avenida de Mayo area—which often required homes to be torn down—led to a dizzying rise in real estate prices in those vicinities in the first decade of the twentieth century, encouraging western migration. Many Jews who could not afford the high prices of the booming city center began to leave in favor of less popular residential areas, including Balvanera, otherwise known as "Once"— which for many years was the quintessential Jewish neighborhood. Once soon became the major business and residential center of the city's Jews. Many of the institutions of the organized community emerged there, including AMIA (Asociación Mutual Israelita Argentina), DAIA (Delegación de Asociaciones Israelitas Argentinas), social and sports clubs and religious associations, and the editorial boards and offices of the most important Yiddish newspapers, *Di Presse* and *Di Idishe Tzaitung* (which, unlike English-language Jewish newspapers, tended to ignore Jewish athletes and ball games).[30] The neighborhood was characterized by visible symbols of Jewish ethnicity, ranging from Ashkenazi temples to stores and delicatessens selling the delicacies of Eastern European cooking. Cultural identity was important; the Jews who left Russia after the failed 1905 revolution maintained community boundaries by building their own synagogue in Paso Street, between Corrientes and Lavalle, rather than attending the Libertad Street synagogue built by immigrants from France and Alsace. Yet even while Jews preserved their ethnic characteristics, affordable rent, cultural and linguistic ties, proximity to the workplace, and a wide range of educational, cultural, and commercial institutions all helped them adapt to Argentine life.

In using the term "ghetto" not even Sofer had in mind physical barriers of any kind that limited Jews to a specific residential area. Rather, he referred to an informal creation of a zone based on economic considerations and voluntary decisions by individuals who preferred to remain close to members of their own ethnic and cultural group and to their own institutions of education, health, social activity, and welfare. Indeed, the segregation indices for Jews in Buenos Aires of the early twentieth century seem to have been much higher than those of Spaniards, French, or Italians, but, as José Moya emphasizes, "Jews in Buenos Aires were less segregated than their coreligionists elsewhere in the diaspora. Moreover, Jewish residential segregation in Buenos Aires also dropped faster and sharper than in most other cities."[31]

The Yiddish language and cultural creation in that language were an inseparable part of the neighborhood scene in Once, at least until the 1940s. However, Jews continued to be a minority in this new neighborhood, where they did not represent more than 10 percent of the population, although their presence was very notable. In 1914, almost 40 percent of the Eastern European Jews who lived in Buenos Aires were concentrated in Once or a contiguous neighborhood, so it is not surprising that this was the first target of the nationalist strike forces during Tragic Week, when they tried to attack Jewish immigrants.[32]

Spanish-speaking Jews and some of those who spoke Judeo-Spanish, or Ladino (Jews originating from North Africa, Turkey, or the Balkans), opted for the Constitución neighborhood, while Jews from Syria (especially from Damascus) settled in Boca, Barracas, or Flores. Nevertheless, some of the Jews from Aleppo preferred to live with the Eastern European Jews in Once rather than mix with the Damascans.

In the three first decades of the twentieth century, Buenos Aires's expansion toward the west began to accelerate. The Vélez Sarsfield neighborhood grew from 4,500 inhabitants in 1895 to 100,000 in 1914; Belgrano, which was annexed to the federal district in 1887, went from some 15,000 residents in 1895 to almost 230,000 in 1936. Another neighborhood that came to form part of the capital in 1887 was Flores, whose population increased tenfold in that same period. Villa Crespo experienced similar growth, partly as a result of the tramway that crossed the neighborhood through Triunvirato and Corrientes Streets, linking Chacarita with the commercial center in just a few minutes. By the mid-1930s the area was already home to some 30,000 Jews, who constituted about one-quarter of all the Jews in the city. This represented the third stage of the urban history of the Jews of Buenos Aires: movement toward the west, and Villa Crespo's transformation into the largest and most important concentration of Jews in the city.

Here, too, some Jews lived in *conventillos*, mingling with other ethnic groups. The most famous *conventillo* was La Paloma, with its 112 one-room apartments and entrances off Serrano and Thames Streets, immortalized in the late 1920s by the renowned play *El Conventillo de La Paloma*, by Alberto Vaccarezza.[33] Its tenants moved once they had gained a foothold in the lower middle class. Unlike the Jews of Once, these Jews were poorer and less likely to be religiously observant.

After World War I, Buenos Aires gradually took on a new look. Streetcars replaced horse-drawn wagons, and the first subway line began operation. Villa Crespo was the destination of choice for the new waves of mostly Polish Jewish immigrants—just as first Plaza Lavalle and then Once had been for earlier immigrants, the majority of whom hailed from the Russian empire.

The last stage defined by Sofer is the dispersion and fragmentation of the community, which began in the mid-1930s as Jews moved to Almagro and Caballito, Floresta, Villa Devoto, or Villa Urquiza, as well as to the north, to Belgrano and Palermo. The post-World War II era saw another shift, toward the suburbs of Buenos Aires (to work, for example, in the textile industry established by Polish Jews in Villa Lynch).[34] Jews now lived in every Buenos

Aires neighborhood. Maneuvering between budgetary limitations and opportunities, many were integrated enough that they no longer needed to live in proximity to other Jews. They had become true *porteños* (Buenos Aires natives), despite all the initial difficulties. However, only Once and Villa Crespo acquired the iconic status of "Jewish neighborhoods." Toward the end of the 1950s and beginning of the 1960s, a joke frequently heard on local radio and later on television went: "What is the capital of Israel? . . . Villa Crespo."

2

THE CRADLE OF TANGO AND FOOTBALL

Villa Crespo and the Essence of Buenos Aires

> Canning and Rivera, Villa Crespo's sentimental intersection, the refuge
> of tramps and cheap philosophers; obligatory passageway of beggars,
> yarmulkes, and Turkish butchers; Canning and Rivera, Palermo Street,
> corner with a suicide's history (a year ago a girl threw herself from a
> third-floor window and was caught in the wires holding up the awning
> of the café, saving her from death), and a café that from early morning is
> filled with unemployed radiotelephone hobbyists.
> —Roberto Arlt, "Canning and Rivera," *Obras*

Before the nineteenth century was halfway over, the area that today encom-
passes the Villa Crespo neighborhood was a verdant plain crossed by a stream.
Toward the end of the century there was a small hamlet there, which grew
day by day until it became one of the city's main urban centers. Traditional
families such as the Peraltas, the Lumbs, the Balcarces, and the Valentín Alsi-
nas began to settle there on individual estates, forming a population nucleus
in the area now known as Corrientes Street. Back in the time of Bernardino
Rivadavia, wide parallel streets were laid down to accommodate vehicles and
provide access to the villages of the inland provinces. Those streets included
the avenues of Santa Fe, Córdoba, and Corrientes. However, as time passed
and the pace of industrialization picked up from the 1880s on, these family
estates began to disappear.[1]

During those years Argentina was fully integrated into the international
market and played a major role as an agro-exporter of raw materials. As a result, national industries began to develop—for example, in leather goods and
shoes.[2] The first businesses to settle in Villa Crespo were European tanner-
ies, an industry that required a large workforce. This demand attracted many
immigrant workers to the area. The Fábrica Nacional de Calzado (National
Shoe Factory) was the first company to set up operations in Villa Crespo, in

1888, attracting hundreds of working families who moved into local tenement housing. The factory employed more than a thousand workers.[3]

Its proximity to the Mercado de Abasto (Buenos Aires's central market) and the recently built Chacarita Cemetery contributed to the region's rapid development, as did the convenient availability of the Arroyo Maldonado, the stream used as a sewer for factory runoff. In the early 1890s, according to the *Memoria de la Municipalidad* (Municipal Report) as reviewed by James Scobie, the neighborhood already had more than four thousand residents.[4]

There are different stories as to how the first neighborhood called "Villa" got its name. According to most sources, Villa Crespo was named by the owners of the Fábrica Nacional de Calzado in honor of the mayor, Dr. Antonio F. Crespo. Another version claims that the name in fact derives from that of the saint of the Italian factory workers, San Crispín, considered the patron saint of shoemakers. Subsequently other "Villa" neighborhoods appeared, including Villa Devoto, Villa Luro, Villa del Parque, and Villa Urquiza.

Some attribute the neighborhood's foundation to the manager of the Fábrica Nacional de Calzado, Salvador Benedit, who was responsible for the creation of such varied public establishments as the Church of San Bernardo, the civil registry, the justice of the peace court, and the local newspaper, *El Progreso*. Benedit was an active politician, a member of the Unión Cívica Party, which was headed by General Bartolomé Mitre. In the days of Manuel Quintana's presidency, Benedit was elected national deputy for the capital, exercising that office from 1898 until his death in 1904. In any case, in turn-of-the-century Villa Crespo, the Fábrica Nacional de Calzado was the backbone of the neighborhood's life and development.[5]

The shoe factory was followed by other industrial concerns that settled in the area and attracted workers from other countries. Gradually a heterogeneous social and ethnic network began to develop, encompassing, among others, Spaniards, Italians, Jews, Arabs, Greeks, Armenians, and Japanese—a real laboratory for the development of a wide variety of hybrid identities.

This process of industrialization and the consequent increase in population impelled the development of infrastructures needed for daily life. One was the channeling and encasing of the Maldonado stream—previously used to carry away industrial waste, which, although convenient for the factories, posed a serious health problem for the population. Other projects included the installation of gas lighting in Corrientes Boulevard, as it was then known (it was renamed Triunvirato in 1893 but regained the name of Corrientes in 1938, at the request of the Juan Bautista Alberdi Public Library); the paving and reinforcement of various streets; and hospitals such as the Hospital Vecinal de San Bernardo, located in Warnes Street between Thames and Godoy Cruz, and the Liga Argentina Médica Asistencial de Villa Crespo (Argentine Medical Assistence League of Villa Crespo). (See Map 2.1.) However, the factors that gave the greatest impetus to the neighborhood's growth were the streetcar line, the subway (Line B), and the railroad. Thanks to these amenities, in the early twentieth century this neighborhood was transformed in a very few years from an area of country estates to an industrialized urban zone.

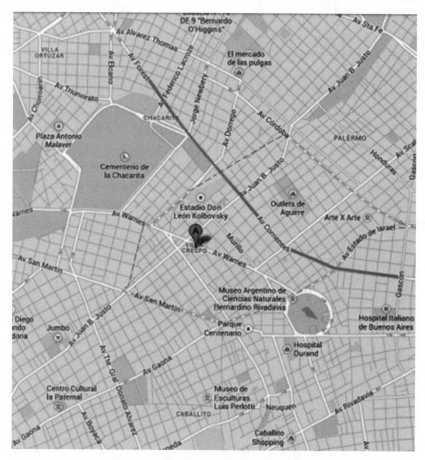

MAP 2.1   Villa Crespo: Corrientes Avenue as the axis of daily life in the neighborhood; Atlanta's stadium on Humboldt Street.

Source: Google Maps.

By the 1920s Villa Crespo was already a neighborhood in which immigrants and Argentine-born residents were well integrated, thanks to daily interaction in social and cultural frameworks, generating a collective identity that was continually undergoing further elaboration and change. These years were also a period of profound transformation for the entire city of Buenos Aires, when modernity coexisted with the lifestyle of the early 1900s.[6] The neighborhood continued to grow right up to the end of the 1970s, when the economic policy of the military dictatorship that took power in 1976 led to the closing down of small and mid-sized businesses, loss of job security, unemployment, and a drop in the quality of life for the socioeconomic group that lived there. In the 1990s, with the indiscriminate opening of the local market to imports, this trend—which began with Martínez de Hoz's anti-industrial policy and reached its apogee with Menem's neoliberalism—intensified, dealing the coup de grâce to many establishments.[7]

The different immigrant groups that flowed into the neighborhood in hopes of achieving a higher standard of living created a cultural mosaic that gave Villa Crespo a distinctive cosmopolitan identity typical of Buenos Aires. This cultural mosaic is reflected in Buenos Aires literature, such as Leopoldo Marechal's *Adán Buenosayres*, published in 1948, in which Villa Crespo is practically one of the protagonists. In it the author highlights different characteristic elements of the neighborhood, such as the *conventillo*, the thug, the stream, the Italian, the Galician, the Jew, and the dance hall—the first and the last being the main points of encounter for people of diverse origins.[8] The multicultural, cosmopolitan character of the neighborhood is also evident from the coat of arms of its charitable and historical organization, the Junta Barrial y de Estudios Históricos, created in 1998. The various symbols on the coat of arms include a temple, the words "coexistence and solidarity," and religious symbols, namely, the cross, the star of David, the crescent moon and star, and the yin-yang.

"Villa Kreplach": Jewish Presence in the Neighborhood

Villa Crespo is known as a neighborhood with a high proportion of Jewish immigrants, who for the most part arrived from Eastern Europe after the waves of Italian and Spanish immigrants. Others included Sephardic Jews who spoke Spanish or Portuguese (or Judeo-Spanish), and some Arabic-speaking Syrio-Lebanese Jews. Most of the Sephardic Jews were from Smyrna, Istanbul,

Salonika, and Rhodes. One point of reference for these groups was their cafés, the most well known being the Izmir, the Oriente, and the Franco.[9]

The peak of the Jewish immigrant influx into the neighborhood was the 1920s through the 1940s, a period in which Jewish influence on economic, social, and cultural life became significant. However, even in 1919 the Jewish presence was notable. That same year Alberto Vaccarezza named one of his plays about Villa Crespo *El barrio de los judíos* (The neighborhood of the Jews). In the pogroms of the Tragic Week, the so-called *niños bien* ("upper-crust boys") of the Patriotic League headed toward Villa Crespo, as well as other neighborhoods, to hunt *"rusos"* ("Russians"—namely, Jews). During the pogrom on January 10, 1919, dubbed "the night of the bonfires," rioters attacked and set fire to many businesses and homes in the Once and Villa Crespo neighborhoods, as well as union and association buildings. Many Jewish men, women, and children were killed, beaten, or tortured, both in the streets and at the police station.[10] By the 1980s, some of the Jewish population had begun to move to other neighborhoods, such as Palermo, Barrio Norte, and Belgrano. Nevertheless, the area retained its image as a "Jewish neighborhood."

The vast majority of Jewish immigrants were laborers, tailors, carpenters, weavers, and peddlers (better known as *cuentenikes*). The latter sold all kinds of merchandise on credit ("on account," or *cuenta*, hence their name), traveling around Villa Crespo on foot and giving working-class families the opportunity to acquire all kinds of products. Once they had more customers, they would move up to a bicycle or a sulky, and ultimately to a permanent location. The second generation, born in Buenos Aires, already included many professionals. A large proportion of the children of immigrants decided on academic careers, and they gradually became a significant presence in the universities. "As usual," explained Carlos Waisman, in the 1950s "the Jews [were] overrepresented in the new industrial middle class and in the left-wing intelligentsia, in new professions such as psychoanalysis and related fields, and in teaching and research within the expanding university system."[11]

A variety of Jewish institutions were established in the neighborhood to accommodate the community's educational, cultural, religious, and social needs. They included a number of Jewish schools, most prominently Scholem Aleijem, one of the most important institutions in the secular Jewish education system since the 1930s.[12] Noteworthy social-welfare organizations included the Asociación Comunidad Israelita Sefaradí de Buenos Aires on

Camargo Street and the Asociación Mutual Israelita de Protección de Enfermos Bikur Jolim.

Both the Ashkenazi and the Sephardic members of the Jewish community integrated fully into the social and cultural life of Villa Crespo, and they actively participated in the development of the three Argentine passions—*fútbol*, cinema, and tango music—as epitomized in the 1933 movie *Los tres berretines*.[13] This is indicated by the number of people of Jewish origin who profoundly influenced the collective cultural oeuvre. One example was Manuel Gleizer, a Jew who had left Russia in 1908 and arrived in Villa Crespo around the 1920s, where he became a patron of the great writers of the neighborhood and the country.[14] After starting various businesses, he decided to open a bookstore at what was then 540 Triunvirato Street, where, as a gathering place for young poets, novelists, and writers, it became a literary center. Gleizer gave some of these young people a chance to publish their works, an action that was the beginning of his own publishing career. Through this legendary bookstore and literary coterie passed such illustrious writers as Alberto Gerchunoff, Manuel Gálvez, Leopoldo Marechal, Raúl Scalabrini Ortiz, Leopoldo Lugones, César Tiempo, Samuel Eichelbaum, Eduardo Mallea, and Jorge Luis Borges. The poet Francisco Luis Bernárdez commented:

> The bookshop that Don Manuel Gleizer kept in Triunvirato Street, perhaps not as a place to sell books so much as to accommodate the leisure and the dreams of a [literary] circle nuanced by Marechal's wild hair, by Nicolás Olivari's lazy cigarette holder, by Pepe Bonomi's asiatic nose, by Ilka Krupkin's unsuitable dinner jacket, and by other elements with which the then new generation began to make its mark throughout the length and breadth of Buenos Aires.[15]

Other major figures in the culture of the neighborhood and the city included the previously mentioned Samuel Eichelbaum, a highly popular playwright in Buenos Aires, and journalist and author Julio Jorge Nelson (Julio I. Rosofsky), director of the old Radio Callao and commentator on tango. However, the real prototype of the Buenos Aires Jew was César Tiempo. Tiempo was born in Ukraine in 1906 as Israel Zeitlin, which was the basis for the pseudonym he later adopted: *zeit* means *tiempo* ("time" in Spanish) in Yiddish and German, while *lin* is the verb *cesar* ("to stop"). Before he was a year old he was already settled in Argentina with his parents, who had fled pogroms and anti-Semitism in czarist Russia. At the age of eighteen he began to attend literary gatherings and wrote his first poems.[16] Two years later he began to publish pieces on Jewish issues in *La Nación*; being Jewish did not prevent his acceptance by a hallowed organ of the Buenos Aires press, any more than it did in the case of the writer Alberto Gerchunoff. Eliahu Toker described his tremendous literary output and creative work in these terms: "hundreds of poems, six, seven volumes of factual or fictional articles, a dozen theatrical works, some fifty screenplays, a thousand articles in newspapers around the world."[17] His sense of social commitment kept drawing him toward *los de abajo* ("the underdogs"), an attraction that would later lead him to embrace Peronism.

In 1930, Tiempo won the First Municipal Prize for Poetry for *Libro para la pausa del sábado*, published by Manuel Gleizer. It was followed by other books in which the Sabbath was a metaphor for the weekly homage that the Jews of Buenos Aires paid to Argentina, which had become their true "promised land": *Sabatión argentino* (1933), *Sábadomingo* (1938), and *Sábado pleno* (1955). In his books as well as his theatrical works he sought to connect Jewish immigrants to the national culture. In fact, all his works exalt the convergence of the Jewish and the Argentine identities. Both identities had equal importance for him, and he was not prepared to sacrifice either to benefit the other. Tiempo's writings also called for pluralism, poeticized the routine of daily life, and described the common people tenderly and compassionately. Many pages are sprinkled with expressions in local slang or Yiddish.

His poem "Sol semita" (Semitic sun) can be considered a tribute to Corrientes Avenue, the axis of the neighborhood and the center of activity in Villa Crespo:

> El Sol delata a ciegas la edad de las mujeres
> embica en las fachadas grises del barrio
> o rueda al subterráneo de la calle Corrientes
> y va a verter su vino dorado a Villa Crespo.
>
> Se baña en el arroyo que cruza Triunvirato,
> gira reverberando sobre el eje del día
> y al promediar la tarde regresa a consignar
> sus redondas monedas en el Banco Israelita
>
> [The Sun blindly reveals women's age
> luffs to the gray façades of the neighborhood
> or rolls into the subway of Corrientes Street
> and goes to pour its golden wine into Villa Crespo.

It bathes in the arroyo that crosses Triunvirato,
Revolves shimmering on the day's axis
And halfway through the afternoon returns to deposit
Its round coins in the Banco Israelita.][18]

Author, composer, and tango musical producer Ben Molar (Moisés Smolarchik Brenner) was another high-profile personality.[19] A key figure in the popularization of tango and in the Argentine recording industry of 1950–70, Molar became one of the symbols of Buenos Aires, and he initiated the movement to establish a National Day of Tango. It is thus no surprise that he was named Illustrious Citizen of Buenos Aires. In the introduction he wrote to José Judkowski's book *El Tango: historia con judíos*, Molar described himself as "that kid from Villa Crespo who at the age of ten was already writing lyrics for carnival musicians," adding "[and] many thanks to Argentina for getting my folks, Don León and Doña Fanny, to start the day and end the evening by singing tangos."[20] Molar and Tiempo were members of the Academia Porteña del Lunfardo (*lunfardo* is the slang of Buenos Aires), a clear indication of their great influence on the shaping and preservation of Buenos Aires identity.

The Jews in the neighborhood were a significant presence, active in all social and cultural frameworks, where they interacted with other immigrant and ethnic groups. The result was the hybrid identity so well portrayed by César Tiempo with his *"casteidish"* (a combination of Castilian Spanish and Yiddish), and it contributed to a better integration of this community into the social life of the neighborhood and the country. It is no wonder, then, that figures emblematic of the Buenos Aires culture should emerge from it.

The neighborhood was typically working class, industrial, and proletarian, shaped by a population of laborers who in earlier years lived crammed into tenements. There, each family had the use of a single room, a small kitchen, and one primitively built bathroom that served the entire building. As a result, the *conventillo* became a place where different migrant groups comingled.

The inhabitants had to put up with both this and a lack of infrastructure that included, for example, poorly maintained roads, no public lighting, a lack of clean water, inadequate hygiene, and other deficiencies. As for local environmental conditions, Villa Crespo, being a highly industrialized area, suffered from the contamination released by local industries such as the tannery—a situation described by Marechal in his novel *Adán Buenosayres*. Villa

Crespo's social makeup made the neighborhood a stronghold of political parties affiliated with the labor movement, such as the Communist Party and, later, the Peronist Party.

All kinds of economic activities were carried out in Villa Crespo. In the industrial sector, new factories were built, such as the Dell'Acqua textile factory, a company belonging to the Italian community, which employed some fourteen hundred workers; the Trillo cigarette factory and the Maspero Brothers metalworking shop; and the aforementioned National Shoe Factory and the La Federal tannery. The budding industry drew new inhabitants to the area, which in turn generated new job possibilities in different fields. The immigrants who arrived in Villa Crespo adapted to all kinds of work—mason, carter, storekeeper, farm laborer, plumber, street sweeper, peddler, pizza baker, grocer, or carpenter—to meet the needs of the growing population.

Commerce played an important role in Villa Crespo's economy, with Corrientes Avenue as the main artery where merchandise of all kinds was sold. Warnes Street was another booming commercial center, identified even then with the automotive sector as a place where any kind of car part could be obtained.

Symbol of Buenos Aires

Villa Crespo is one of the neighborhoods most representative of what is considered the "true essence" of Buenos Aires. During the 1930s it became almost a synonym for tango and soccer, two of the pillars of the city's urban identity, and its rich cultural and social life has made it emblematic of what it means to be a native of Buenos Aires. Accordingly, it has given rise to many icons of Argentine culture, in both literature and music. Notable examples are the tango, the creole *sainete* (a one-act comic opera), the dance saloon, and various writers of world renown.

The tango was born in the obscure, impoverished, humble areas of the city, such as the banks of the Maldonado Arroyo; it was only in the 1920s that this genre made its appearance in the downtown cabarets.[21] Villa Crespo was one of the most fitting environments for tango, the most distinctive musical genre of the city of Buenos Aires, and some even claim the neighborhood was its birthplace. A verse from "Cuna de Tango" (Cradle of the tango), by Salvador Llamas, is a good example:

> El viejo farol de la esquina,
> de luz mortecina,
> me dice que es cierto
> que el tango nació en Villa Crespo.
>
> [The old streetlamp on the corner,
> with its failing light,
> tells me it is true
> that the tango was born in Villa Crespo.][22]

Although the tango's birthplace is a matter of debate and the honor is claimed by many, this verse does indicate Villa Crespo's importance in the development of one of the most important symbols of urban culture. The popular song was influential in the neighborhood and was danced to and sung devotedly in the dance halls and numerous cafés. A large number of the traditional tango *boliches* (dance clubs) were also located in Villa Crespo, such as the ABC Café, which was dubbed "the house of tango." Legendary popular dance halls such as Salón Peracca or Salón San Jorge were places where poets and tango lyricists met. Salón Peracca in particular was a symbol of Buenos Aires nightlife, the place where the most characteristic tango, the *arrabalero* ("slum-dweller" tango), was danced. The poet and tango author Enrique Cadícamo, in his book *Viento que lleva y trae* (1945), dedicated a poem to it called "Salón Peracca."[23] Villa Crespo's renown as a bastion of the most traditional school of the 2–4 rhythm attracted tango dancers from around the country to its dance halls and cafés.

Among the tango notables who were part of the neighborhood was Paquita Bernardo, the first woman to perform on the *bandoneón* (a type of large concertina), previously considered to be an exclusively male instrument. Better known was the musician, pianist, composer, and conductor Osvaldo Pugliese. His long musical career, punctuated by boycotts and other barriers raised by his Communist sympathies, ensured him a preeminent place in the pantheon of Argentine tango. A sculpture of Pugliese and his orchestra can be enjoyed in the heart of Villa Crespo, almost at the corner of Corrientes and Scalabrini Ortiz.

In the literary sphere, Villa Crespo was a nurturing environment for the creole *sainete*, providing local color for these stories that recounted Buenos Aires daily life. Among the practitioners of this genre, Alberto Vaccarezza is one of the best known. Classified as "the master of the Buenos Aires *sainete*,"

Vaccarezza was a prolific author whose works include *Las chicas de Gurruchaga* (1917), *El barrio de los judíos* (1919), *El Arroyo Maldonado* (1922), *Chacarita* (1924), and *El Conventillo de La Paloma* (1929). The last-named play was performed at the National Theater with the internationally renowned actress Libertad Lamarque in the principal role—a role she would play another thousand times.

Other writers and celebrities of the cultural world very closely associated with the identity of the city and the neighborhood were Baldomero Fernández Moreno and the playwright, narrator, poet, and essayist Leopoldo Marechal. The latter was famous for his novel *Adán Buenosayres*, which, praised by Julio Cortázar in 1949 in an essay in the journal *Realidad*, focuses on the neighborhood of Villa Crespo and emphasizes the main features of the Buenos Aires identity.[24] Ángel Magaña, the famous actor of the golden age of Argentine cinema, and José Gobello, who was a linguist and expert in *lunfardo*, a slang that originated in the Río de la Plata region, should be added to this list as well.

Villa Crespo's heterogeneous socioeconomic network was what gave it its strong Buenos Aires identity, a network based on the characteristic elements that continually recur in tango and *sainete* lyrics—for example, the ruffian, the slum, the immigrants, and the *conventillo*. Thus, cultural media managed to turn these elements into characteristic symbols of *porteñidad* (Buenos Aires "nativeness").

The vitality of Villa Crespo civil society was reflected in the varied socioeconomic activity that took place in different spheres. These included the typical Buenos Aires cafés, the movie theaters, the newspapers, the libraries, and even the tenements. The San Bernardo Bar y Billares café, a favorite of many Atlanta fans for decades, played a central role in the neighborhood. In the early 1930s it had the biggest billiard room in the area, with more than twenty pool tables. Especially notable, however, were the neighborhood's dance halls and social clubs; they were a meeting place for the new inhabitants of the burgeoning community, shaping the unique cultural identity that would eventually characterize the city of Buenos Aires.

During the 1940s and 1950s, the dancing halls were used for public dances. Admission cost was very little, which allowed people of different social origins to take part in what were mass events—the larger clubs might admit thousands of people. One of the most popular halls was Salón Villa Crespo, which was used for family celebrations, conferences, concerts, and theatrical events. There were also dance academies that taught people to dance, particularly the tango, which was generally danced by men. Often, however, these "academies" were actually a front for a different kind of physical activity.

A number of clubs were established and developed in Villa Crespo for social or sporting purposes. The National Shoe Factory also influenced the social life of the neighborhood, its manager having created one of Villa Crespo's first social institutions, called La Nacional. Here management, clerks, and laborers mingled, sharing the experience of social and sporting events.

Another such club was the Club Social y Deportivo Villa Malcolm, which held both sports activities and social events such as dances and concerts. This club was popular with the middle classes, but often bands and singers associated with the working class were brought in, underlining the comingling between social groups.[25] Others, such as the Club Social y Deportivo Fulgor de Villa Crespo, managed to set up their facilities in rambling old houses where they used the space for soccer fields, basketball or bocce courts and had rooms for social games such as chess, dice, dominos, or cards. The Sporting Social Club, founded in August 1930, won renown on the basketball court in later years. Social and cultural life was so vibrant in the neighborhood in the 1940s and 1950s that the traditional tango orchestras ceaselessly made the rounds of the various clubs, societies, and dance halls.

Another sphere of activity for this kind of club was loaning space to social institutions. One example is the Club Social y Deportivo Villa Crespo, which besides offering sports activities like any other club, also hosted, among others, the Rotary Club, the Junta de Estudios Históricos (a historical research organization), and the Ateneo Cultural de Villa Crespo (a cultural center).

Besides institutions intended for the general public, there were clubs affiliated with specific social groups, such as the Club Social Israelita Sefaradí (Sephardic Jewish Social Club), the Círculo Israelita de Villa Crespo (Jewish Circle of Villa Crespo), and the Círculo Italiano de Villa Crespo (Italian Circle of Villa Crespo). Still others specialized in various sports, such as the Círculo de Ajedrez de Villa Crespo (Chess Circle of Villa Crespo) or the Club Ciclista Nacional (National Cycling Club, of which Vicente Auterio, Argentine biking champion at the time, was a member).

The working-class, industrial, proletarian nature of the neighborhood up to the mid-twentieth century made it particularly important to the Socialist movement and the Communist Party. In the 1920s and 1930s, the Buenos Aires Communist unions in the garment industry, for example, were dominated by Jews, owing to the huge number of Jewish textile workers. (See Figure 2.1.)

FIGURE 2.1 Jews dominated the city's textile industry:
The list of the founders of the Unión de Sastres Talleristas includes
the name of the author's grandfather-in-law, J. Bichman.

Source: Photo by Julio Bichman.

In some unions the original constitution and bylaws were written in Yiddish. The largest was the Sindicato de Obreros Sastres y Anexos (Union of Tailors and Related Workers), which had a strong presence in Once and Villa Crespo.[26] The Socialist contribution to neighborhood culture should not be overlooked, either. The library of the Centro Socialista was one manifestation of this. However, the Alberdi Public Library and the Ateneo Cultural de Villa Crespo were both central pillars of cultural life in the neighborhood. The library of the Asociación Cervantes also played a significant role.

Another very active cultural sphere was the local press. The major newspapers included the Bartolomé Mitre-influenced *El Progreso*, founded in 1895 by Salvador Benedit and Julián Bourdeu, and considered in the 1970s as the "doyen of Buenos Aires local journalism"; the independent *El Látigo*, established in 1928, which lasted ten years; and *La Voz de Villa Crespo*, which debuted in 1922 and, like the other two papers, pulled no punches in describing the social reality of the neighborhood, an approach that gave it the tone of a crusading paper.

The main artery of Villa Crespo was Corrientes Street, which bustled with economic, cultural, and social activity.[27] Along and around it clustered many cafés and in particular the three movie theaters of the neighborhood, which were gathering places for young people. These movie theaters were the Rivoli, at 5312 Corrientes; Villa Crespo, two blocks further; and the combination movie theater-playhouse Cine-Teatro Mitre, located at what used to be 726 Triunvirato. The cafés were the center of bohemian life in Villa Crespo and the heart of the neighborhood's intellectual life. Corrientes Street was also famous for its carnival parades, events that involved a great deal of social effort and provided an arena in which local residents from all walks of life intermingled.

Football in Villa Crespo

In the first decade of the twentieth century there was still a clear gap between the densely populated neighborhoods in the city center and the periphery, where football was just beginning to gain popularity—a popularity that by the 1920s would spread to the older neighborhoods (see Figure 2.2). Histories of

FIGURE 2.2   Football became a central activity for Jewish Argentine children
in Buenos Aires from at least the early 1920s.

Source: Courtesy of Marcelo Fleker.

the sport in Argentina are peppered with anecdotes by players of how in the first third of the century they played in the streets and vacant lots or any other available space, with balls made out of rags, sometimes replaced by rubber ones. The game was not yet encouraged in the schools, and playing was prohibited in the plazas and parks.[28]

These informal matches led to the birth of amateur football clubs, which gradually began to compete in the framework of independent leagues. This process resulted in the establishment by the leagues of rules governing football fields. It was only at the beginning of the 1930s that professional football was institutionalized in Argentina; at that time various sports were already recognized as a "healthy" activity that deserved the support of the authorities, whether municipal, provincial, or national.[29]

Long before Atlanta appeared in Villa Crespo, local residents were passionate about football, which was played in several of the neighborhood social-athletic institutions. Both native-born and immigrant young people, Jews being no exception, took to football with obvious enthusiasm. If indeed, as Jeffrey William Richey claims, in the early twentieth century "soccer became a key vehicle for Argentine politicians, intellectuals, and players to widely disseminate a version of cultural nationhood that excluded non-European elements of the national population,"[30] then embracing football was an additional way for Jewish Argentines to ensure that they were included in the European and white category. At the workplace or the café, a Jew could not talk with his Gentile friends about religion or traditional practices, explained one of my informants, but *fútbol* was a topic of common interest that allowed them to conduct a conversation. In other words, by participating in soccer—as players, spectators, or simply readers of the sports columns and magazines— Jewish Argentines sought to carve out their own position in society.

For the most part these early soccer clubs were not up to the challenges of professional football and never achieved national fame. Before we examine the Atlanta club, its history, and its connections with Villa Crespo, we ought to mention two other football clubs that had early links to the neighborhood: Chacarita Juniors and Argentinos Juniors.

In the early 1900s the neighborhood already had two football clubs. One was called Los Mártires de Chicago (The Martyrs of Chicago), in honor of the anarchist workers who were condemned to death after the Haymarket revolt in that American city in May 1886. The other was made up of young Socialists and was called El Sol de la Victoria (The Sun of Victory). In 1904, the same year that saw the birth elsewhere of the Club Atlético Atlanta, the two existing clubs decided to merge into a single club under the name Asociación Atlética y Futbolística Argentinos Unidos de Villa Crespo (United Argentine Football and Athletic Association of Villa Crespo). Since this name was too long to fit on the club's official seal, it was shortened to Asociación Atlética Argentinos Juniors.[31]

This club's first headquarters was established in the home of the Agostini brothers at 450 Aráoz Street. The new club adopted red and white as its colors, in homage to the Socialist Party, which that same year had managed to elect the first Socialist legislator in America, Dr. Alfredo Palacios.

After getting the club set up and resolving the issue of the seal, the young club members had to find a field on which to play. Initially they rotated between the neighborhoods of Caballito and Villa Crespo, playing often on a field near Cid Campeador. Then they broadened their search for a good, permanent place to play, scoping out Villa Ballester, Villa Urquiza, Villa Crespo again, and Chacarita. Finally, in 1926, Argentinos Juniors would seek their fortunes in the Paternal area, building their new soccer field at the intersection of Avenida San Martín and Punta Arenas.

There was another team in the neighborhood, called Defensores de Villa Crespo (Defenders of Villa Crespo), composed mostly of players from the neighboring area of Chacarita. On May 1, 1906, the Chacarita members met at the headquarters of Section 17 of the Socialist Party, at the corner of Dorrego and Giribone Streets, for the purpose of breaking away from the club to create a new one, to be called Chacarita Juniors.

The founders of Chacarita Juniors held their first meetings in the back room of a tobacco shop in Rivera y Leones Street, but its first "clubhouse" was actually a dairy shop at 3636 Jorge Newbery Street, an improvised location in the office of a dairy belonging to a Basque who decided to let the young club founders have it for their meetings. The treasurer, Antonio Fernández, gave the club a shed around the back of his house at Charlone and Estado Streets in which to meet on rainy days.[32]

We have more legendary anecdotes than documentation concerning the early days of Chacarita Juniors. One story goes that to raise money to buy the club seal, the members collected old newspapers at houses around the neighborhood and sold them to a business in Villa Crespo, making enough on the deal to buy the desired rubber stamp. The money to buy a ball was donated by a local commissioner on condition that the club play a game against his former club, Defensores de Villa Crespo. Reportedly the match lasted less than half an hour because the ball burst.

In April 1907, the club officers decided to build the club's first playing field in an empty lot at the corner of Federico Lacroze and Álvarez Thomas, although the municipality was planning to turn the lot into a road and the rickety facilities there had been dismantled. Clearly, for the young founders of Chacarita, neighborhood boundaries were insignificant, and the club's stomping grounds in those early days encompassed both Chacarita and Villa Crespo.

Chacarita's first years were difficult, especially since the club lacked a permanent playing field. It was getting its income from running carnivals and playing football. In 1915 a group of members and players switched to the Platense club in the Núñez neighborhood, leaving Chacarita in danger of extinction as much of its activity had to be canceled. Most of the seceding group returned a few years later, however, and in 1919 the club reorganized and began to meet weekly in the Café de la Curva at the corner of Jorge Newbery and Gribone. That same year, after four years of inactivity, the club resumed its athletic activities.

After joining the Argentine Football Association in 1920, Chacarita set up its headquarters in the Dell'Acqua factory in Villa Crespo. Lacking a pitch of its own, Chacarita had been playing on Club Enigma's field in Los Andes Park. Construction on the club's first official stadium began in 1925, in the block encompassed by Humboldt, Murillo, Padilla, and Darwin Streets, and the stadium was inaugurated two years later. By this time Club Atlético Atlanta had already settled in Villa Crespo. Thanks to Chacarita's growing fan base in those years and the requirements of professionalism, the club was obliged to build a new stadium, this time at 300 Humboldt, a street it shared with Atlanta's football field. The new stadium, accommodating some forty thousand people, was inaugurated February 19, 1932, with a game against Montevideo's Nacional, in which the local team won 3 to 0.[33] By then the Jewish youngsters of Villa Crespo would rather go to Humboldt Street on Shabbat than to one of the neighborhood's synagogues. Football had became a secular faith for many Jews, who saw traditional Saturday rituals as outmoded.

Chacarita occupied the Humboldt Street stadium for about a decade, its eternal rival, Atlanta, being one of the reasons it had to move. The land where Chacarita's stadium was located was rented to Atlanta. In 1943, the Sociedad de Tierras de Villa Crespo (Villa Crespo Land Company), which was affiliated with Atlanta, bought the Humboldt property and evicted Chacarita from their stadium. The last match played on that field paradoxically did not involve Chacarita, but pitted Colegiales against Temperley on December 16, 1944.

Chararita's new home was the town of San Martín, or more precisely the neighborhood of Villa Diehl.[34] The stadium was inaugurated on July 8, 1945, with a friendly game between Chacarita and Montevideo's Nacional, which Chacarita (nicknamed "*los funebreros*," or "undertakers" because of the Chacarita Cemetery) won by a hair. Thanks to its move, Chacarita managed to increase its membership from 4,960 in 1944 to almost 8,000 by the end of 1945—mainly because its new location was in an area devoid of any other sports club.[35]

3

"THE WANDERING JEW"

Atlanta in Search of a Playing Field

In the early 1900s, football clubs were linked to customs of social interaction in Buenos Aires civil society. Like the public libraries or community-improvement societies, sports clubs, too, played an important role in the communities that were forming in different neighborhoods, developing their own social imaginary, collective identity, and local loyalties. Buenos Aires was in the midst of a process of accelerated urban modernization, which was accompanied by a boom in community associations arising from grassroots initiatives and pressures on one hand, and on the other promotion of the same by state or municipal authorities, as well as by charitable associations, health and burial societies, and even professional organizations.[1]

However, football clubs were not created by the state or by the municipality, but by groups of boys in various neighborhoods of the capital and its suburbs—adolescents who wanted to play soccer and, to that end, sought one of the many unoccupied fields in the city. In the meantime, they played in streets, plazas, and vacant lots. They were the original members, leaders, players, and fans all rolled into one. They wanted to compete against other young men, including teams from the English private schools. Accordingly, they organized and played in different independent leagues, parallel to the "official" league they wanted to join.[2]

During the first decade of the twentieth century, football ceased to be the exclusive province of the schools of English immigrants and the elite (as did the sports of cycling, archery, cricket, and fencing) and was rapidly appropriated by locals who made "*fútbol*" their own. Football became a sport identified with the working and lower middle classes as well as with the Argentine character. Innumerable clubs were founded in those years, many of which did not survive because of their precarious resources. Among those that did, Club Atlético River Plate was founded in 1901,[3] followed during the same decade by Boca Juniors, Racing, Independiente, San Lorenzo, Huracán, Atlanta, Argentinos Juniors, Chacarita Juniors, Platense, and Ferrocarril Oeste, among others. According to Julio Frydenberg, in 1907 more than three hundred club teams, mostly neighborhood affiliated, played in the independent leagues.[4] At the time, Buenos Aires, Montevideo, and London were the cities that boasted the largest number of clubs and stadiums for this sport; football had come to form an integral part of Buenos Aires life—masculine life, at any rate. At the inauguration of the River Plate stadium in 1917, it was the Atlanta team that was invited to play in the first game. As the figure below shows, the game attracted a huge crowd. (See Figure 3.1.)

Football had been played in Argentina since the 1860s, and during the first half of the 1890s the first official league was formed.[5] Among the clubs that were not associated with the English immigrant community, the pioneer was the Club Atlético Porteño, founded in 1895. The city authorities supported the establishment of athletic clubs, considering physical exercise and sports

FIGURE 3.1 The inauguration of the River Plate stadium in 1917;
Atlanta defeated the home team 3–1 on this occasion.

Source: http://www.sentimientobohemio.com.ar/100_previariver.htm.

essential for moral development and personal hygiene, as well as a good way to keep young people away from the evils of urban life, such as drinking and gambling. From the end of the nineteenth century, doctors, educators, social reformers, military officers, politicians, and essayists advocated strengthening the body as a guarantee of physical and moral health and to prevent biological and social diseases.[6] As early as 1885 the Argentine president and intellectual Domingo F. Sarmiento promoted the idea of "educating the body."[7] The following years saw increasing approval of the practice of, first, individual sports and, subsequently, team sports of English origin. The latter were considered to encourage discipline, cooperation, solidarity, mutual respect, healthy ambition, and self-control. Apparently everyone enthusiastically recommended physical exercise. This is exactly why the word *atlético* (athletic) appears in the names of so many football clubs founded during that period, including Atlanta.[8]

In 1900, Club Porteño requested from the municipal authorities and obtained, in early 1901, a free lot in the Tres de Febrero Park for "open air games." The municipality would use this lot in 1910 as the site of an industrial fair that was part of the festivities celebrating the independence centennial. That year, 1901, was also the year that Club Atlético de Estudiantes obtained its playing field, an achievement duplicated in 1904 by Club de Almagro.

Analyzing the minutes of the city council of Buenos Aires, Rodrigo Daskal came up with a list of subsidies granted by the council in 1909. Of the twenty-three subsidies, eight went to charitable associations, six to individuals, four to religious institutions, two to educational bodies, two to physical exercise and sports institutions, and one to a commemorative project.[9]

Many football clubs were set up by hardly more than eleven members—the players—and were characterized by their ephemeral existence or precarious resources. The lack of a home playing field was a common problem, forcing teams to change fields, use the fields of other teams even for local games, or always play as the visiting team.

Statistics on the growing number of spectators at football games in Buenos Aires during the first third of the twentieth century are hard to come by, but it is interesting to note that as early as August 1928 a sports writer for *El Gráfico* was contending that the clubs should be helped to expand. "We could aim at 40,000 spectators for the most attractive international matches," he explained. "Stadium capacity has to be increased."[10] Indeed, in mid-1932, the football magazine *La Cancha* described a match between Racing Club and River Plate attended by fifty-five thousand spectators, with another twenty thousand left outside the Avellaneda stadium unable to get tickets and thousands more who decided not to go at all, for fear they would not be able to get inside.[11]

By the 1920s, as Julio Frydenberg has noted, "football occupied a central place in the local life of the district, in masculine sociability in the street, on the corner and in the café and in family life—that is, it occupied part of the public space and also part of daily life in the home."[12] One indication of the rapid growth in the importance of football was a remark by Radical deputy Le Breton in 1915 describing football as a sport that facilitated "physical and moral development," and that should accordingly be encouraged at school.[13] Although it would be many years before elementary education incorporated football into its curriculum, the game's importance and its moral and physical benefits were recognized by many as early as the second decade of the twentieth century.[14]

The first media that contributed to the identification of the clubs with the inhabitants of the neighborhoods where they were based were *La Mañana*, *La Argentina*, and *Última Hora*. A more important role in this process was played by the daily *Crítica*, which in the 1920s became the Spanish-language paper with the biggest circulation (its founder and owner, Natalio Botana, briefly served as the president of the Argentine Football Association in 1926),[15] and the sports weeklies *El Gráfico*, which debuted in 1918,[16] and *La Cancha*, which appeared a decade later. The radio was another factor in strengthening this link. Buenos Aires had enjoyed regular radio broadcasts since 1920, and the first sporting event to be transmitted over the air was the boxing match between Luis A. Firpo and Jack Dempsey in 1923.[17] Two years later the first broadcast of a football game was transmitted by a pioneering Buenos Aires station, even before the broadcasters of London or Paris attempted it. Gradually, the popular social imaginary began to associate a certain neighborhood with the most prominent club in that area. Often clubs fought for the right to be considered as the representatives of their neighborhoods in that collective urban consciousness.[18]

Foundation and First Steps of Club Atlético Atlanta

In those early years of the twentieth century, when football was just getting started, a group of fans of the game from the Buenos Aires neighborhood of Monserrat decided to create a neighborhood soccer club and named it Club

Atlético Atlanta. On October 12, 1904, Benigno Larrive, Héctor Franco, Trifón Piaggio, Juan Escribano, Luis Sagardoy, Juan José Enrich (see Figure 3.2), H. Rapallo, and Fabián Orradre met at the home of Tomás Elías Sanz, a businessman in the Constitución neighborhood, with the intention of founding a club.[19] Since there were not enough chairs in Sanz's house, the meeting moved to a nearby plaza. Before the meeting was over, at Trifón Piaggio's suggestion, a collection was taken up to buy a leather ball and a pump: eleven pesos were donated, the equivalent of two days' wages for a laborer.

According to some authors, as well as the club's official website, the reason the Día de la Raza (Day of the Race), October 12, was chosen as the day to start the club was that the founders wanted a significant date to commemorate the club's creation.[20] However, President Hipólito Yrigoyen instituted the Día de la Raza in Argentina by means of a decree that was not published until October 1917.[21] From then on the date acquired growing importance and significance in Buenos Aires. Accordingly, it appears that the emphasis that some fans place on this date is part of an effort to create a heroic legend around the club's foundation and to invent a tradition worthy of a "major" club.

To compete in the independent leagues this group of youngsters needed a name, a jersey, an office, a minute book, a board of directors, and an emblem. There are two main stories concerning the origin of the club's name. One version says it was designed to honor the United States city of Atlanta, in the southern state of Georgia, in memory of a natural disaster that occurred there in those years.[22] This version lacks verisimilitude, since no such occurrence has been recorded in that period. The second, more likely, version is that the club was named after the United States warship USS *Atlanta*,[23] which arrived in Buenos Aires port for the inauguration of the Manuel Quintana–José

FIGURE 3.2 Lifetime membership of Juan José Enrich, one of the founding members of Club Atlético Atlanta, 1942.

Source: http://www.sentimientobohemio.com.ar/nota_enrich.htm.

Figueroa Alcorta ticket, the administration that succeeded President Julio Argentino Roca.[24] This warship was the second of five of the same name, the third of which was the most famous owing to its action in the Second World War. This particular ship, however, inspired the young men of the Montserrat neighborhood by its arrival in 1901 and the broad journalistic coverage it received as a result of a series of baseball games played between members of the Atlanta's crew and US citizens residing in Argentina.[25]

The club's choice of colors has also given rise to two competing stories. The vertical yellow and blue stripes evoke the awnings typical of Buenos Aires shops at the time, goes one version.[26] The other version attributes the choice to the colors of the Swedish flag on a boat noticed by one of the club's founders during a routine stroll through the Riachuelo area.[27] The early years of the club are not well documented and accordingly offer considerable scope for a mythical narrative of the past.

The first field where Atlanta played was at the intersection of Juan Bautista Alberdi and Escalada Streets in Floresta.[28] Here the club members built their first field house from wooden crates they had smuggled out of Hirschberg & Co., where several of the club's officers worked; they even improvised a bathroom. However, their stay was short, owing to the rising rents of the time, and they soon moved to another field, at Alberdi and Lacarra. This time the Isola company provided the wood needed to build a combination field house–locker room. Once again, however, the club's occupation proved temporary. Atlanta had to move numerous times to different neighborhoods in the capital, including Villa Lugano, Villa Luro, Flores, and Parque Chacabuco, before finally settling down, in the 1920s, at 540 Humboldt Street, on the border between Villa Crespo and Chacarita.[29] Throughout its early years Atlanta was relatively nomadic. Because of its erratic wanderings and lack of any geographical anchor, the CAA acquired the nickname of "*bohemios*" (gypsies).[30] In recent decades, this nickname has become popularly associated with the concept of the "wandering Jew," although some claim that it was initially an expression of disdain for "gypsies," the homeless wanderers from the region of Bohemia who were often marginalized as pariahs and aliens wherever they went. In 1934, for example, *La Cancha* referred to "*los bohemios*, that race of gypsies, white as the snow of their mountains."[31] The same issue described Atlanta as "a dry little leaf that the cyclone cannot rip from the branch." In other words, the club lived in precarious conditions, but had the fighting spirit it needed to survive.

As for the club's first headquarters, they were located in a plaza near the home of Elías Sanz—appointed the club's first president—at Bernardo de Irigoyen and Independence Streets, but the members soon decided to return to the building kindly provided by Sanz. After this apartment was abandoned, the club's first "office" was the assembly room of the *La Prensa* daily newspaper, where they held their important meetings. At those meetings they made such decisions as the resolution to retain blue and yellow as Atlanta's distinctive colors and the prohibition on holding membership in another club concurrently with membership in Atlanta.[32]

In 1906 the club had only twenty members, most of them laborers at Isola. Yet even then it drew the attention of the press. After Atlanta defeated River Plate 9–0, a sports writer wrote:

> Atlanta and River Plate yesterday played a match that, judging by its actions, will go down in history for the fans of the former. At the call of the referee, Mr. Federico Silvestre Pérez, the gold and blue team came out of the locker room. . . . Eight minutes later Miranda made the first goal, then Castromán, Noseda, and Barbetti scored. The first half ended with the partial triumph of Atlanta, 4 to 0. In the second half goals were scored by Castromán (2), Bernáldez (2) and Siriani (1). Atlanta has one of the most homogeneous teams around, and time after time it has been demonstrating its real capacity in this diabolical English game.[33]

The following year Atlanta destroyed Independiente, 21–0, after "a proud, brilliant, and positive performance," as one journalist put it.[34]

The fledgling club also decided to expand its activities with a program of competitions for members that included a needle-threading race, a 100-meter dash, a sack race, a relay race, and a 50-meter egg-and-spoon race.[35] However, the club leaders' greatest concern was acquiring a field for the club and a stadium of their own. They had to worry about paying rent for the grounds and the expiration or renewal of rental contracts. The possibility of having to move again was the focus of discussions among board members. "[Talking about the field] we find ourselves in worse conditions than other clubs," complained one member, according to the club minutes.[36] It was only in 1920, after rejecting offers for the sports field belonging to Club del Plata in Pereyra Park, that the board of directors finally found a suitable lot, the property of Juan Dufour on Humboldt Street between Camargo and Padilla. It was in fact Elías Sanz who signed the papers "as joint guarantor and primary debtor" for this property. The endorsement of Atlanta's new president, Alberto Chissotti, was also required.

The list of Atlanta's founders does not include a single name that can be identified as Jewish. Moreover, Atlanta was in fact not considered "the Jews' club" until the 1940s or 1950s. It is interesting, however, that although the founders of Club Atlético River Plate, a club that was established in 1901 in the Boca neighborhood, did include a Jew, and this club has, over the years, had more Jewish players and many more Jewish fans, it has never had any sort of Jewish image or associations—unlike Atlanta.[37] In fact, very few people in Argentina know that Leopoldo Bard, the first captain and president of River Plate (1901–8), was Jewish.

In its early years, Atlanta's principal activity as an institution was football. Although it did organize various social and cultural activities almost from the beginning, it became a social and sports club only in the 1930s. Until then, football was paramount. The founders decided to join the Argentine Football Association (Asociación del Fútbol Argentina, AFA) in 1906 and began to establish themselves in the leagues. Besides official football, Atlanta, like other clubs of the era, had several teams that competed in different leagues and friendly matches, using alternative names such as Oriente, Atlanta Extra, Sabañón, and Viruta.[38] Meanwhile, the club was not growing: it had only twenty members, who all worked at the Isola company—as did the players and club officers.[39]

Wanting a football stadium where it could play as the local team, in 1906 Atlanta tried twice to merge with other teams that might provide a solution to this problem. The first attempt involved Club Atlético Olivos, but the proposal went nowhere. The second approach was to Club Atlético del Oeste. At first it looked as though an arrangement might materialize. The merger between the two "brands" reflected the great challenges that many clubs of the era had to face. The leadership of Atlanta considered Club del Oeste's thirty members a great advantage, since they would increase the institution's membership substantially. By that time, Atlanta actually had more members, but not so many that it could afford to scorn thirty additional ones. In this merger, Atlanta contributed its colors and Oeste its field, located in Chacabuco Park. For two years Atlanta had two playing fields: the one at Floresta and the one in Chacabuco Park, which it rented to other teams that did not have pitches of their own. In 1908 it sold the Floresta field for sixty current pesos (m$n 60), retaining the Chacabuco Park lot as its sole field.

However, the union between the two clubs did not prosper, since the Club del Oeste officers insisted that both teams drop their own names and take the name of Club Atlético Chacabuco—a demand that was one of the main reasons that the Atlanta representatives ultimately rejected the merger.[40]

In the years leading up to the centennial of the May Revolution, Atlanta had to abandon its Chacabuco Park field temporarily as a result of a ruling by the Buenos Aires municipality directing the construction of an amusement park in that location for the centennial celebrations. Accordingly, the club played in the fields belonging to the Banco Nación and Ferrocarril Oeste clubs before eventually returning to Chacabuco Park. Moreover, at the same time that its pitch was constantly switching around, so were its club headquarters, with frequent moves around Palermo, Congreso, Once, and other neighborhoods.[41] Despite this instability, however, the club was beginning to develop an orderly institutional structure, creating five subcommittees in 1911 in charge of Atlanta's different social and athletic activities—specifically football, celebrations, administration, facilities maintenance, and the club library.[42]

The importance Atlanta was gradually gaining in the social and political spheres was reflected in the celebration of its tenth anniversary, which was attended by the minister of foreign affairs, José Luis Muratore; the minister of war, General Ángel Allaria; and the minister of public education, Tomás R. Cullen. Other notable guests were Ricardo C. Aldao, president of the Argentine Football Federation (1912–14) and of the Argentine Football Association (1918–19); the mayor, Joaquín de Anchorena; and the president of the Chamber of Deputies, Marco Aurelio Avellaneda.[43]

In 1912, Atlanta decided to leave the Argentine Football Association and join the Argentine Football Federation, thereby ascending to the first division.[44] In 1915, after the two associations had reunited, the club rejoined the Argentine Football Association. Four years later this association divided once again and Atlanta joined the Asociación Amateurs de Football (Amateur Football Association).[45]

The "progressive" image that Atlanta would project in the 1960s and 1970s did not exist in the club's early years. In April 1916, the daily La Mañana published a piece "canvassing the clubs about the national elections." According to the paper, most of the players in Racing were going to vote for the Conservatives; in Independiente some of the players were Radicals, and many others were more moderate national Socialists or more revolutionary international Socialists. The picture was quite similar in Boca Juniors—that is, Radicals and Socialists. The players of San Lorenzo, still according to the *La Mañana* reporter, were mostly Socialists; those of Porteño, Radicals, and those of Gimnasia y Esgrima of Buenos Aires planned to vote for the Partido Demócrata Socialista. In Atlanta there was a wide range of views, said the article, and it named the Radical players (Miró, Bolinches, Lessa, Negri, and Perazza), the international Socialist Valentini, and the Argentine Socialists Ceppi, Pereyra, Conti, and Fredes.[46]

After its eviction by municipal order from the Chacabuco Park pitch where it had played from 1912 to 1919, Atlanta began to play on the field owned by the Ferrocarril Oeste club, at 250 Martín Gainza Street (formerly Caballito Street), and in 1920 it played on the now defunct pitch of Club Atlético Banco de la Nación Argentina. The culmination of this phase of the club's history came in 1922, when after years of wandering from one playing field to the next and one clubhouse to the next—the peregrination that earned the members the nickname of "*bohemios*"—the club found a permanent home in the neighborhood of Villa Crespo.[47]

Villa Crespo had been in flux since the beginning of the century, distinguished by its dynamism and its mass of new immigrants, many of them Jews. The club's arrival in this quarter, where it rented its playing field from Señor Dufour, also marked a boom in its membership. From 1921 to 1922 the number of members quadrupled (in August 1922 the club register showed 503 names), and it continued to grow by fits and starts up to 1929, when it reached a total of 1,508.[48] In the early 1920s Atlanta's renown in the world of Argentine football was great enough to inspire the foundation of a club with the same name in the city of La Plata. The Buenos Aires club resolved "to provide moral and material support to that entity, to donate a flag and send a football."[49] This was a common practice in the 1910s and 1920s: the dominance of the *porteño* soccer culture in Argentina was reflected in the decision of many provincial clubs to adopt names in homage to the successful clubs of the federal capital, Atlanta being one of them.[50]

In those years, the popular press tended to use certain adjectives or nicknames to refer to the football clubs, occasionally not mentioning the club's actual name at all. While the players and fans of Atlanta were called "*los bohemios*" and, eventually, "*los de Villa Crespo*" (the Villa Crespians),

Gimnasia y Esgrima of La Plata came to be known as *"mens sana"* or *"los trip-eros"* ("the gluttons"). Racing was called *"la academia"* ("the academy"), and its rivals from Independiente were *"los diablos rojos"* ("the red devils") or *"los rojos de Avellaneda"* ("the reds from Avellaneda"). The Chacarita club members were *"los funebreros"* ("the undertakers") because of the club's proximity to the local cemetery; Vélez Sársfield was *"el fortín"* ("the little fort") or *"los de Villa Luro"* ("the Villa Lurians"); River Plate was *"los millonarios"* ("the millionaires"); Huracán, *"el globito"* ("the little balloon"); Platense, *"los cala-mares"* ("the squid") or *"los de Saavedra"* ("the Saavedrans"); San Lorenzo, *"la escuadra de Boedo"* ("the Boedo squad"), *"el ciclón"* ("the cyclone"), *"los cuervos"* ("the crows"), or *"los santos"* ("the saints"); and Quilmes was *"los cerveceros"* ("the brewers"). *"Bohemios"* was acknowledged as Atlanta's nick-name for the first time in 1929, according to the club minutes—ironically, after the club had already been permanently based in Villa Crespo for several years and was really no longer a "gypsy" club.[51] From then on Atlanta would be *bohemio* by origin and by choice, to emphasize its previous years of precarious existence.

Atlanta's pitch was on Humboldt Street, between Camargo and Padilla.[52] The club's 1920 report records the discovery of a field that "owing to its location will be without a doubt one of the best situated fields, surrounded by a dense population that has lacked a sports club to give the young people of the neighborhood the perspective of exercise for normal physical development."[53] The stadium was inaugurated with a game between Atlanta and River Plate, which ended in a tie of 1–1. However, the great number of spectators who came to watch it was significant, reflecting the club's importance. Moreover, the number of club members and spectators continued to increase, soon necessitating the construction of new bleachers.[54] From its beginnings the stadium remained imbued with a strong symbolic value, becoming a constitutive hub for the club and its fans.

According to data published by the daily *La Nación*, in 1931 the stadium with the largest capacity was the San Lorenzo stadium (73,000 seats), followed by the River stadium (58,000) and Boca (55,000). Next came the Huracán stadium (41,000 seats), Sportivo Barracas (33,000), Almagro (19,000), Vélez (16,000), Platense (14,000), and Argentinos Juniors (10,000). The stadiums that accommodated fewer than 10,000 spectators included Excursionistas, Chacarita Juniors, and Ferrocarril Oeste (8,000); Barracas Central (7,000); Defensores de Belgrano (6,000); and Atlanta (5,000) (see Table 3.1).[55]

TABLE 3.1   Biggest stadiums in Buenos Aires in the early 1930s

Stadium	Capacity
San Lorenzo	73,000
River	58,000
Boca	55,000
Huracán	41,000
Sportivo Barracas	33,000
Almagro	19,000
Vélez	16,000
Platense	14,000
Argentinos Juniors	10,000
Stadiums with a Capacity Below 10,000	
Excursionistas	8,000
Chacarita Juniors	8,000
Ferrocarril Oeste	8,000
Barracas Central	7,000
Defensores de Belgrano	6,000
Atlanta	5,000

Source: Author's elaboration, based on various issues of *La Nación*, 1931.

Although some clubs had a permanent home stadium before Atlanta, such as Ferrocarril Oeste in 1904 or Sportivo Barracas in 1920, many clubs did not reach their final locations until after Atlanta, notably Independiente in 1928 (the first stadium built out of concrete); San Lorenzo in 1929; River Plate in 1938; Argentinos Juniors, Boca Juniors, and Nueva Chicago in 1940; Vélez Sársfield in 1943 (a stadium replaced by one of concrete in 1951); and Chacarita Juniors in 1945.

Atlanta's new location also brought together the two teams that would be archrivals, Atlanta and Chacarita Juniors. At the time it was not unusual for two major football clubs, in addition to other, smaller, ones, to coexist in the same neighborhood. However, in most cases only one would be considered to represent the neighborhood. From 1922 on, Atlanta and Chacarita competed for that status. In the world of football, rivals are normally seen as enemies, and the closer they are geographically, the greater their mutual enmity and hostility. The relations between River and Boca, Independiente and Racing, and Huracán and San Lorenzo are examples of this phenomenon. Atlanta and Chacarita are another notable instance.

Consolidation and the Beginnings
of Professionalism

The lack of a home soccer pitch meant that Atlanta was unable to consolidate its membership during the first two decades of its existence. Many other clubs facing similar challenges simply disappeared. Atlanta, too, teetered on the brink of extinction until it gained its foothold in Villa Crespo. Ever since then, the tradition of this club of humble beginnings managing to establish itself "by the skin of its teeth" has been a source of pride for its fans.

In the early 1920s, Atlanta was headquartered at 3587 Garay Street, where the decision was made to install additional bleachers in the stadium on Humboldt Street to accommodate the crowds of fans, which were growing from one day to the next. In moving to Villa Crespo club officers had hoped to boost the number of the club's members and sympathizers, and their hopes were realized within the first few years at the new location. The first year alone saw a rise of 400 percent in the roster of members. In absolute terms the number was not particularly impressive, but it was a substantial increase compared with Atlanta's previous membership. By 1923, the club had 783 members.[56] Beginning in 1924 the meetings of the board of directors took place at the club's now permanent headquarters at 470 Humboldt Street. It was time to begin developing social and cultural networks in the neighborhood. In 1927 activities other than football were beginning to emerge, yet football continued to be the main sport in Atlanta, which was entering the last phase of its amateur period.

In its eighteen years of amateur status, which ended in 1930, Atlanta played nineteen tournaments. It won its biggest landslide victory in the 1920 tournament in which, as the away team, it beat Sportivo Buenos Aires 9–0. In contrast, its most devastating defeat was in a game against Boca Juniors that it lost 0–8. By the end of the era, Atlanta had managed to attract almost fifteen hundred members, while the largest club in Argentina was River Plate, with nearly fifteen thousand.[57]

Throughout this period, the club leaders were looking for ways to increase club revenue, whether through ticket sales; increased membership fees; contracts for radio broadcasts, commercials over the stadium loudspeakers, or advertising posters on the pitch; refreshment concessions; loans and donations from the members; or friendly games. Thus, for example, in March 1914, Atlanta played a game against an Uruguayan team on the football field of Gimnasia y Esgrima of Buenos Aires, collecting the substantial sum of 5,323 pesos. In 1923, for the purpose of building more stadium stands, the club issued 2,500 coupons at a price of 2 pesos each to raffle off to members and their friends. One-hundred winning coupons were drawn on the first Sunday of each month, before the football game.

Atlanta's relations with government authorities were particularly important in this regard. Atlanta was one of the first football clubs to receive support from the Buenos Aires municipality. As early as 1910 the town council granted it a subsidy, and in 1913 provided land to be used for playing fields.[58] The president of Atlanta in the years 1926–27, Alberto Sanguinetti, was also a city councilor. Of course, dependence on public funds meant that Atlanta's officers, like those of other clubs, had to maintain good relations with whatever government was in power, be it civilian or military, Peronist or anti-Peronist.

The competitive pressure to ensure victories gave rise to various cases of corruption in Argentine football even before the sport went professional. Atlanta was not immune to accusations of shady behavior. In mid-1925, Natalio Botana's daily paper, *Crítica*—which at the time was selling hundreds of thousands of copies a day—published a series of editorials that turned into a crusade against football administrators who, according to the newspaper, were corrupt and interested only in making money. An editorial published on June 9 that year said, "Atlanta's managers are the same as Lanús's: after a few lucky wins they get giddy and think they already have everything it takes to win a tournament. . . . [T]here's no way they're willing to lose. On Sundays, since the other team was good, they had recourse to unsportsmanlike means to annihilate their opponents, and it seemed almost more like a human slaughterhouse than a football game."[59]

The professional era of local football formally began on May 31, 1931 (although in the 1920s there were cases where clubs bought players from other parts of the country and brought them to the capital, in open violation of the rules of amateur sports). Thus, the Asociación Amateurs Argentina de Football disappeared and the Liga Argentina de Football (Argentine Football League) was born.[60] Club presidents would now aim at maximizing profits, building massive infrastructure projects, and expanding membership. Sports magazines became very popular, and journalists contributed to the elaboration of myths about *fútbol*, national identity, neighborhood loyalties, and masculinity.

Atlanta played its first professional game against River Plate and was defeated 0–1, but later beat its eternal rival, Chacarita Juniors, 3–1. In the second year of professional soccer, the major teams began to buy up the best players from the lower-ranking teams, with the result that those teams had to find new people to fill their empty spots. Atlanta decided to fill its own vacancies by buying players from clubs in the provinces or from neighboring countries. That same year, 1931, Atlanta's officers tried in vain to hire all the players of the Uruguayan team that had established itself as the world champion. The following year they took on nine Paraguayan players, hoping to improve their performance. These transactions ultimately generated conflict within the club, since they failed to produce the results Atlanta craved. Some of these players returned to their own country; others moved to different teams in Argentina.

Even in this early stage of Atlanta's history, toward the end of the period of "*amateurismo marrón*" (or pseudo-amateurism, when although players were not yet officially allowed to accept payment, most clubs were in fact paying many of them indirectly or secretly), Atlanta had begun the practice of selling its homegrown talent—for example, players Célico, Tarasconi, Paternoster, Médicis, Nunin, and De Césari, who made names for themselves after moving to more important teams. In the 1930s, the print media was already referring to Atlanta as a club that "exported" players.

At that time the gap between Chacarita Juniors and its neighbor Atlanta seemed huge. In mid-1933, as Atlanta was struggling to balance its budget, Chacarita inaugurated its new 25,000-square-meter field with renovated stands and space for a variety of athletic activities. Sports magazines like *La Cancha* and *Alumni* celebrated the constructions that transformed Chacarita into "a powerful institution." There was much excitement during the first game played in the new stadium (against the Uruguayan team Nacional de Montevideo) as an enormous hot-air balloon and five military airplanes flew over the field in celebration.[61] Still, the *bohemios* were proud of their own club, and when Atlanta celebrated its anniversary on October 12, 1933, goalkeeper Mapelli declared that "the discovery of America" and the establishment of Club Atlético Atlanta were two major events of similar importance.[62]

Teetering on the Brink of Extinction: The Failure of the Merger with Argentinos Juniors

In 1934 an event took place that would determine the club's direction in the following years. The newly constituted Argentine Football Association decided to merge Atlanta with Argentinos Juniors, the club that had deep roots in Villa Crespo.[63] This initiative was motivated in part by the big clubs trying to eliminate the small clubs that were allegedly undercutting the business of professional football and reducing the earnings of the larger clubs. Accordingly, some clubs in the first division were downgraded (Tigre and Quilmes), and others were forced to merge (besides Atlanta and Argentinos Juniors, Lanús and Talleres were combined). This policy elicited a whole range of reactions and criticisms. *El Gráfico* reflected the prevailing climate when it published an article that strongly criticized the initiative as abuse, claiming that it was covering up the fact that "the greatest responsibility for the powerful clubs' bad finances lies with the clubs themselves, which in their zeal to monopolize champions have not hesitated to pay bonuses and high salaries. This has had more influence on their deficits or meager earnings than the trifling box office takings when they have had to play against weak teams with little popular appeal."[64]

The year 1934, according to the club minutes, found Atlanta doing well in its football games, but reduced to only 887 members and in terrible economic straits. Reportedly, on many occasions there were only eleven jerseys for three teams, and socks, "of which they only had the upper part, since the sole was made of paper," were passed around among players. Perhaps for this reason the club became involved in activities unrelated to sports. In July 1932, *La Cancha* reported that Atlanta could not renovate its stadium since it was in arrears with its rent.[65]

At times, as a result of its merger, Atlanta seemed to be in danger of returning to its "gypsy" ways. In any case, the attempted merger with Argentinos Juniors was not achieving its purpose; the combined team had a terrible season, winning only two out of thirty-nine games.[66] The Jewish goalkeeper for Argentinos Juniors, Jaime José Rotman, nicknamed *"El rusito"* ("the little Russian") by *La Cancha*, stood out from the rest of this team (later, in 1942, he would play a season for Atlanta).[67] In the stadium, the fans of the two clubs did not mix and cheered only their "own" players.

In September 1934, the AFA decided to intervene in the club and suspended its affiliation on the grounds that clandestine gambling was going on at the club headquarters. The resolution stated that "a study of the books and records . . . shows that the leaders of the club . . . have not adhered to the barest minimum of consistency in their administration, to the point where it is impossible to establish with any exactitude the sum of its current debt and the number and situation of its members."[68]

Under these circumstances, it was apparently impossible to comply with the requirements of the Atlanta–Argentinos Juniors articles of consolidation, dated February 26 of that year, which also "reveal a state of disorganization in the first of the clubs mentioned that is incompatible with the standards of responsibility and propriety that should govern the lives of the affiliated institutions." Accordingly, the Assembly of the Argentine Football League resolved to "disaffiliate 'Club Atlético Atlanta Argentinos Juniors' and grant affiliation to 'Asociación Atlética Argentinos Juniors'."[69] According to *La Cancha*, "so much for real news . . . it was known several months ago . . . Atlanta is suspended until February [1935], but the word is that several leaders swore they would not let it back in. . . . [I]t has not been much work to pull Atlanta out of the Argentine League. The difficulty will be to bring them back into the fold."

The resolution effectively gave Atlanta the opportunity to "rejoin [the League] in the first division, at the annual ordinary Assembly of February 1935 . . . if within 90 days of that date it demonstrates that it had reorganized itself socially and administratively, excluding the people who have managed it since and including 1932, who shall be ineligible for managerial positions in affiliated clubs for a period of five years. . . . "[70]

The former president of Racing and future president of the AFA, Ernesto F. Malbec, was appointed *interventor* (temporary administrator) in Atlanta, and he succeeded in reorganizing the club in accordance with the conditions imposed by the league. In his report on the intervention, he analyzed the abortive merger with Argentinos Juniors as well as the restructuring of Atlanta's administration. Malbec, a plastic surgeon by profession, described the difficulty of determining the financial results of the merger, since "the accounts were limited to one cash ledger, which partially recorded revenue and expenditures." The information contained in this ledger was registered "under inexact rubrics, and the minutes book did not show the terms under which the players had been hired, the wages paid to employees, bonuses, authorized expenditures, etc."[71] As a result, the organization's liabilities, revenue, and outlays could not be determined with any exactitude. The documentary irregularities were connected to "the improper way in which receipts were issued, especially those for payments to players, staff, groundsmen, etc."[72] Responsibility for the irregularities lay mainly with the board of directors, president, vice president, secretary, and treasurer who had administered the club and who remained disqualified for two years.

Malbec's conclusions were that "the causes of the merger's failure" had to do with the bad finances and the "moral discredit that these situations imply for sports institutions." He finished by saying, "Complementing this financial anarchy was the patent hostility of the Clubs' representatives to the merger, shown at every opportunity, which prevented them from finding the solution indispensible to the smooth operation of the Club." On the subject of Atlanta's situation when the intervention began, Malbec emphasized "the abnormal legal situation that Club Atlético Atlanta was going through, asserted before the Inspección General [Corporate Records Office] itself by a number of members, who, pointing out various irregularities, petitioned for a legal intervention by the office."[73]

After only two months of intervention, the ambitious Malbec (already eyeing the presidency of the national football association) was able to inform the Assembly of the Argentine Football League that the situation now met the relevant legal requirements, congratulating himself on the accomplishment of an intervention that was "highly beneficial to the Club." Malbec published a notice in all the Buenos Aires dailies and radio stations to the club's creditors, and promoted a complete re-registration of all the members. A club roster dated September 20, 1934, contained 1,728 names. However, the dues collected during the time of the merger with Argentinos Juniors indicated that the real number of members varied between 800 and 900, taking into account delinquent payers. It was ascertained that over 500 individuals, despite not having paid any dues at all in 1933, continued to appear on the members' register. The spirit of renewal that the intervention gave the members was evident almost immediately. After sixty days, the new club register listed some 2,500 members, whose identities and other details had been duly verified by the new authorities.

Successful though Malbec's management had been, Atlanta still needed funds in order to recover from its long history of impecunity. The normal development of professional football activities was very difficult when the club dues barely covered general expenses, rents, wages, and the like, leaving nothing to pay down even the most pressing debts. Some members of the board of directors publicly undertook to pay off some of the debts out of their own pockets. The *interventor* asked the league for an indirect contribution of $10,000—that is, by directly paying off the club's most pressing debts (for example, outstanding fees and wages, past-due documented invoices, and so forth). The club officers also decided to organize various events to commemorate Atlanta's thirty-second anniversary, allocating the revenue to the club's coffers. The end-of-the-year celebrations were a substantial source of income, since they involved dances with music performed by the Willi Memory Jazz Band.[74]

Thus Atlanta rose like the phoenix from its ashes, more vigorous than before. The new management expressed its "deep gratitude to the members, who have with diligence, perseverance, and capability defended the Club in the difficult moments when it faced enormous peril as an institution, so much so that its demise had been decreed by those who had the power to make it happen."[75] To thank the former *interventor*, Malbec, for his work, the club honored him with a dance held on March 2, 1935. During the first-division game in Villa Crespo against Club Atlético Lanús, it bestowed on him a ceremonial scroll and a gold medal.

In the club's first season after its reaffiliation, the performance of its elite football team left much to be desired. Despite this disappointment, however, its standing was still better than it had been all the years since the institution of professionalism. In this early professional period, the doubts and dilemmas of the club managers concerning investment in the players' salaries were evident. The club's annual report published at the beginning of 1936 said, "It is clear that the clubs that are best placed logically presupposes [*sic*] more effective players, who in recognition for their performance should be better paid, which in consequence increases this line item; but examination of the accounts of the different clubs shows a clear anarchy in this respect; it might therefore be more equitable to pay the players according to their collective capacity or performance."[76] Still under the traumatic shadow of the forced merger with Argentinos Juniors and the short disaffiliation from the league, the board of directors complained about the policy of the big clubs that endangered the existence of the smaller ones, saying that

> with respect to expenses some clubs have behaved rashly, committing large amounts of money to acquire players. It is clear that if we look only to our own interests we should encourage that policy in the hopes of being favored by some transfer [of players] but from a general perspective such excessive investments are antieconomical and stir up these institutions, making them think that the solution to the consequences of their own mistakes lies in eliminating the clubs they call "small," perhaps forgetting that they themselves began exactly the same way.[77]

Using a mixture of biologistic jargon—in vogue during the 1930s—and social and sports discourse, the 1936 club report claimed to be the voice of the less influential clubs, explaining:

> If the first-division clubs must be pared down, it cannot be done violently, but rather by a natural attrition, resulting in the phenomenon we see in biology and which governs the relations of beings in nature, where the most fit survive

and predominate in the struggle for life. Thus, the survival of the fittest will take place naturally.

The "big" clubs need the competition of the "little" clubs because it is the action of the latter that allows the former to be big. Without the small clubs, some of those clubs that are now big would have to take the place of the small clubs, with the natural consequences that this implies.

Nature, which is a wise teacher, has permitted beauty in all the manifestations of life so that it can be differentiated from ugliness; good from bad; light from dark; and everything is ruled by the law of contrasts, so that, for there to be "big," there has to be "small."[78]

All these remarks reflect mixed feelings due to the lack of funds and the threat represented by the large clubs together with the aftertaste left by the era of amateur football, with its greater emphasis on the team as a whole rather than the individual players. It was a defensive reaction and a resistance to the commercialization of sports and leisure.

Toward the end of the 1930s, Atlanta went on a South American tour. Between December 1939 and February 1940 it played seven games in Chile and Colombia, losing only one. In 1940 various suspicions of bribery arose in a scandal in which Atlanta's leadership was probably involved in some way. The scandal had to do with the promotion of the Banfield team after a confirmed bribe to two players from Barracas Central. Nonetheless, the AFA ratified the promotion even though it counted Banfield's first five games as defeats.

Around this time Atlanta began to develop a social life, together with an openness toward playing other sports besides football. In 1937 boxing was added, with the idea of organizing exhibitions in cooperation with the Comisión Municipal de Box (Municipal Boxing Commission). In the social sphere, Atlanta's carnival dances were making a splash, constituting by 1935 "something serious, prestigious, and important."[79] The end-of-the-year dances were held on December 21, 24, 28, and 31, 1935, and January 4, 1936. According to the board of directors, "although the pecuniary utility of these dances was meager, this B.D. is happy to have held them, because [they] allowed members to meet in acts of healthy social recreation." In 1937 massively attended costume balls were held. The 1936 club report includes a photograph of "a select group of little girls who honored our carnival dances" and another of a crowd standing and listening to the orchestra. These images underline Atlanta's growing social and local importance for women and children as much as men, and its heterogeneous social and ethnic base.

For the last year of the 1930s, on the club's thirty-fifth anniversary, it was decided to wrap up the festivities with a dance at the Círculo Israelita de Villa Crespo (a Jewish community organization), a decision that highlighted the importance of this community in Atlanta and the neighborhood. Between 1936 and 1947, the Jewish population of Villa Crespo grew by 67 percent, and it is from this period that Jewish membership in the club's board of directors was uninterrupted, although still relatively sparse.

The number of Jewish players in Atlanta during the 1930s and 1940s was small. One of the more notable ones was José Liztherman, a player from Rosario hired in 1938 and transferred to Boca Juniors the following year in exchange for the sum of twenty thousand pesos, a friendly game, and the transfer of two players valued at four thousand pesos each.

The history of the Lighterman family, sometimes written Lizhterman, is a fascinating one and illustrates the way sports helped Jews integrate into the Argentine nation. Coming from a Jewish Argentine family of Rosario, the three sons, José, Rubén, and Ernesto, all became well-known football players. Born in Rosario in 1914, José was a center forward and a high scorer. The fact that he was nicknamed "Jaime" to highlight his Jewish origins might in itself serve as a good starting point for a discussion of sports and ethnicity in Argentina.[80] The Irish Jew Louis Bookman had a similar experience when he came to play for the Bradford City Football Club in England in 1912. His City teammates immediately dubbed him "Abraham." A few years later, when Bert Goodman started to play on the Tottenham team (known for its strong Jewish support), he was soon nicknamed "Kosher" by the other players.

José Lighterman came to Atlanta from the ranks of the Belgrano de Rosario team and wore the Bohemian jersey for two seasons, 1938 and 1944. His younger brother, Rubén, born in 1922, was also a center forward, but only played one match on Atlanta's elite team, in 1940. He then moved to the Acassuso club in the Boulogne Sur Mer District of San Isidro Partido, Greater Buenos Aires. The third brother, Ernesto, played for Chacarita as well as the national team.[81] This family serves as a good starting point for a discussion of sports and ethnicity in Argentina, exemplifying the importance of football in the lives of many Jews in South America. Atlanta had Sephardic fans and players as well, not just Ashkenazi Jews. Goalkeeper Bensión Moscona (who moved from the Club Atlético Excursionistas to Atlanta in 1940) was one of them.

4

VILLA CRESPO

The Promised Land

Once settled in Villa Crespo, Atlanta began a long campaign to gain members and oust Chacarita from the coveted position of neighborhood representative. The so-called "big five" football clubs—River Plate, Boca Juniors, Racing, Independiente, and San Lorenzo—had greater drawing power and collected more revenue; consequently, they were becoming enormous institutions with thousands of members, leaving Atlanta in the dust. According to Julio Frydenberg, in 1920 among the clubs of the Asociación Amateurs, Racing and River Plate accounted for 37 percent of football revenue. With Independiente, San Lorenzo, Atlanta, and Platense the amount rose to 63.6 percent. The fifteen remaining teams got the other 36 percent.[1]

Even in Villa Crespo itself, Atlanta was unable to dethrone Chacarita. Frydenberg provides statistics on the number of members in the Buenos Aires football clubs of the 1930s. During the first half of that decade, River became the biggest club. From almost 15,000 members in 1931, it grew to more than 30,000 in 1935. San Lorenzo, which had a similar number of members at the beginning of the decade, reached almost 20,000 in 1935. Boca Juniors grew during the same period from 8,500 members to 22,450, Racing from 6,400 to 19,460, Independiente from 5,400 to 15,000. In the same period, Atlanta doubled its membership—but it was dealing with much smaller figures, from 1,400 to 2,850, while Chacarita more than tripled its member register, from 1,300 to 5,450.[2] (See Table 4.1.)

In the small clubs, the expenses of professional football drew criticisms of all kinds. In the annual report published at the beginning of 1937, Atlanta officials explained defensively to the members: "The players are paid too much, but we have to keep up this pace or we'll go under, since the possibility of relegation makes everyone worry about warding off those perspectives [sic]. Moreover, the players who earn the most are not always the most efficient, and

TABLE 4.1 Membership of leading football clubs, 1910–1940

	San Lorenzo	River Plate	Boca Juniors	Independiente	Vélez Sarsfield	Huracán	Racing	Argentinos Juniors
1910					41			
1911					58	80		
1912					84			
1913					114	400		
1914		475			75			
1915		665			95			
1916		781			136			
1917		1045			239			
1918		1645			358	400		
1919	203				409			
1920	465	762			436			
1921	1073	1080			497			
1922	1342	3493			471			
1923	1492	5002			733			
1924	1616	3795			872			
1925	1817	3358			916			
1926	2337	3733	3020	2600	1250	1641	2600	
1927					1230			927
1928					1210			1008
1929					1190			760
1930					1290			669
1931		19714	8500	4200	1340	2986	6400	
1932		22327	12900	5700	3200		8300	144
1933	15108	27195	23200	7300	5200		13500	
1934	16400	30165	22100	8700	6680		14000	
1935	19655		22400		6420	6700	19400	
1936	19110		20400		4920		19600	
1937	17200		19200		3390		20200	
1938	17256		15300		3230		16400	
1939	20256		17500		3200		15900	
1940	20640		29600		3390	16385		

Source: Julio D. Frydenberg, "Los sectores populares: porteños y el fútbol durante las tres primeras décadas del siglo XX" (PhD diss., Universidad de Buenos Aires, 2008), 194–95.

various factors are involved here that sometimes necessitate actions that are not very fair."

They finished up by saying, "The players, between bonuses, salaries, and prizes, receive respectable salaries that have no equal in any other human activity relative to the amount of time spent doing it."[3] This judgment, although still true to this day, resonated more during the 1930s, among the first generation of Buenos Aires natives in the professional era.

Although football was the main activity for most of the clubs, including Atlanta, and football ticket sales provided most of their revenue, the club officials gradually found they had to broaden "the sports horizon of their members"—that is, include other disciplines in order to attract a more diverse population, including women and children, to their activities. Since the 1920s, sports had gradually become part of the lives of a growing number of women. In a book titled *Moral y deporte* (1937), Próspero Alemandri, an educator and member of the club Gimnasia y Esgrima of Buenos Aires, recommended that women indulge moderately in "tennis, golf, horseback riding, cycling, skating, swimming, basketball, dancing, and using exercise equipment."[4] This idea was embraced by an increasing number of advocates.

In 1937, Atlanta added boxing to its activities—among other reasons, so that it could organize exhibitions and make money from this popular and lucrative sport.[5] Accordingly, the club joined the Federación Argentina de Box (Argentine Boxing Federation). The first boxing festival was held at the end of that year, "with the contribution of ringside seats by Chacarita Juniors."[6] In return, Atlanta offered free tickets to Chacarita fans. In 1939, a boxer from the club, Oscar Pino, competed in the Argentine championship tournament (Campeonato Argentino) and made it to the finals.[7]

At the same time, the club continued to expand its social and cultural activities in an effort to strengthen its identification with the neighborhood, create personal networks and trust, and increase membership (thereby also increasing the income from membership dues). Atlanta was not the only club to make such efforts. In 1926 Dr. Beltrán, president of Club Colegiales, explained that his institution was not just a sports club but also "participates in the life of the neighborhood."[8]

The club became a social sphere, establishing itself as an axis of the collective imaginary. Only some of the inhabitants of any given neighborhood habitually attended football games, and the number of actual club members was even smaller, but most of the neighborhood residents identified themselves as sympathizers or fans of the main local football club. This was the case, for example, with San Lorenzo in Boedo, Nueva Chicago in Mataderos, and Vélez Sarsfield in Villa Luro.[9] It would also be the case with Atlanta in Villa Crespo, but only from 1943 onward. (See Table 4.2.)

Many other football clubs had embarked on a similar process of strengthening ties in the barrio and expanding social activities or accommodating additional sports. From the 1910s on, the Buenos Aires middle class began to take over spheres of public recreation that were once the prerogative of the elite—including both sports and social activities. The clubs met the new

TABLE 4.2 Neighborhood football clubs

Barrio	Number of Football Clubs	Representative Football Club
Almagro	6	Almagro
Villa Crespo Chacarita	15	Atlanta Chacarita Juniors
Boedo	6	San Lorenzo
Caballito	3	Ferrocarril Oeste
Boca		Boca Juniors
Belgrano	6	Defensores de Belgrano Excursionistas
Saavedra		Platense
Paternal		Argentinos Juniors
Floresta	3	All Boys
Villa Luro		Vélez Sársfield
Parque Patricios Pompeya	7	Huracán
Mataderos	12	Nueva Chicago
San Telmo		San Telmo
Barracas	8	Sportivo Barracas Barracas Central
Villa Urquiza	4	
Santa Rita	6	
Villa Devoto	15	
Total	91	17

Source: Julio D. Frydenberg, "Los sectores populares: porteños y el fútbol durante las tres primeras décadas del siglo XX" (PhD diss., Universidad de Buenos Aires, 2008), 179–80.

demands in many ways. In their study of the social dimension of Club Atlético River Plate in the early twentieth century, Rodrigo Daskal and Mariano
Gruschetsky mention various practices adopted by the club, such as giving
other institutions the use of its land as a means of legitimizing the club's local
rights. It was a way of validating its place in the neighborhood vis-à-vis both
the local population and the public authorities. This is how River Plate, for
instance, was able, after moving to the Alvear y Tagle Stadium, to successfully
transfer its previous identification with La Boca to its new neighborhood, Palermo. In Atlanta's case this policy can be seen even more clearly in its decision
to rent space to Chacarita when the rival club needed it.

Around this time all the clubs were similarly engaged in developing various social activities and additional sports; Independiente was one example.[10]
However this process also gave rise to internal friction when it came to setting club priorities, pitting those who were interested in nothing but football
against those who also attributed importance to the club's role as a social center. When this conflict came up in the aforementioned Club Independiente in
1925, it was decided to give priority to acquiring property for a soccer pitch,
but once construction of the pitch was completed in 1928 the club's board of
directors focused its efforts on building a clubhouse, an objective they accomplished in 1936 when they inaugurated the current building in Avenida Mitre.
The new clubhouse was equipped with a covered pool, an indoor ball court, a
gym, and a café.

Anniversaries, Patriotic Commemorations, and Dance Parties

In Atlanta in the early 1920s one of the officers was still insisting that "since our
institution is one of those that only specialize in the sport of football," other
activities were of lesser importance.[11] This view would not disappear in the following years, but after the club's move to Villa Crespo those who favored the
idea of developing other activities gained the upper hand.

Before it had celebrated its fifth anniversary, the club decided to diver-
sify its activities with a program of competitions for members that included
a needle-threading race, a 100-meter dash, a sack race, a relay race, and a 50-
meter egg-and-spoon race. In 1910, the year of Argentina's centenary, the daily
La Nación donated a collection of books for the club library. In August of
that year negotiations were undertaken to acquire property at the corner of

Rivadavia and Muñiz for the establishment of a library and clubhouse. This deal, promoted by Manuel Montes de Oca, a senior government official, came to nothing, but it did mark the beginning of further development of social and cultural activities in the club.

Anniversary celebrations have been a recurrent activity in all the sports clubs, a symbolic means of constructing and maintaining collective identities. They began at a very early stage and helped popularize football and build neighborhood loyalties. In 1914 Atlanta celebrated its first decade, with the collaboration of several other clubs. A series of athletic events were held, culminating on the night of October 12 with a banquet held in the rooms of the Hotel de Mayo. This was the beginning of a tradition of celebrating anniversaries. In 1929 the club celebrated its silver jubilee. "It is a glorious date that obliges us to look at the past, understanding the enormous, titanic labor of those who preceded us," explained one of the directors.[12] The festivities included a theatrical soiree and a banquet to which sports writers were invited.

Patriotic commemorations were also opportunities to call the faithful together. In 1911 five subcommissions were appointed in Atlanta. One, obviously, focused on football; another on administrative matters, requests, and authorizations; the third dealt with the playing field; the fourth consisted of two librarians; and the fifth, precisely, was in charge of organizing celebrations in the form of festivals, tournaments, and patriotic demonstrations. In 1914, in order to raise funds to improve the facilities at the club's pitch—which at the time was still in Parque Chacabuco—a festival was organized on the historic site of the Buenos Aires Frontón (Córdoba and Libertad Streets), with popular dance music provided by a group of serenaders.

In the 1930s, each football club had its own anthem. The Chacarita Juniors song ended like this:

> Chacarita Juniors, clamores de triunfo
> será el gran campeón
> arriba, compañeros
> alta la frente
> de cara al sol.
> Chacarita Juniors, clamor de triunfo
> con fe, fuerza y valor
> sabrá romper las vallas
> luchando siempre
> por el honor.

[Chacaritas Juniors, cries of triumph
it will be the great champion
up comrades
head high
face to the sun.
Chacarita Juniors
cries of triumph
with faith, strength, and valor
will know how to break down the walls
always fighting for honor.][13]

Atlanta's first anthem in fact dates back to 1908. Ricardo Pérez Camino, who composed the music for it, was one of the members of Atlanta's board of directors at the time. However, Atlanta's best-known anthem was composed three decades later by the musician Juan Bava, a former member of the club (Atlanta membership card number 31) and a *bandoneón* player who directed a well-known dance band for many years. Of Italian immigrant descent, Bava was born in 1901 in Villa Crespo (at 37 Loyola Street). He had been a musician since childhood and had one of the first tango bands in the city, before the era of Troilo and others. His own band accompanied him in both the pseudo-cabarets and the neighborhood sports clubs, as was customary in those days. As a result, he played at Atlanta on numerous occasions.[14]

According to the club's 1943 annual report, on July 2 of that year Atlanta adopted as its official march a song composed by member Juan Bava with lyrics by Floreal. Atlanta's president at the time was Fernando Saccone, assisted by Alberto Chissotti as vice president and Luis Bianchi as secretary. The march was recorded on vinyl in 1938 with the voice of Carlos Bermúdez, who was the vocalist with Juan Bava's band. It was the first recording made by the man who also sang with Ciriaco Ortiz, Pedro Láurenz, and Horacio Salgán.

Marcha del Club Atlético Atlanta

Con la altivez de un buen varón
Quiero rendir un homenaje a tus colores.
¡O, viejo club! que al resurgir
Sabrás mostrar de tu pujanza los colores.
Pues hoy espera la afición
Que vuelva a brillar con bellos fulgores
Tu fiel pabellón y lleno de honores

Puedas afrontar con fe el porvenir.

¡Vamos, viejo club!

Alza tu voz cubierta de esplendores

¡Vamos a luchar

que el triunfo ideal te va a coronar!

¡Vamos, que el Sol del porvenir

habrá de cubrir tu marcha triunfal!

¡Vamos a la lucha, vamos viejo Atlanta

Que siempre mi aplauso te habrá de alentar!

[Atlanta Athletic Club March

With the pride of a good man

I want to pay tribute to your colors.

Oh, old club! that coming back to life

You will know how to show the colors of your strength.

For today the fans are expecting

Your trusty and honorable banner

To shine once again with beautiful brilliance

May you face the future with faith.

Come on, old club!

Raise your splendid voice

We will fight

that you may be crowned by the ideal triumph!

Come on, may the sun of the future

have to cover your triumphal march!

Let's join the struggle, let's go, old Atlanta

My applause must always encourage you!]

This march was played for many years over the stadium's loudspeakers before each game.

Another very common practice in the clubs from an early stage—and Atlanta was no exception—was the organization of friendly games and other events for the benefit of different associations, including dances, sports fairs, and artistic festivals. The purpose of many of these events was to raise money in order to pay for stadium improvements or other club projects. In fact, from the 1920s on all the clubs regularly held dances, called variously dance festivals, family dances, dancing matinées, or dancing soirées.[15]

As for the infrastructure of the clubs, from the 1920s through the 1940s there were two priorities: the playing field and the club headquarters or clubhouse, in that order. In this respect, Atlanta underwent something of a change between the mid-1930s and the mid-1940s, during the presidencies of Fernando Saccone and Alberto Chissotti. Thanks to the vision of various board members, the clubhouse began to take on greater importance. In 1933 the municipality closed half of Padilla Street, and Atlanta seized the opportunity to build a bocce court there. In the following years bocce would be one of the club's most representative sports—possibly an indication of the significant presence of Argentines of Italian descent both in the neighborhood and in the club. Atlanta also contracted with a consortium to build a cafeteria, a restaurant, a hall for dances and social functions, and a skating rink and dance floor. A group of members fought hard against this initiative and the signed contract, arguing that football had to remain the absolute priority.

The club's 1936 report stated that the plan to build a social and sports annex had been achieved with the construction of this facility on the lot adjoining the stadium. "We have already been able to hold the carnival and end-of-year dance parties there, in a setting consistent with the importance and prestige that these events have acquired."[16] The speedy construction of a tennis court, skating rink, children's playground, and other amenities was promised. The premises measured 4,500 square meters, surrounded by a stone wall. The property was landscaped with trees and flowering plants. In one part of the annex a basketball court had already been installed. "Given the great number of supporters this game has been gaining," explained the report, "we believe it will be a big success with the Club members."[17] In 1938 the Campeonato Relámpago de Cadetes (Cadets' Lightning Tournament) was organized in the club, drawing the participation of several basketball teams and the attendance of a substantial audience. Club Sportivo Barracas took home the top honors. The following year the club's anniversary was celebrated with a dance, a boxing festival, and a women's basketball tournament. In 1940 the club's report mentioned very proudly (if somewhat paternalistically):

A significant event of transcendental importance for the course of this sport has taken place this year in Women's Basketball. We are referring to the Novicias team, which, after a successful season in which they remained undefeated, won the championship in their category, thus winning the right to compete in the 1st Division. The fact that the women's team was made up of players who had learned most of what they knew of the sport in our institution, and that they put into these friendly skirmishes all the affection they feel for it, makes their already worthy triumph even more pleasing and valid.[18]

The importance of Atlanta's "dance parties" was growing noticeably in each new season, as they attracted an enormous and heterogeneous attendance. These parties offered young people opportunities for socializing and courtship with the opposite sex. In the case of the young Jews in the neighborhood, they also provided a possible avenue for meeting and dating young people of other ethnicities.

The year 1936, according to the club's financial report, began with a 40 percent increase in the number of participants at these dances. Their significance lay in the fact that "besides being an enjoyable show for the members, it is a substantial source of funds."[19] The following year the club officers could already boast that the popularity gained by these events "gives our dances a prominent place among all those in the Capital."[20] In response to criticism from some of the members who saw football and nothing else as the club's purpose, the leadership defended its actions by emphasizing the "healthy social recreation" constituted by these events and noting that the New Year's and Epiphany celebrations were particularly important for "gathering the families of all the members in our clubhouse for the traditional holidays."

Analysis of the club's income in 1936 and 1937 shows the economic importance of these social gatherings. The carnival dances of 1936 earned the club 13,640.64 pesos, which, added to the 1,665.30 pesos raised by the festivals, totaled 15,305.94 compared with 17,673.47 pesos in 1937—the result of an organized advertising campaign and the importance that these festivities had gained over time. In contrast, the income from football games came to $64,761.17, compared to $49,762.22 in 1936.[21] In other words, the income from the dances represented between one-quarter and one-third of the income from professional football—no paltry sum. The club's 1938 report is clouded by pessimism as it discusses the club's financial situation, the dwindling number of members (who at year's end totaled fewer than three thousand), and an athletic capacity that did not augur well for a brighter future enhanced by ever-higher honors. The only ray of light appeared during carnival time, when the usual dances were held in the social-sports annex. This grand event, attended by celebrities from the radio and the cultural scene, once again proved itself as an outstanding fund-raiser.[22]

Thus, by the second half of the 1930s Atlanta had become known for its big fiestas and dances accompanied by major orchestras and bands: Feliciano Brunelli, Osvaldo Pugliese, Rodolfo O. Biaggi, Maffia, Láurenz, the Santa Paula Serenaders, Juan D'Arienzo, and others. President Saccone ordered the construction of an enormous wooden dance floor that covered the entire football field in addition to the open-air tracks and the hall and basketball court—all with wood from the Saccone y Borla company.

The 1940s was the decade in which tango and the great tango orchestras flourished; young people commonly followed their favorite bands to any club where they were performing.[23] In Atlanta the aforementioned open-air dance floor attracted the most popular tango groups and their followers—including bands such as Juan D'Arienzo, Alfredo de Angelis, Canaro, Tanturi, and Di Sarli.[24] Seeing how successful the club's social life was, President Fernando Saccone decided to extend the dance floor, a move he never had cause to regret.[25] In the following decades many nationally known figures appeared on that floor, including Leopoldo Marechal, Ben Molar, Osvaldo Pugliese, Paquita Bernardo, Alberto Vaccarezza, Esteban Celedonio Flores, and the charming Discepolín.[26] All this gave Atlanta a unique importance in the formation of the Buenos Aires identity, as one of the most distinctive clubs in the capital city.

In the early 1940s the club's development and advancement were a source of great satisfaction for the officers as well as the members. In the annual reports a tone of optimism replaced the pessimism that often colored the statements of the 1930s; insecurity gave way to self-confidence. The increased number of members, which now exceeded six thousand, the expansion of sports activities, the beginning of construction on a new clubhouse, and the purchase of land for a new stadium all contributed to "a fundamental change in the aspect of the club."[27] In 1941 a banquet was organized to honor the former presidents of the club. They included the first standard-bearer, Elías Sanz (1904–5); Trifón Poggio (1906); *La Nación* journalist Augusto De Muro (1907–9); Juan J. Enrich (1910–18); physician and former councilor of the federal capital Alberto J. Sanguinetti (1926–27); José Minutto (1929), who had significantly increased the number of members; Francisco A. Rocca (1932), the social reformer (whose proposal to build the clubhouse outside the neighborhood in Segurola Street, on land he himself owned, had been rejected); the last president of the era before the advent of foreign players, Antonio Sturla (1932); Fernando Saccone (1936–38), who during his presidency came to the club's rescue with strong financial support; Damián Ciancio (1939); and the incumbent president, Santiago Bascialla.

In one of the speeches made on this occasion, the veteran partner and life member Jacinto Boix emphasized that

> Club Atlanta has taken a transcendentally important step in its sporting life by getting its own field, acquired by a group of partners. . . . Today begins a new era that allows us to look towards the future with optimism; we will cease to be a Club that passes its years without ambitions, without ideals, vegetating in the practice of football; we have a more important role to play, to provide Villa Crespo with the great social institution of sports, to carry it to the same heights as the greatest in the country. . . . [28]

On May 21, 1942, Club Atlético Atlanta's new clubhouse in Humboldt Street was officially inaugurated, with various activities and sports demonstrations.[29] The banquet guests included the president of the Argentine Football Association, Ramón Castillo (Jr.) (son of the vice president of the Republic, Ramón S. Castillo, who would become president upon the death of Roberto Ortiz in mid-July); the president of the South American Sports Confederation; and the president of the Football Association of Chile, Luis Valenzuela.[30] The festivities organized to celebrate the club's thirty-eighth anniversary that year reflected both a vibrant and diverse civil society and the club's own importance and deep social roots in the community. Atlanta sponsored the First Great Olympics of Villa Crespo, held on October 10, 11, and 12. In these competitions all the clubs active in the area met under the blue-and-gold banner: Club Social Villa Crespo, Círculo Israelita de Villa Crespo, Agrupación Juvenil y Democrática Alerta, Peñarol, Argentino, Social y Deportivo Michael Doura, Social y Deportivo Fulgor, Social Febo, Palermo Juniors, Círculo Gurruchaga, Acción Argentina (Sec. Juv. V. Crespo), Social Suipacha, Social Morfones, Social y Deportivo Monte Carlo, Social y Deportivo Bernardino Rivadavia, Maldonado Foot-Ball Club, Darwin Foot-Ball Club, Club Villa Malcolm, Social y Deportivo Los Indios, and Ciclón de Warnes. Several clubs from other districts sent representatives to these celebratory games, including River Plate, Huracán, Racing, and Asociación Hebrea Macabi. These "Olympics" included football, basketball, table tennis, fencing, gymnastics, judo, hockey, bicycle races, figure-skating exhibitions, weightlifting, and others.

That same year saw the inauguration of the skating rink, at the time considered one of the largest on the continent, and a venue for large-scale events.

The inauguration ceremony was attended by representatives of clubs that were already practicing figure skating, such as River Plate, Boca Juniors, and Racing. In 1943 handball was added to the sports activities offered by Atlanta. Thus, in the early 1940s the club was affiliated with the Argentine Football Association, the Argentine Boxing Federation, and the Argentine Skating Federation, and it had applied for membership in the Bocce Federation, the Argentine Tennis Federation, the Argentine Table Tennis Federation, and the Chess Federation.[31] In an effort to promote the latter, Atlanta participated in the Campeonato de Ajedrez Interclubs de Foot-Ball (a chess tournament between football clubs) in 1942. It also organized the first children's drawing contest.[32]

Around that time the club also became involved in track and field, with 100- to 10,000-meter races, 4 × 100-meter and 4 × 400-meter relay races, javelin throwing, and shot put, among other events. In addition, at the end of the 1930s Atlanta was represented in the International Grand Prix and the Argentine Grand Prix races, the most important car races of the time, by three racing drivers: Osvaldo Parmigiani, Rosendo Hernández, and Domingo Marimón.[33]

By this time the club's policy of expanding the range of sports played by its members was well established. In 1940 it declared "The board considers that without ceasing to devote every attention needed to football, it is imperative, in order to curry the interest of some and gain new support, to include other sports and intensify [sic] the existing ones,"[34] which, in this case, meant tennis, volleyball, bocce, skating, and roller hockey.

Nonetheless, professional football was clearly still the most popular sport. The club leadership called it "a semaphore" that signaled the level of the institution's progress and prestige. At the same time, football represented an enormous investment:

> Professional football is the modern ten-headed dragon. It demands, always demands. Powerful team, victories, elements that raise the team's standing, big salaries, big prizes. Members want to experience victories, joys repeated Sunday after Sunday, and to satisfy this desire the teams must be given potentiality, and the pace imposed by professionalism requires the acquisition of valuable players that provide that power, and to do this the pesos reach amounts representing expenditures that absorb everything football yields, without ever attaining the income needed to satisfy its maintenance and renovation needs. . . . [35]

In this context it is worth noting the growing emphasis on amateur football—the source of players who could fill in on the professional team, thereby
avoiding some of the expenses of contracting players from other clubs.

Since Atlanta's first entry into professionalism, the achievements of its first-
division team had not been impressive. During 1931 and 1932, it placed eighteenth among the eighteen clubs, and sixteenth in 1933. In 1934 it placed last of
the fourteen contending clubs. In 1935 it was in fifteenth place out of eighteen.
Its best year in this period was 1936, when it placed sixth. The following year it
fell to thirteenth out of eighteen, in 1938 it was ninth out of seventeen, and in
the last year of the decade it was sixteenth out of eighteen clubs. It repeated this
performance in 1940. In 1941 it finished in eleventh place (out of sixteen clubs),
in 1942 it was in fifteenth place, and in 1943 it once again occupied the eleventh
place among the sixteen clubs competing in the first division. (See Table 4.3.)

The club officers could draw some consolation from the growing number
of members, "the cornerstone whereon rests the grandeur" of a sports institution; from 2,984 at the end of 1938 the total increased to 3,771 at the end of 1939
and 4,818 in 1940.

To finish up this chapter in the life of the club, mention should be made
of the forced move of Chacarita Juniors from the Villa Crespo neighborhood,
after Atlanta bought the land on which the rival team was headquartered.[36]
This was the end of an era in which both clubs shared the neighborhood, and
the beginning of a new phase in which Atlanta was the only football team to
rule in Villa Crespo.

TABLE 4.3   Atlanta's rankings, 1931–1943

Year	Clubs	Rank
1931	18	18
1932	18	18
1933	18	16
1934	14	14
1935	18	15
1936	18	6
1937	18	13
1938	17	9
1939	18	16
1940	18	16
1941	16	11
1942	16	15
1943	16	11

Source: Author's elaboration.

Atlanta's humble origins and its nickname of "*bohemio*" assured the club of the sympathy of the lower middle class in Villa Crespo, on the one hand, and intellectuals and leftists, on the other. After all, gypsies supposedly scorn material possessions, value simple habits, and are dedicated to the artistic or the intellectual life. The presence of Communist directors in the club, especially León Kolbowski, imposed this image of a progressive club from which it would benefit for several decades.

The Origins of the Rivalry Between Atlanta and Chacarita Juniors

On May 1, 1906, the former members of the recently defunct Club Defensores de Villa Crespo decided to meet at the hall belonging to the Socialist Party at the intersection of Dorrego Street and Córdoba Avenue and create Club Chacarita Juniors. It was named after the home neighborhood of the club's founders, although in 1919 other names were proposed: "Jorge Newbery," in honor of the pioneer of Argentine aviation; "General Soler"; or "Defensores de Maldonado." In the end they kept the name Chacarita Juniors.[37]

The fact that the club's founders met on the premises of the Socialist Party is not unique, but neither is it axiomatic. The left-wing movements' views on football at the end of the nineteenth century and beginning of the twentieth were characteristically ambivalent. The anarchists, for example, argued that "you can't fight against exploitation by kicking a ball."[38] Not a few Socialists and Communists warned of the danger of "bourgeois employers' clubs," and in the 1920s and 1930s they fought against "the snares of professionalism" and promoted an alternative sports culture, "healthy workers' sports" or "emancipating red sports."[39]

The founders of Chacarita Juniors chose for their jersey the colors red, white, and black—a choice that, according to one version, was motivated by a gift from the prominent Gath & Chaves department store where several of the members worked. The official explanation, however, is that the color red denotes the blood of the people, white is for purity, and black is for the cemetery that is one of the neighborhood's central landmarks.[40]

Initially Chacarita seemed to be facing the same destiny as its future neighbors, the destiny that earned Atlanta the nickname "gypsies": the inability to find a permanent home. Nevertheless, the club stayed in the same neighborhood, and in the early 1920s it acquired the land encompassed by

Murillo, Darwin, Padilla, and Humboldt Streets. This field was only one hundred meters away from Atlanta's old soccer pitch and across from its current stadium; there Chacarita played its home games until 1930. This was how the two clubs first encountered each other, but since the two teams competed in different divisions, it was not until 1927 that they actually played each other, in a game that Chacarita won 2–0.[41] On June 4, 1931, in the early stages of professional football, the two neighbors confronted each other again, this time victory going 3–1 to Atlanta, the visiting team.

As Chacarita kept gaining more fans, the club decided to build a stadium large enough to accommodate them. Construction began at 300 Humboldt Street (a block away from Atlanta), reaching completion in 1932, when the new stadium was inaugurated with a game against Nacional de Montevideo, which the local team won 3–0.[42]

The supporters of both Chacarita Juniors and Atlanta lived and mingled in the same part of Buenos Aires, Atlanta having more fans in the Villa Crespo neighborhood and Chacarita dominating in the neighborhood from which it took its name—the reason being that Atlanta, unlike Chacarita, retained its headquarters in Villa Crespo.[43] However, Atlanta differed from Chacarita not only in the number of its supporters, but also in its social base. Atlanta had apparently won the passion and allegiance of the residents of the area around Avenida Corrientes, that is, middle-class and lower-middle-class people, frequently Socialist in outlook, who lived in rented rooms and *conventillos* and trusted that progress would bring social mobility to them and to their children. Chacarita, by contrast, if we may generalize, was more strongly rooted in the area of *la cueva* ("the cave"), which crossed Dorrego Street and the railroad lines, a poorer area occupied by a more underdeveloped population living in public housing. However, of these two neighboring clubs, the older brother was Chacarita. During the 1930s, the magazine *La Cancha* promoted a series of jigsaw puzzles made from the photographs of the eight most important squads of Argentine football, which included none from Atlanta, but did include Chacarita.

Atlanta was none too pleased with the fact that two football teams shared the same neighborhood, with their playing fields right next to each other. Moreover, throughout the 1930s there was friction with the owner of the field that Atlanta had rented since 1922, Mr. Dufour. Thus, for example, July 1938 saw the occurrence of

an event as serious as it was unexpected, when the owner went to court requesting, on the grounds of two months' arrears in the rent, the cancellation
of the rental contract and our eviction from the premises, which were highly
coveted by two major companies—we are certain—a fact that may have been
behind Mr. Owner's unadvised attitude. All of this raised the fear that we
would not be able to reach a satisfactory solution, even by complying with the
exorbitant demand made upon us.[44]

Once more the threat of having to find and move to a new home loomed
on the horizon. The contract in force until then was due to expire in 1942.
After a series of negotiations by the club's officers, a new contract was signed
that amended the previous one with respect to both the rent, which increased
by some 10 percent to one thousand pesos a month including taxes and sewer
fees, and the term, which would now run until 1945.

Toward the end of 1941 an opportunity arose to buy the adjacent properties,
which Chacarita Juniors occupied by municipal license. At the time there were
two lawsuits pending between the owner of the land and Chacarita, one for eviction for failure to pay the rent and the other to determine the rent due. Atlanta
leaped at this opportunity. To finance the purchase of the field and construction
of a new stadium, the Sociedad de Tierras de Villa Crespo (Villa Crespo Land
Company) was created. It was affiliated with the club, and many local residents
were stockholders. On November 12, the Society signed a sales contract. The deal
cost a total of some 475,000 pesos, including a down payment of 34,000 pesos
at the time of signing, 64,000 pesos to be paid when the deed of ownership was
signed, and the rest to be paid in five annual payments of 75,000 pesos each.

For Atlanta it was extremely important to emphasize from the moment it
bought the property that in doing so it had "intended no harm to Club Chacarita Juniors; rather the main motive behind the operation was the circum-
stance of being able to provide our club with a proper stadium, and the public
fact that the neighboring institution had been sued for eviction, and besides
said property had been offered to a major industry by the intermediary of the
Banco Francés del Río de la Plata."[45]

Less important than the veracity or accuracy of this version is the fact that
for Chacarita's fans at the time and those who came after them the sale looked
like a legally dubious operation carried out by stealth, "an operation never
well explained by those with better memories, nor by the club minutes, nor by
the communication media of the time."[46]

The commentary published in the daily *La Nación* described the land purchase as carried out "on a weekday, without stridency, in the greatest silence, a silence that can sometimes also be fertile." Reference was made to "a project that has come to maturation with surprising speed," accomplished by a group of prominent members, some of them veterans of the club's earliest days, each one agreeing to contribute a certain monthly sum, up to 2,500 pesos, thus creating in effect a corporation.[47] Atlanta decided to keep the property it was renting to use for practice, lower-division games, and other activities. Atlanta's leadership was very aware from the beginning of the possible interpretation of its purchase, and so to clarify its position it felt obliged to publish a statement through its representative in the Argentine Football Association rejecting the accusations expressed by Chacarita Juniors. This document is important enough to warrant quoting a few paragraphs:

> In recognition of various rumors circulating relative to the sale of the property . . . which are completely unfounded, Club Atlético Atlanta feels it necessary to reestablish the truth . . .
>
> It is inexact that the main thought of the directors of Club Atlético Atlanta . . . was the memory of the events of September 1934, when the delegate of Club Chacarita Juniors, in his character as member of a special commission, drafted and defended the report ruling that all the members of the Argentine Football Association should sign an undertaking expelling Club Atlético Atlanta from its ranks.
>
> This measure was not carried out because those representing our Club at the time demonstrated the inconsistency of the accusations expressed, and were perfectly understood by the other clubs, which decided to name Dr. Ernesto F. Malbec as *interventor* in our institution.
>
> This episode has been completely forgotten by Club Atlanta, which is steadfast in its intention to strengthen as much as possible the cordial relations it maintains with all the institutions that form the Argentine Football Association.[48]

The aversion toward Chacarita is clearly reflected in Atlanta's club minutes. In 1943, when the club's directors were discussing ways to settle Atlanta's debts, they spoke of possibly raising club dues, recruiting new members, "and greater box office receipts from football games, as long as only one institution is active in the Villa Zona area."[49] One of the members, Rodolfo Duchini, opined on this occasion that "whatever investment might have been made to oust Chacarita Juniors . . . would be negligible if you take into account the moral and material ways in which [Chacarita] helped injure the institution in 1934." Duchini was referring once more to the supposed role that Chacarita had played in the pressure the AFA brought to bear on the small clubs, including Atlanta, in the mid-1930s when it was trying to merge the professional and amateur leagues. That is, Atlanta was convinced that for some years Chacarita had been working to evict it from the neighborhood.

When it comes to the conflict between the two Villa Crespo rivals, it seems that much water has run through the Maldonado stream, at least during the decade before the purchase of Chacarita's playing field. In any case, that purchase evicted Chacarita from its stadium and forced it to move to a new place.[50] The acquisition of this property meant that a dream long nurtured by Atlanta finally came true, and this was also what opened the way for the young vice president of the Land Company, León Kolbowski, to take his place among the directors of the club, where he promoted the project of building a new stadium.

Chacarita Juniors' new home was the neighborhood of Villa Diehl, in the San Martín district,[51] but its clubhouse remained in the Chacarita barrio. Seventeen years later, Atlanta built a stadium on the site of Chacarita's old stadium.[52] According to Ariel Korob:

> It is on the basis of [Atlanta's] always precarious situation that the most "unprecedented" idea for survival arose: the destruction of the enemy. . . . [T]he overvaluation of the stadium and territorial roots have been the godparents to Chacarita Juniors' disappearance from the neighborhood. There has been perhaps no previous occasion in professional football where the fiercest adversary has been eliminated so successfully. This has been the case with Chacarita, which by its proximity was considered to be the greatest threat to Atlanta's existence—an emotional climate generating fears that contributed to the production of fantasies that resulted in Chacarita's expulsion from the neighborhood once the opportunity arose.[53]

Having its own playing field was very important to Atlanta in its efforts to be considered a true Club, with a capital "C." After all, one of the conditions that the AFA imposed on its affiliate clubs was having a soccer pitch of their own. From the beginning, it was a fundamental requirement for entry into professional football. Accordingly, when Atlanta finally achieved this milestone, it exaggerated its importance—as if all the existential fears caused by the long absence of a home stadium had disappeared with the stroke of a pen. As it happened, the club would end up investing most of its energy during the years up to 1943 in improving and maintaining this small stadium (known as "*el cajoncito*," or "the little box," as well as "*el pañuelito*," or "the little handkerchief"), since the precariousness of its facilities kept it in constant danger of being closed down.

In the meantime, for the next two years Chacarita continued to play its games in a field owned by its most hated neighbor, before it finally moved to San Martín. During this period the money taken in for the sale of seats at the games went to Club Atlanta, but Chacarita Juniors' board members and subscribers were allowed in free. At least a few people in Atlanta apparently felt rather satisfied by this supposed humiliation of Chacarita. In any case, Atlanta's acquisition of land of its own on which to build its stadium was considered "the most important, transcendent deed accomplished by the Club since its foundation." The club's 1945 report contained the following statement: "Atlanta . . . has been alive for 40 years and only now, it may be said, is beginning to live."[54]

5

IN THE SHADOW OF PERONISM

The 1940s were a time of prosperity for the Atlanta football club, particularly after Juan Perón assumed the nation's presidency in 1946. Even before that, the CAA had been gradually increasing its institutional estate; it inaugurated its clubhouse in 1942 and bought the adjoining land that Chacarita Juniors had been renting. Building a clubhouse greatly benefited the club because it gave the members a meeting place, provided amenities, and allowed membership to grow, which was a fundamental factor in any club's development. The member roster listed nine thousand names. It is true that eliminating all those in arrears with their dues reduced this number, but there were still a good six thousand left.

The club report published in early 1943 reflected a level of satisfaction and self-confidence unknown in the 1930s: "Atlanta, whose progress is eloquently revealed, continues to develop at a dizzying rate and in a manner very satisfying to those who have fondly continued to follow its evolution. . . . [T]he healthy direction of its finances has impelled the institution forward, allowing it to work in new directions oriented towards channeling its extensive construction program . . . [which] confirm[s] our optimism concerning the future of the institution."[1] The club's sights were set on building a new stadium, and the modest successes of the first-division team did not diminish these hopes.

Another expression of Atlanta's prestige could be seen in the foundation of an eponymous club, Club Atlanta de Rosario, in the city of Rosario. At the beginning of 1943 the veteran Atlanta donated a cup to its namesake, to be contested for in that city. On the occasion of a game with Newells Old Boys in Rosario, a reception was held in honor of the Buenos Aires Atlanta's officers. In April of the same year a support group, the Círculo Bohemio del Abasto, had been founded. A small group of members who worked in the Almagro neighborhood market presented a plan to the board of directors detailing ways they could help promote the club's progress, adopting the motto, "For a great Atlanta." And they did indeed contribute to the recruitment of new members.[2]

In addition to the dances that helped raise funds and strengthen connections with the neighborhood population, a film festival was organized in the Villa Crespo movie theater to benefit Atlanta's social department fund. The event, held in September 1944, enjoyed the participation of noted radio personalities such as Osvaldo Miranda and Elías Fort, the poet and artist Héctor Gagliardi, and the orchestra of Pedro Láurenz and singer Roberto Quiroga. The festival culminated with a showing of the film *La Guerra Gaucha*, which premiered in November 1942 and was directed by Lucas Demare, with a screenplay by Homero Manzi and Ulyses Petit de Murat. Based on the book of the same name by Leopoldo Lugones (1905), it is considered one of the most successful films of Argentine cinema. As a result, this festival "constituted an absolute triumph, both socially and economically."[3] The following year the film festival included a less "nationalistic" film: *Romeo and Juliet*.

Football's national and patriotic character was especially notable in the celebrations of the club's thirty-ninth anniversary, which took place between October 9–12, 1943, under the new, de facto military government that had assumed power in June.[4] The program included football, basketball, and roller-hockey games, figure skating, a parade and show by gymnastic groups, native dances and recreational games, track-and-field events, a fencing exhibition, Charlie Chaplin imitations by Amar Montaño, and the famous evening dances, as well as the blessing of the national flag and an open-air mass accompanied by the military brass band of the General San Martín Grenadiers Regiment. The ceremonial "queen" was a club member, Selma Filomena de Arata, and the ceremonial "king" was none other than the president of Chacarita Juniors, Jesús Pravia. The Círculo Criollo El Rodeo, a cultural heritage organization, put on a parade, and there were also equestrian displays and regional songs and dances.

In 1944 the football team managed to improve its performance, achieving the eighth slot in the league table, as shown in Table 5.1 below. The goalkeeper Jaime Rotman had left the club, but scorer José Lighterman contributed to the "brilliant performance of the first-division team" with seven goals.[5]

In the mid-1940s, the club expanded its athletic activities and added new sports. It diversified its offerings to members by adding amateur football, micro soccer (the field for this was built out of wood donated by member Felipe Caletrio), track and field, skating, basketball, handball, hockey, and chess.

TABLE 5.1   Atlanta's rankings, 1944–1958

Year	Clubs	Rank	Division
1944	16	8	First
1945	16	11	First
1946	16	15	First
1947	16	16	First
1948		Tournament suspended by players' strike. Atlanta was promoted to the first division that year (there is no data on the final rankings and number of teams in the tournament).	Second
1949	18	14	First
1950	19	14	First
1951	17	15	First
1952	16	16	First
1953	18	2	Second
1954	18	4	Second
1955	18	5	Second
1956	18	1	Second
1957	16	12	First
1958	16	4	First

Source: Author's elaboration.

Atlanta's track-and-field team was noted for its achievements, which earned it praise from the magazine *La Cancha* in October 1945: "Club A. Atlanta has achieved a rank in freestyle track and field that places it on a nearly exclusive level in this activity, and all thanks to the obvious quality of its athletes."[6] The same year saw the triumph of Pedro Caffa of Atlanta in the twelfth Barrios Marathon (Maratón de los Barrios), an event organized every year by the magazine *El Gráfico* and in which Caffa beat almost six hundred rivals from all over Argentina as well as neighboring countries.[7]

In 1944 the Department of Intellectual Education was created for the purpose of the "cultural improvement of all children, especially members and offspring of the Institution who desire it."[8] To this end schoolteachers and university professors were recruited from among the club membership. A couple of years later a small playground was inaugurated at the club's center.

In mid-1946 the deed transferring the property at 300–400 Humboldt Street was signed. The Villa Crespo Land Company proceeded to carry out its mandate, ceding to Club Atlético Atlanta, upon payment of 625,000 pesos, all the rights vested in that property. Then, having fulfilled the purpose for which it had been created—acquiring this land as a site for the club's new sports facility—the company ceased to operate.

The transfer to Atlanta of the River Plate idol Adolfo Pedernera in 1947 created a huge sensation in Argentine football. However, the enthusiasm did not last long, since at the end of that season the club was relegated to the second division for the first time in its history. Fortunately, its stay there was brief because the AFA cancelled relegations in all the divisions in 1948 and decreed the promotion of Atlanta and Ferro to the top flight.

In addition to the thrill of returning to the first division, the club was enjoying a rich social and cultural life. That same year the carnivals benefited from the collaboration of tango artist Osvaldo Pugliese, who played at eight dances. These kinds of events were very popular not only in the neighborhood but throughout the city, attracting prominent artists and media coverage. In the carnivals of the following two years the festivities were conducted by the comic actor José Marrone and the *bandoneón* player Alberto Mancione.

Atlanta's popularity was further boosted by the growing state support of all sports typical of the Peronist decade (1946–55). In fact, so notable was that support that one of the first steps taken by the self-proclaimed Liberating Revolution that overthrew General Perón in September 1955 and tried to eradicate every vestige of the deposed regime was a "de-Peronization of sports." This consisted in boycotting some of the most prominent athletes of the country, identified with the Peronist "tyranny," and intervening in the Football Association and the Argentine Olympic Committee, as well as other institutions. One of the last measures taken by the military officers who led that de facto government, shortly before the general elections of 1958 and the transfer of command to a civil government, was to shut down the Dirección de Deportes y Educación Física (the sports and physical education department) in the Ministry of Education and Justice. In the decree published by the minister of education, the following reasons were given for this step:

> The deposed government turned the organization and teaching of physical education and sports into an instrument of political propaganda, corrupting and subverting their true values and significance. . . .
>
> Physical education, as a subject of instruction, does not merit preferential treatment or treatment different from that extended to other school subjects.

> On the contrary, [in Argentina] physical education has never been considered a compulsory subject or been included in the core curriculum, and pupils attending gymnastics practice [outside of school] or whose health might suffer were excused from it.[9]

These measures reflected the anti-Peronists' sweeping identification of athletic activity in general, and sports for children and young people in particular, with "the deposed regime." The opponents of the Peronist regime saw the regime's encouragement and promotion of sports during the years 1946–55 as additional proof of its "Nazi-Fascist" character. Again and again they recalled the way the Nazis in Germany and the Fascists in Italy had tried to exploit sport for political purposes. When the Peronist regime successfully organized the World Basketball Championship in 1950 and, a year later, the first Pan-American Games, in Buenos Aires, critics lost no time in comparing these events to the world soccer tournament organized by Benito Mussolini in 1934 or the Olympics hosted by Adolf Hitler's regime in Berlin in 1936.[10]

Although the regime's enemies, seeking to demonize Peronism in every way possible, were obviously exaggerating, certainly no Argentine government prior to Perón—and probably none since—invested as much effort and as many resources both in the development and encouragement of sports and in the effort to earn political dividends from this policy.[11] Peronism used sports for the dual purpose of reshaping the Argentine national consciousness in the spirit of *justicialismo* (as the Peronist ideology was called, from the word *justicia*, or "justice"), and mobilizing support for and loyalty to the regime and the personality cult of the president known as "el Primer Deportista" ("the First Athlete").

However, sports, like the education system during these years, was also an accommodating channel for democratization and popularization as well as political socialization and indoctrination. The regime encouraged amateur and competitive sports of various kinds for children and adults of both genders, not only in the capital but also in the provinces and national territories. This expansion of athletic activity was an expression of the regime's populist character.

In fact, as one of the spokespeople of the justicialist regime remarked with some exaggeration, Perón turned the country into one immense, clamorous stadium.[12] Various sports associations were allocated budgets from public funds. Tens of thousands of children from all over the Republic participated in the young people's tournaments named after Evita Perón. On many occasions Peronist deputies introduced motions in the National Congress to provide support for one provincial sports club or another.[13]

Peronism's promotion of sports should be seen as part of an effort to rehabilitate popular culture, characteristic of Latin American populist movements.[14] It must be remembered that sports—especially some branches, such as football—were part of the mass culture, creating a very broad common denominator. Sports were also a means of upholding the idea of social mobility, so important in Peronist Argentina. Outstanding athletes of humble origins helped emphasize, through their own accomplishments, that in the New Argentina it was an individual's talent, skill, and ability that determined his or her status, not social background.[15]

The vision Peronist Argentina upheld was of a modern, urban, industrialized society. For its leaders, sports represented progress and modernity, since sports activities in the twentieth century involved secularism, equal opportunity (to compete), bureaucratization (that is, administration and guidance), specialization, rationalization, and measurability (rules are set, ability is measured in terms of targets and achievement, and athletes train in order to make the most of their abilities).[16]

From the turn of the century up to the 1940s, sporting activity in Argentina was largely a private effort by various sports associations, while the state was conspicuous by its absence or apathy. Perón, in contrast, systematized state involvement in this sphere, and sought to establish a centralized supervisory system overseeing all sports. Measures to this end included the foundation of a new organization merging the Argentine Sports Confederation (Confederación Argentina Deportiva) with the Argentine Olympic Committee (Comité Olímpico Argentino) and known by the two bodies' combined acronym, CADCOA, as well as the appointment of Peronist activists to head the different sports associations and federations.[17]

Of course, in Peronist Argentina the encouragement of sports was also intended to serve the same purpose it had originally served in European countries since the turn of the century—namely, as a means of both controlling the masses, ensuring that they continued to perform their productive role in the economic system, and eradicating their "revolutionary potential." Sports competitions generally operated (and still do) as constructive, nonviolent outlets for instincts and urges that could be dangerous in political contexts. Sports became one of the central leisure pastimes of the urban working class.

Peronism seems to have promised workers bread (improved wages and working conditions) and circuses (harmless athletic activity). Years later the weekly
Primera Plana described the situation: "It was better [for the regime] that fa-
natics fought for sports trophies rather than political ones, that people remained divided in clubs and not in parties. The limitations Perón imposed on
political activities were thus compensated for by his solid support for sports,
in which Peronists and opposition members intermingled."[18]

One of Peronism's main goals was the establishment of "national unity,"[19]
and the "gospel of Peronist sports"—like the mobilization of the entire education system—was perceived as one of the more effective means to achieve that
goal and shape "the New Argentine" in "the New Argentina." Efforts were
made to weave sport into the fabric of Argentine society. Since various sports
clubs were traditionally linked with different groups of immigrants, Perón's
sports policy was also designed to encourage their cultural integration in the
national melting pot. Thus, Perón promoted sport as a mechanism for trans-
forming original identities in order to create both national unity and political loyalty to the regime. In January 1948 Perón declared, "As it happens, the
sporting environment is where differences disappear, where a camaraderie
superior to any other is born, and where a nobility and greatness of spirit are
formed that must be human beings' sole objective."[20]

Perón's interest in the subject was due, first, to the fact that he himself had
practiced many sports since childhood, especially after entering the Colegio
Militar (National Military College). A military fencing champion from 1918 to
1928,[21] Perón was slated to participate in the Olympic Games in Paris in 1924
and was greatly disappointed when Minister of War Agustín P. Justo refused
to authorize his trip. The young officer also organized several boxing competitions and in 1914 helped found a boxing club in Paraná, the first of its kind
outside Buenos Aires. In the following years he participated, to one extent or
another, in a wide range of sports, both in Argentina and abroad where he
served as a military attaché: gymnastics, horseback riding, rowing, football,
basketball, shooting, the high jump and the broad jump, boxing, polo, skiing,
and even fox hunting.

In addition to his own long-standing affinity for sports, early in his career as a statesman Perón realized the political potential they offered. This is
particularly evident in his attitude to the most popular of them all: football.
Football was not of any particular interest to him personally; boxing was
much more his "thing," and he preferred to be in the first rows of the Luna

Park ring where the major boxing tournaments were usually held rather than in the stands at a football pitch. Nonetheless, he allocated many resources and a great deal of attention to football, since week after week the stadiums attracted great crowds of people, a setup that, in addition to the emotion and drama generated by the game itself, was a convenient forum for disseminating propaganda and mobilizing these masses for political purposes.

Although it can hardly be contended that Perón preferred any particular club (unlike President Justo, a known fan of Boca Juniors),[22] in those years the regime was identified in particular with two popular teams: Racing, from Avellaneda, which won the championship three years in a row (1949, 1950, and 1951); and Boca Juniors, whose fans would maintain their Peronist links for decades. Ramón Cereijo, the finance minister, was a fan of Racing Club, which earned that team the nickname of "Deportivo Cereijo."

It was Cereijo who approved funding to various clubs to finance building and renovation projects. The most famous loan was made, predictably, to Racing for the construction of its stadium, named "Presidente Juan Domingo Perón" and officially opened in 1950. This impressive stadium boasted one hundred thousand seats and was a key venue for Argentina's staging of the first Pan-American Games.[23] In the first years of Peronism other stadiums were built as well, namely, those of Huracán (inaugurated in 1947) and Vélez Sarsfield (1950) in the federal capital, and that of Sarmiento in the city of Junín, Evita's hometown.[24] Statistics show a considerable increase in the number of spectators at football matches in those years.

Another major construction project, inaugurated in 1952, was the automobile racetrack in Buenos Aires, named "17 October" after the founding date of the Peronist movement.[25] The custom of naming stadiums, sports facilities, competitions, tournaments, and trophies after Juan or Eva Perón or using terms and concepts associated with justicialism constantly expanded during the Peronist decade.

Although Peronism preached the moral, esthetic, and healthful value of sports, it focused primarily on their potential to inspire fraternity, cooperation, social solidarity, national identity, discipline, and loyalty. Athletic activities were supposed to reflect the social achievements of Peronism, since it was the improvement in living conditions effected by Peronism that gave citizens of all social sectors—not just the middle and upper classes—the possibility of participating in sports.[26]

The nationalist, anti-imperialist dimension of the Peronist doctrine was a regular feature of official discourse on the importance of sports. Although most of the sports practiced in Argentina, including football, had been imported from other countries, Peronist Argentina wanted to be considered sovereign and independent in athletics as well as politics. In a 1949 speech, Perón called for the establishment of a separate, national, Argentine system for sports, claiming, "We have an Argentine cuisine, and we cannot accustom ourselves to other food; we have a music of our own. By the same token, we must have physical training and sports that are adapted to our people."[27]

Unsurprisingly, every Argentine achievement in the international athletic sphere was enthusiastically celebrated. This was especially true of the May 14, 1953, Argentine national football team's victory over England in Buenos Aires. A crowd of eighty-five thousand people, including Perón himself, filled the River Plate stadium and gave a standing ovation to the national team, which won 3–1. The goal scored by Ernesto Grillo is still remembered in Argentina, and since then May 14 has been celebrated as the Día del Futbolista (Day of the Football Player).[28]

Club Atlético Atlanta was, inevitably, influenced by national politics as it weathered first the military regime and then the first two Peronist governments. Although views and political loyalties in the Villa Crespo neighborhood were divided between the Peronists and those who continued to support the Unión Cívica Radical (UCR, Radical Civic Union) or the traditional parties of the left, the club's leaders understood the need to adapt to the behavior patterns expected by the national authorities.

The San Juan Earthquake: Atlanta Mobilizes

The bond between Atlanta and Juan and Evita Perón dated back to the beginning of 1944, when club members took up a collection to assist the victims of the San Juan earthquake. They were part of a nationwide wave of solidarity with the population of the province of San Juan, which suffered the loss of many lives as well as devastating material damage. In his book *The Ruins of the New Argentina*, Mark A. Healey argues that this disaster and the project to rebuild the province and particularly its capital transformed not only the province but also the nation. The earthquake was a stirring and galvanizing watershed event, an accusation against the old established social order and an open invitation to change it.[29]

Perón launched a campaign to mitigate the effects of the catastrophe and quickly initiated plans to rebuild the devastated province. This campaign proved to be a great success and a springboard for the public career of its director, who would soon found a movement, become president of the Republic, and transform the political and social structure of the country. Perón recruited radio personalities and local film stars to roam the streets of Buenos Aires collecting donations. Barely a week after the earthquake he organized a gala concert at Luna Park Stadium benefiting the earthquake victims. That night the celebrated announcer Roberto Galán introduced him to a radio soap opera actress named Eva Duarte, who from that moment would play a central role in the military man's ascending political career. Perón managed to mobilize the support of businessmen, union leaders, journalists, and athletes. He coordinated a wide range of fund-raising activities, including fashion shows, art exhibits, film showings, special opera and ballet events, and, of course, football games, the revenue from which went to charity. This last category even included Brazilian players, who contributed very generously.

A festival organized by Radio Belgrano at the Atlanta clubhouse raised the sum of 4,278 pesos, handed over to the Secretaría de Trabajo y Previsión (Secretariat of Labor and Social Welfare) headed by Colonel Juan Domingo Perón, for the relief of the San Juan victims. This was Atlanta's effort to mitigate the distress of the victims of the San Juan earthquake, which had left some ten thousand dead and one hundred thousand homeless.

It is notable that in 1945 Atlanta's board of directors gave permission for the Committee for Assistance to Italy to hold an arts festival to benefit the victims of World War II in that country, and another festival to raise funds to help the many families injured by the flood that hit Villa Crespo in November of that year. In early 1946 a friendly game was held between the traditional adversaries (since both remained committed to the neighborhood), Chacarita Juniors and Atlanta, to benefit those harmed by the Villa Crespo flood. The game was held on the field of Club Atlético Platense, which donated the use of its facilities.

In 1943 Atlanta's board of directors decided to make the general director of Tiro y Gimnasia (the army department concerned with marksmanship and physical education), Major General Adolfo Arana, an honorary member of the club. The following year they extended the same honor to the quartermaster of Campo de Mayo and Palomar, Major-General Eduardo Jorge Ávalos.[30] The club also adapted to the new social policy emanating from the new Secretaría de Trabajo y Previsión. On December 1, 1944, Atlanta's president signed an agreement with the presidents of other sports organizations, the board of the Mutualidad de Empleados de Entidades Deportivas (a benefit society for employees of sports organizations), and the aforementioned Secretaría de Trabajo.

During the events of the club's "fortieth-anniversary week," celebrated in October 1944, telegrams of congratulations poured in from, among others, Colonel Perón himself, who was now vice president of the nation, and his aide-de-camp, Major Solanas Pacheco; the state undersecretary of intelligence and the press, Lieutenant-Colonel Carrocella; the commander of the first horse artillery regiment; other officers of the same regiment; and the mayor, Lieutenant-Colonel Caccia (as well as the manager of the Banco Israelita, Jacinto C. Armando).

In 1946 Atlanta formed a pro-stadium commission, consisting of an honorary committee and an executive committee. The honorary committee was presided over by no less a personage than the chief of the federal police, General Juan Filomeno Velazco, a pro-Franco nationalistic Hispanophile of the extreme right (whom Perón removed from office in mid-1947), and included the minister of foreign affairs, Juan Atilio Bramuglia (who switched from Socialism to Peronism while Perón was in charge of the Secretaría de Trabajo y Previsión), as well as the president of the national chamber of deputies, Ricardo C. Guardo.

Even more interesting is the fact that the two vice presidents of the prostadium executive committee were both veteran members of Atlanta who had recently been elected as national deputies in the Peronist camp, and that from this time on they served as liaisons between the club and the authorities. They were Manuel García (Labor Party) and Manuel Álvarez Pereyra (Radical Civic Union—Junta Renovadora), an Yrigoyenist former soldier who in 1931 had participated in the Chaco uprising against President José Félix Uriburu. Álvarez Pereyra was a veteran *socio* of Atlanta. He joined the club in 1907 and became vice president in 1929. In 1934 he challenged one of the leaders of Racing to a duel because he offended Atlanta. He actually served as Atlanta's president from December 1, 1946, until he resigned at the end of October the following year.

According to the club's archives: "Distinguished members of the club, who have the signal honor to represent the Nation in the Most Excellent National Chamber of Deputies, discerned the patriotic desire of Atlanta members and the public necessity represented by the construction of the sports facility on our lot, [and] undertook active and commendable arrangements committed to promoting sports, allocating a substantial sum of money."[31] (See Figure 5.1.)

It is hardly surprising, then, that 1946 was considered the best financial year the club had ever had in all its long life. However, this financial situation did not produce the desired results in the club's performance in professional football. (One of the few players to distinguish himself during this period was the Jewish Argentine Santiago Kaufman.) Nor did the club's brief economic prosperity translate into any notable increase in the number of members. The support offered by the Peronist regime allowed Atlanta's leadership to enjoy a brief period of optimism. The club's 1947 report included a statement that "sports, social, and cultural activity carried out in this fiscal year has surpassed [that in] all other eras in the history of the Club."[32] Atlanta's reports during these years were filled with Peronist rhetoric about *justicialismo* and the New Argentina, together with tributes to the government and its policy of assisting sports entities in general and Atlanta in particular. In 1947 a loan of 1.5 million pesos for the purpose of building Atlanta's new stadium was announced (Decree No. 37.729, signed by President Perón and Finance Minister Ramón Cereijo). Immediately afterward the board of directors passed a resolution to appoint Perón as honorary president of the club. The president's wife, María Eva Duarte de Perón, Minister Cereijo, and the former chief of the federal police, Velazco, were all made honorary members in recognition of their efforts on behalf of Argentine football. This was a common practice at the time. The AFA, as well as leading clubs such as River Plate or Boca Juniors, also acknowledged government support by calling Perón Presidente del fútbol argentino (President of Argentine football) or *"primer hincha"* ("no. 1 fan").

At the same time, the club leaders never took any responsibility for the less than sterling performance of their football team in some seasons, instead alluding vaguely to bad luck or hazily described external factors beyond the board's control. This attitude was clearly discernible when the board claimed, in 1947:

> Atlanta was not overcome in fair contests on the field: factors and currents set in motion against our colors by who knows whom and for what shameful purposes ended up triumphant, and not our club defeated. . . .
>
> Every opportunity was cleverly exploited. . . . Bribery chooses its victims. Atlanta was the martyr of this period . . . the rulings of the referees who demonstrated malicious intentions on some occasions and incompetence or ignorance of the rules on others.

CLUB ATLETICO
"ATLANTA"
Sociedad Civil

Fundado el 12 de Octubre de 1904

★

FUTURO ESTADIO

Memoria y Balance

42º EJERCICIO

Diciembre 1º de 1945 - Noviembre 30 de 1946

★

Secretaria: HUMBOLDT 540
U. T. 54, Darwin 4371

Estadio: HUMBOLDT 408
B U E N O S   A I R E S

FIGURE 5.1 Cover of the 1946 annual report showing
a sketch of the projected new stadium.

Source: Memoria y Balance: 42º ejercicio, 1º de diciembre 1945
al 30 de noviembre 1946 (Buenos Aires, 1946).

Accordingly, it described the season as "the most shameful parody carried out in the contest that we had no chance of winning."[33]

November 1948 saw an intervention in the club that lasted until April 28, 1951, when Carlos Urien, an official in the justice department, called elections. The list headed by Major Juan Iacapraro defeated that of Ángel Peralta, and on May 4 the victors assumed control of the institution. Shortly afterward, the club's board of directors authorized and organized a mass convoy to Mar del Plata and then to Government House to show support for President Perón's reelection. This was not unusual. Many other civilian associations met with Perón at the time and urged him to run for a second presidential term. Iacapraro bestowed upon Perón the title of honorary president of Atlanta. Iacapraro's own presidency did not last long. A few months after assuming office he had to request a furlough owing to commitments imposed by his political and military career, and Vice President Lieutenant-Colonel Antonio Castro took over as acting president.

A Stadium Called Eva Perón?

On July 9, 1951, the Eva Perón Stadium was inaugurated in Junín, with funds provided by the president's office. Club Atlanta sent a large delegation to the opening. The club's new president, Antonio Castro, decided that the new stadium that Atlanta was going to build on the club's adjoining empty lot would also be named after Eva Perón—a decision that was never acted upon.

In early April of 1952 the country's vice president, Hortensio J. Quijano, a Radical Party politician who had embraced Peronism at an early stage, passed away before he could begin his second vice-presidential term. Atlanta's board of directors made several gestures of respect: they suspended all sports and social activities for two days; they sent a condolence card to Quijano's family as well as a floral offering; and they attended the wake and the burial, inviting club members to do the same. In retrospect, it was a dress rehearsal for the imminent demise of Eva Perón.

The first months of 1952 were characterized by a general concern for the health of the first lady. On June 4 Perón's second inauguration was celebrated. Although cancer was destroying her from within, Evita was determined to participate in the festivities. It turned out to be her last public appearance before her death, which occurred on July 26. The funeral procession from the presidential residence to the Ministry of Labor attracted an enormous crowd despite the unremitting rain. This was the first of many mass expressions of sorrow and grief recorded in the following weeks. A mixture of spontaneous outbursts and a campaign orchestrated by the government impelled two million Argentines to flood the Plaza del Congreso on Sunday, August 10, when the coffin containing the remains of the young former actress-cum-social leader was transferred to the Confederación General del Trabajo (CGT, the General Confederation of Labor) building.[34]

The Club Atlético Atlanta naturally joined all the other associations across the Republic in expressing their sorrow over the death of the "spiritual Head of the Nation." On the very day of Evita's death, the board of directors met in an extraordinary session presided over by Major Juan A. Iacapraro and the first vice president, Lieutenant-Colonel Antonio S. Castro. The members of the board stood in homage to the deceased and then published a resolution that explained the means taken "in response to the sad news of the death of Mrs. Eva Perón, an altruistic and selfless lady who sacrificed her life for the sake of the people, and taking into account that this event moves the entire Nation and extends universally to the most remote places, wherever the torch burning with faith and love has reached."[35]

The board of directors decided to suspend sports and social activities from July 26–29, to fly the national flag at half-mast, to send a floral offering, to send a telegram and condolence card to President Perón and also to the Peronist Women's Party and the Eva Perón Foundation, and to attend the wake and burial all together, inviting club members to do the same. That year they also decided formally to "build the monumental Sports Stadium, to be called 'Eva Perón' as a posthumous homage to the woman who was a beloved honorary member of the Institution. It is also decided that the children's section of the new Stadium will be called 'Evita.'"[36] The club's annual report included a full-page photo of Eva Perón, "eternal in the soul of her people. Perpetual member," and another of the "President of the Argentine Nation, Army General Don Juan Domingo Perón, Honorary President of our institution." The club's leadership took yet another step to show its commitment to the Peronist regime:

> Rendering just homage to the person who has struggled so mightily for the happiness of the people, this Institution donated thirty copies of the book *La Razón de mi Vida*, by our unforgettable fellow member Mrs. Eva Perón, to each of the Cooperative Associations of Schools No. 1, 2, 4, 17, 18, 21, 22, and 27; fifty copies to the Pro-Hogar Policial de la Seccional 29 [a social welfare organization]; and one copy to each of the members of the different subcommittees in the various athletic groups and to all the administrative and maintenance staff.

That year Atlanta also began lending its support to the Evita children's tournaments. Back in 1948 the then-first lady had adopted and sponsored the initiative of Emilio Rubio, editor of the sports section of evening paper *Noticias Gráficas*, to organize a children's football championship. One of its objectives, as expressed by President Perón at the opening ceremony for the Huracán stadium, was "[to remove] our young people from vice and from the places where men do not gain in health or virtue, to turn them into athletes who start preparing their souls and bodies to be virtuous and honorable citizens."[37]

In the following years, the children's tournaments became one of the most prominent and successful enterprises of the Eva Perón Foundation—another way of recruiting and training young people as the generation that would give continuity to Peronism. There are no precise statistics on the number of children who participated or the amounts of money invested. According to various accounts, in the first championship 11,483 young athletes signed up from the federal capital and another 3,722 from greater Buenos Aires. The scope of these tournaments gradually expanded to include the entire nation, and by 1950 the number of participants exceeded one hundred thousand. Beginning in 1951 the competitions extended beyond football alone to include such disciplines as track and field, gymnastics, basketball, swimming, and water polo. The following year similar championships for girls were instituted. In 1953, the year that the Juan Perón Children's Championships were launched, the number of participants exceeded two hundred thousand.[38] The weeklies *Mundo Deportivo*, *Mundo Peronista*, and *Mundo Infantil* were all enlisted in the cause of the mass propagandizing of the Evita tournaments, to encourage the participation of children and teenagers.[39]

According to Alberto Luchetti, the chairman of the Argentine Olympic Committee in those years and Perón's former fencing coach, the financial investment in these sports tournaments rose steadily, from 478,000 pesos in 1948 to three times that amount in 1950 and five times that in 1951. In 1952, 4 million pesos were invested in this project, rising to more than 8 million in 1953. To these sums must be added, of course, subsidiary government aid channeled into the organization of these sports events by various means. The fact that the finance minister, Ramon Cereijo, was one of the originators of the Eva Perón Foundation's sports policy facilitated the transfer of government funds for various purposes connected with these sports competitions and indicated the great importance Peronism attributed to sport. Deputies of the majority faction in Congress voted appropriations every year to support the foundation's sports activities, to the open disapproval of the opposition. In 1955 deputies Alfredo Alonso, Angel Miel Asquia, and others proposed the allocation of additional sums of money for this purpose.[40]

These sports rallies were an additional example of popular festivals heavily imbued with Peronist and national symbolism, like the events of October 17 or May 1. In the last two years of the regime, up to the military coup of September 1955, the foundation sports competitions reached their apex in the form of the Children's and Young People's Olympics, in which representatives from neighboring countries participated.[41]

By 1952 Atlanta had achieved economic independence, thanks to its definitive ownership and control of its land—together with everything built and planted on it. Moreover, once its contract with the Viñales Hnos. company had expired, the club recovered the rights of enjoyment and usufruct in the sales of drinks and snacks in the stands and at the snack bar, advertising, and the profits from the dances held at the clubhouse, as well as the bar, lunchroom, and café services. However, it was a difficult year financially for Atlanta, and the club managed to lobby the public authorities successfully for an increase to their original loan, bringing the total to 1,800,000 pesos, with which the club intended to pay off its debts or convert short-term debts into long-term ones. According to the club officers, the loan was "obvious confirmation that General Perón continues to offer the most fervent support to sports entities, to provide them with opportunities to develop and to play the social role required by the justicialist doctrine."[42] That same year the list of honorary members included the names of the two ministers in charge of the national economy: Ramón A. Cereijo and Alfredo Gómez Morales.

Displayed on the cover of Atlanta's 1954 annual report was the motto, "We support the [Peronist] Second Five-Year Plan." The list of board members included General Perón as honorary president. María Eva Duarte (lifetime member) headed the list of honorary members, which, again, included the economic ministers of the second Peronist government, Ramón Cereijo and Alfredo Gómez Morales. The president was Ventura Cozzo (until his retirement at the end of July of that year). These appointments are the basis of Ariel Korob's statement that "[d]uring the 1940s and 1950s members of Atlanta's boards of directors on several occasions were helped to their positions by the [Peronist-dominated] AFA."[43]

The next yearly report was published shortly after Perón's overthrow. Once again the club's leadership had to adapt to new circumstances, erasing all its previous links with the "deposed tyrant" in order to ensure the survival of the institution. A small group of old leaders was now at the club's helm: Santiago Bascialla as president; Alberto Chissotti as vice president; and Isaac Slinin as secretary. The whole category of "honorary members," which included Evita and other Peronist figures, disappeared from the annual report. In addition, the new leadership tried to start a new chapter without causing a rupture in the club, despite the deep divisions in contemporary Argentine society and the persecution of those identified with the defeated regime (former Atlanta president Álvarez Pereyra was jailed and former president Antonio Castro had to retire from the army). The annual report avoided "casting a shadow over the former authorities, since all of us, directors and members, bear our own share of guilt in any mistakes, and everyone who did much or little for their greater glory . . . deserves the gratitude of the new supporters."[44]

Other football clubs also had to dissociate themselves from Peronism and learn how to navigate the years when all mentions of Peronism and the former president were outlawed. They watched anxiously as the new regime arrested Carlos Aloé, the former mayor of Buenos Aires who was editor of *Mundo Deportivo* and the organizer of the Evita youth tournaments, and investigated Ramón Cereijo, the former minister considered a patron of soccer in general and Racing in particular. The new AFA *interventor*, Arturo Bullrich, was given the task of purging Peronist influences from professional football. Club Atlético Sarmiento, which had named its new stadium after Eva Perón in 1951, now had to rename it Sarmiento Stadium. The annual reports of the club in the early 1950s sang the praises of Peronism, Perón himself, Evita, and her brother Juan Duarte; in the 1955 *Memoria y Balance* all references to Perón were gone.[45]

The Price of "Loyalty"

The last two years of the Peronist decade were not good for Atlanta's football team. In the 1954 season it did everything possible to move up to the first division, but its efforts failed, and by the end of the season it had managed to reach only the fourth slot of the Primera B [First B] national league. The club's archives document 1955 as "one of its gravest periods." Apparently the discouragement of remaining in the lower division led many members to abandon the club, and there were not enough new members to replace them. Moreover, an aborted project to build a new swimming pool had left the club coping with both the absence of a pool and the destruction and debris left by the excavations. The club lost income from member dues and possible vendor concessions. As though that were not enough, the delay in the start of the football championship and the revolutionary events that suspended tournament activities for several weeks meant an extraordinary drop in football revenue.

This situation was further exacerbated by the closing of the Villa Crespo stadium, a measure that was motivated, according to some members, by political considerations. The collapse of the stands in another club's stadium in August 1955 prompted a series of inspections in the Atlanta stadium as well. Under the "pretext" (as the *bohemios* saw it) of the deplorable condition of some of the iron girders supporting the benches, the *"cajoncito"* on Humboldt Street was ordered to be closed. According to the club's officers, the situation was "brilliantly used to cause us such great harm."[46] After all, went the argument at Atlanta, such defects were common at most stadiums, especially those that were not in the Primera A (the highest league division). The fact that only Atlanta's stadium had been shut down completely, when at other clubs' stadiums just the damaged sections were closed off, was interpreted as a political punishment for a club that was supposedly too closely identified with Peronism. Years later, in conversations I had with old fans of Atlanta, they talked about the "rancor and vengeance" of some of the people in the reorganized AFA in the era of the Liberating Revolution.[47]

The Jewish image of the neighborhood, and, by extension, of Club Atlanta, may have contributed somewhat to a certain attitude of suspicion and mistrust on the part of the new national authorities, particularly since at the time nationalistic Catholic groups were distributing anti-Semitic pamphlets that included accusations against the Jews and Masons who supposedly surrounded President Perón and were responsible for the conflict between the regime and the Catholic Church in general and the attempt to separate the church from the state in particular. One of these pamphlets, dated May 1955, described Perón as a Mason and a puppet in the hands of the secret Jewish lodges. In late 1954, in the city of Córdoba—always considered a bastion of militant Catholicism—the police broke up a demonstration of Catholics carrying placards reading, "Down with Perón and his Jewish friends."[48] The conspicuous presence of Rabbi Amram Blum in the president's inner circle had been particularly irritating for many Catholic militants. In the atmosphere created by these tensions, many Jews realized that, in fact, the anti-Semitic threat came not from Perón's regime, but from its Catholic and conservative opponents. The fear was that, as in other times and places, Jews would once again find themselves scapegoats and victims of a politico-cultural war.[49] Atlanta was obviously not a Jewish club, but its location in the middle of a "Jewish neighborhood" and its increasing number of Jewish members and leaders may have been seen as an issue in this anti-Peronist, anti-Jewish climate.

The club's stadium was repaired and reopened, but this episode helped accelerate proceedings related to the construction of the coveted new stadium. Since the early 1940s, when the Villa Crespo Land Company was formed and began the process of acquiring the lot at 300 Humboldt Street, it had been clear that this would be the site of the club's future stadium. A few years later, the company ceded the property to Atlanta.

As Edgardo Imas explains, the small dimensions of the "*cajoncito*"—built at 400 Humboldt Street and inaugurated in 1922—and the fact that the land under it did not yet belong to Atlanta prompted successive boards of directors to keep restating the goal of a new stadium.[50] Later, after Chacarita Juniors had left the neighborhood, various plans and committees were formed.

Accordingly, there was talk of a stadium made of concrete in 1946, and a model of it was included on the cover of the club's annual report that year. However, all the plans, including those of Peronist inspiration, ran aground as a result of insufficient financial resources to begin the monumental work, political ups and downs in the organization and in the country, divisional relegations in football, and competing priorities.

In 1956, however, the plan was brought back to life, revived by Atlanta's promotion to the first division that season and by the ad hoc subcommittee chaired by Alberto Chissottti and including club member León Kolbowski. Two years later work began in the empty lot next to the stadium that Atlanta was using at the time. This was the beginning of the stadium that would be inaugurated in June 1960 and, decades later, named after León Kolbowski.

Meanwhile, the club continued its other activities. In the early 1950s a company was created (Sociedad Atlanta S.A.) for the purpose of purchasing the land next to the clubhouse which belonged to the San Martín railway—this was achieved in 1952. It should also be noted that around this time the club was affiliated with the Argentine Football Association, the Argentine Basketball Association, and the Argentine Track and Field Federation, the Argentine Women's Basketball Federation, and the Argentine Skating, Handball, Table Tennis, Wrestling, and Weightlifting Federations, as well as the Argentine Boxing Federation. In the mid-1950s, the board presided over by

Alberto Chissotti began to expand the club's sports facilities, remodeling the clubhouse and finally completing the construction of the swimming pool. Sports activities were added, and the practice of basketball, although not yet well established, soon bore its first fruits when the club won the metropolitan championship in 1958.

To return to football, after laboring for four consecutive years in the second division, Atlanta returned to the top category in 1956, while its archrival Chacarita was moved down. Only two years after returning to the top, Atlanta played its best season yet, ending up fourth in the league table and winning the Copa Suecia (Sweden Cup) by beating Racing Club 3–1 in the final.[51]

6

THE RISE AND FALL OF A
NEIGHBORHOOD CAUDILLO

One of Atlanta's golden ages was, undoubtedly, the presidency of León Kolbowski, which lasted from the second half of the 1950s to nearly the end of the
1960s. During this time the image of Atlanta as a "Jewish" and "progressive"
institution was reinforced. Kolbowski's inauguration as president marked the
culmination of a process that had begun in 1922 with Osvaldo Simón Piackin,
the first Jewish member of Atlanta's board of directors. In 1968, in what turned
out to be the last year of León Kolbowski's presidency, Jewish Argentines became a majority among the board members for the first time: twelve out of
twenty-two. (See Table 6.1.)

The very fact of Kolbowski's involvement in CAA activities might seem
surprising at first. Nothing in his public or business career would seem to indicate any special interest in football. However, it was actually his political identity and Communist militancy that directed his steps to Humboldt Street. The
Argentine Communist Party (Partido Comunista Argentino, PCA), which had
a strong bulwark and significant presence in Villa Crespo in the 1920s, sought
ways of increasing its influence in the neighborhood.[1] During the Peronist
decade and the years of the Liberating Revolution it had to maintain a cau-
tiously low profile, but the election of Arturo Frondizi as the nation's president
in February 1958 created new conditions.[2] The new tenant of the presidential
palace came to power as the head of a heterogeneous coalition of supporters
that included the Communists, a situation that the PCA exploited by, among
other things, venturing into social spheres not previously identified with it.

The story of Kolbowski's life was summed up by his son, Jorge Kolbowski,
with the sentence: "My father was first Orthodox, then Communist (the hor-
ror!), and subsequently a football fan; and, in addition, Jewish!!!"[3]

León Kolbowski was born in Baranowicz, Poland, on April 12, 1912, and
immigrated to Buenos Aires at the age of fifteen with his parents and siblings.
The Kolbowskis, like thousands of other Jewish families, had decided to leave

TABLE 6.1 Atlanta club members and number of Jews on the Board of Directors, 1904–1969

Year	Total Members	Jews on the Board of Directors	Percentage of Board
1904–21		0	0
1922	503	1 of 11	9
1923	604	1 of 22	4.5
1924	624	0 of 20	0
1925		1 of 14	7
1926	460 (source: Iwanczuk1993)	0 of 23	0
1927		1 of 17	6
1928	763	1 of 13	7
1929	1,508	0 of 17	0
1930		0 of 17	0
1931		0 of 17	0
1932		0 of 9	0
1933		0 of 19	0
1934	887 (according to *Libro de Actas Para Asambleas 1934–1952*, p. 7)	1 of 22	4.5
1935	merged with Argentinos Juniors		
1936		1 of 13	7
1937		2 of 21	9.5
1938		1 of 21	
1939	1,400 (according to the 1944 Annual Report)	2 of 14	14
1940		3 of 22	13
1941	2,473 (according to *Libro de Actas Para Asambleas 1934–1952*, p. 41)	2 of 22	9
1942		1 of 22	4.5
1943		5 of 22	22
1944	3,800	4 of 23	17
1945		3 of 22	13
1946	4,300	4 of 25	16
1947	7,800	3 of 26	11.5
1948–50			
1951	11,323	1 of 26	4
1952		1 of 24	4
1953	"a little lower than last year," the Annual Report and financial statement says, without specifying an amount.	4 of 20	20
1954		4 of 20	20
1955		6 of 25	20
1956		6 of 20	30
1957			
1958	3,462	8 of 27	29
1959	1,579 (following a general clean-up of membership records)	8 of 26	30
1960	4,500 (calculation based on the Annual Report and financial statement)		
1961	7,241	11 of 27	40
1962	8,515	7 of 19	36
1963	4,500 (estimate based on Annual Report)	7 of 18	38
1964	more than 6,000 (according to the Annual Report)	11 of 28	39
1965	8,300 (deduced from the membership dues recorded in the Annual Report)	9 of 22	40
1966	7,800 (deduced from the membership dues recorded in the Annual Report)	12 of 28	42
1967	5,100 (deduced from the membership dues recorded in the Annual Report)	12 of 26	46
1968	6,000 (deduced from the membership dues recorded in the Annual Report)	12 of 22	54
1969	7,500 (deduced from the membership dues recorded in the Annual Report)	8 of 28	28

Source: Ariel Korob, "Procesos identitarios e imaginarios locales. Atlanta: bohemios y judíos" (MA thesis, Universidad de Buenos Aires, 1998).

Eastern Europe under the pressure of poverty, discrimination, anti-Semitism, and pogroms, and they headed to the Río de la Plata. Upon arriving in Buenos Aires, the family first settled in the Once district, but in 1933 they moved to Villa Crespo. By profession a portrait retoucher, León married "a 16-year-old Romanian, tiny, beautiful," as Jorge tells it. One of León's brothers chose to return to his native Poland and was killed in the Holocaust. León's father was religiously observant. He had a furniture store in the neighborhood and also served as *shamash* (beadle) in the Murillo Street synagogue, a lay office that required him to deal with the logistics of the temple's daily operations.

In the 1930s, León Kolbowski founded and directed several mutual funds that served as a source of aid for immigrants all over the Republic. If you needed to paint your house, marry off a son or daughter, meet some family or health need, or obtain assistance for your small business, you could request a loan from these small institutions. The banks did not normally extend financial assistance for such trivial needs. Kolbowski began this line of business with the establishment of the Sociedad Mutual de Residentes de Baranowicz y sus Alrededores (Mutual Society of Residents of Baranowicz and Its Surroundings), Baranowicz being his home town in Poland, and his pioneering business venture lasted for several decades. Kolbowski's fluency in Polish, Yiddish, Spanish, and probably some knowledge of Hebrew facilitated his work. According to Jorge Kolbowski, "I am certain I have heard him speak the Polish language, but later I am more certain that it was no longer spoken at home. There were probably reasons for forgetting."

Beginning in the 1940s, cooperatives began to replace mutual societies; they had greater financial capacity and margin for maneuver.[4] Kolbowski founded and directed several of them: Mutual de Villa Crespo, Primera Caja Mercantil, Caja Popular Lavalle, Once de Septiembre, and Los Andes. In the following decade he was cofounder of the Instituto Movilizador de Fondos Cooperativos, a national institution. Through this entity he promoted an enormous number of credit, consumer, production, and other cooperatives in the federal capital, Buenos Aires province, and the interior of the country. Even the orchestra of Communist Osvaldo Pugliese was set up as a cooperative of this kind. Pugliese, a member of the Argentine Communist Party since 1936, was thrown into jail for his "Bolshevik" attitudes several times in the late 1940s and early 1950s, during Juan Perón's first administration. The composer of such popular tangos as "Negracha," "La Yumba," and "Malandrada," Pugliese enjoyed much popularity in Atlanta during the Kolbowski presidency.[5]

The PCA Seeks to Expand Its
Influence in the Neighborhood

All this activity had a clear ideological tinge. Kolbowski, like many other Jews, became a Communist during World War II, when Nazi Germany invaded the Soviet Union. From that moment on, as his son Jorge put it, "The Communist Party was behind, in front, and to the sides." Kolbowski *père* remained loyal to his leftist activities for a quarter of a century. In the 1940s he played an important role in the Communist Party's fund-raising campaign, and in the elections of the AMIA in October 1955, Kolbowski was a member of List No. 2, headed by Pinie Katz.[6] Katz was a laborer from Russia who became an eminent journalist and free thinker in Argentina.[7] Founder of the morning Yiddish-language daily *Di Presse*, he was the most prominent figure in the Yiddishist section of the Communist Party and, later, one of the most well-known intellectuals among the Argentine adherents to the Idischer Cultur Farband (ICUF, Federation of Yiddish Cultures, the Argentine branch of a international, Yiddish-based, left-wing politico-cultural organization).

In fact, it was precisely the Communist Party that impelled Kolbowski to get involved in the Atlanta sports club in the mid-1950s, with the aim of expanding party influence in the neighborhood. This initiative of the PCA should come as no surprise. The clubs in Argentina had cultivated ties with the main actors in national politics since the earliest days of *fútbol*. During the first third of the twentieth century, the practice of this sport was present in some form in all the major institutions: the church, the political parties, the armed forces, companies, and unions. Moreover, as Rodrigo Daskal has pointed out, often the boundaries between the administration in a club and the political activity outside it were rather permeable; in many cases club officers took advantage of their institutional positions to become directly involved in the political arena.[8] Many observers were unhappy with this politicization of football, and an editorial in the magazine *La Cancha* complained in September 1928, "Politics should not seep into the clubs. The latter cannot be Yrigoyenist, or Socialist, or Conservative, without threatening the purpose of these institutions."[9]

Communists at the time, for their part, viewed activity in the football clubs with some suspicion. They were greatly angered, for example, when a group of athletes introduced the conservative candidates Leopoldo Melo and Vicente Gallo in the Coliseo Theater. An editorial published in *La Internacional* toward the end of March 1928, on the eve of the presidential elections, clearly expressed its opposition to politics in sports:

In its meeting on the 27th of this month, the Congreso Directivo de la Federación Deportiva Obrera [the governing body of the Workers' Sports Federa-
tion] finds it necessary to denounce to proletariat youth the farce constituted
by bourgeois sports and the alleged "sports for sports' sake." In the capitalist
regime sports, like education and the army, constitutes an organization designed to distract the minds of young workers, to remove them from unions
and working-class organisms.... The declaration of the candidacy of the agricultural and animal-husbandry bourgeois by a so-called committee of athletes
is the most egregious case not only of the corruption of bourgeois politics but
also of the sports of official institutions.... [10]

Also worthy of attention is the close relationship between the PCA and
a progressive sector of the Jewish community, a relationship notable since
the very birth of the party, especially in the language-based sections that
were created for the purpose of recruiting party militants from different immigrant groups. From the very beginning the Argentine Communist Party
had a Jewish section that carried out activities in its own language (Yiddish)
and enjoyed autonomy in specifically Jewish matters. This was because the
Communist sector, although quantitatively insignificant within the local Jewish community, was nevertheless influential there since it was constant and
consistent. The PCA, like the anarchists and, for a short time, the Socialist
Party, had language sections—including a Yiddish section—designed to recruit immigrant workers. As Edgardo Bilsky explains, "Communist activity
among Jews began with the recognition of the ethnic characteristics of the
Jewish worker, but, unlike the Bund, it denied him any 'national' character
and sharply criticized Zionism."[11] The Jewish Section was second only to the
numerous Italian Section in importance, representing 14 percent of all members of the Communist Party in 1927.[12] Like the other language sections, the
Jewish Section promoted neighborhood and cultural activities.

Villa Crespo, owing to its socioeconomic characteristics and notable Jewish
presence, has long been the site of a major PCA branch. In the 1920s and 1930s
the Communist Party was popular in Villa Crespo and enjoyed a strong following in various organizations that included large numbers of Jewish members,
such as those related to the clothing and tailoring industries, which operated
within the framework of the Unión Sindical Argentina (Argentine Syndical
Union). The Jewish influence was so great in these associations that their stat-
utes were written in Yiddish, the largest being the Sindicato de Obreros Sastres
y Anexos (the Union of Tailors and Related Workers). Another Communist

union in Villa Crespo in which Jews were numerous and influential was the Textile Workers' Federation, the Federación Obrera de la Industria Textil.[13]

The Communist Party promoted education and recreation in the neighborhood through a network of libraries, cultural centers, schools, and sports clubs. The party also organized activities for children, artistic events, and celebrations. All these activities were targeted at the working class, since this was a way of penetrating that sector of society.

Naturally, sports—especially football—were an important way of gaining the interest of workers. In the 1920s and 1930s in particular, the Communist Party created a large number of football clubs in the city of Buenos Aires, including the neighborhood of Villa Crespo. Their names were taken from Communist culture—for example, Rosa Luxemburgo, Sportivo Lenin, Hoz y Martillo (hammer and sickle), Primero de Mayo (1st of May), Hijos del Pueblo (Sons of the People), La Internacional, and so on.[14] In July 1924, these clubs joined forces to create the Federación Deportiva Obrera (FDO, Workers' Sports Federation). Each time this body organized an important football match, it used the facilities of Club Atlético Atlanta. One such occasion was a game between the FDO and the Federación Roja del Deporte del Uruguay (Red Sports Federation of Uruguay) in October 1925, attended by some two thousand spectators.

The Communist Party succeeded in founding some ten "workers' schools" in the city of Buenos Aires. Most of them were set up by Communists of Jewish background and were located in the areas of Paternal and Villa Crespo. The intention was to create a school network independent of the state system that would be more suitable, useful, and accessible to the children of workers. There were also Communist-oriented Jewish educational institutions, namely, the Borokhov schools run by the Poalei Tzion Party and the Arbeter Shuln of the Arbsholorg (an organization of workers' schools), which were coordinated through the Idsketzie (the Jewish section of the Communist Party) and located in heavily Jewish neighborhoods such as Villa Crespo.[15]

Back in the mid-1950s, Kolbowski was already a well-known neighborhood figure thanks to his famous shop, Galería Durero; ads for this enterprise used to appear in the newspaper *Tribuna*, which belonged to the ICUF and was associated with the sectors of the community that represented the Communist ideology.[16] He was also known for his role in the credit cooperatives and the Sholem Aleijem School. Photographs from this era show a man of imposing physical presence: tall and wide-shouldered, with a mustache. (See Figure 6.1.)

FIGURE 6.1 León Kolbowski giving a speech to Atlanta fans.
Source: Courtesy of Jorge Kolbowski's archive.

This rapidly integrating immigrant never abandoned his Jewish identity. Despite his identification with the left, he continued to honor his Orthodox religious background at home by celebrating the Jewish holidays—such as Passover and Rosh Hashana—with prayer and traditional songs. "It was obligatory for him to read the prayers of Yom Kippur in Hebrew," his son Jorge told us. "Yiddish was the language spoken at home and I heard it so much that some of it stuck with me." Since we are what we eat and drink, it was interesting to hear his description of his father's outings with a cousin:

> Afterwards they would go to the León bar, which was at Corrientes and Pueyrredón, and have tea with "*limene*" [lemon]. The tea was served in a very delicate glass, with sugar cubes. The lump of sugar was held firmly between the upper and lower molars, sweetening the tea as it was sipped. It took a lot of experience (imported from Russia) to keep the sugar lump from dissolving with the first sip.[17]

Don León frequented places where Jewish Argentines met to talk, do business, or play. He never abandoned or changed his Jewish surname, and in the newspaper items published about his activity in Club Atlanta, the biography of the "Pole" born in Baranowicz was often mentioned.[18] He had a strong Jewish-Polish accent when he spoke Spanish, which more than once caused smiles among club members, especially his pronunciation of the double "r." The difference between Kolbowski and Leopoldo Bard, the first captain and president of Club Atlético River Plate, is notable, among other reasons because in Bard's case few people knew (or know even now) that he was Jewish.[19]

Kolbowski's involvement in Atlanta's administration began in 1955. According to some sources, Kolbowski first came to the club at the invitation of Eduardo Aruj and Luis Izcovichi, who wanted him to give the club the benefit of his administrative experience and advise the board of directors. His first job was as director of the club's amateur football division, and he soon joined the professional football committee. He was president of Atlanta from 1959 to 1969, a period in which the football team—"the basis and foundation of our existence," as the 1963 annual report said[20]—turned in a commendable performance. It was a season that made history, guided by coaches Spinetto, Giudice, Zubeldía, and eminent trainers such as Adolfo Mogilevsky, Amándola, and Miri, to name a few, who trained Marcelo Echegaray, Galvanese, Alberto de Zorzi, Osvaldo Zubeldía, Hugo Gatti, Biasutto, Caffaro, Bertoni, Néstor Errea, Gonzalito, Carlos Griguol, Luis Artime, Salomone, Raimondo, and many others. Just like Salo Muller, the Holocaust survivor who became the much-loved physical therapist of the Ajax Dutch football club between the years 1959–73, Mogilevsky was admired for years by Atlanta's management, players and fans, and also contributed to the Jewish image of Atlanta.[21]

In 1958–59 the Atlanta team, trained by Mogilevsky, managed to win its only first-division tournament, the Copa Suecia, organized during a suspension of the official championship, "our team being the main host." (See Figure 6.2.) It defeated Racing Club and won a title and the handsome sum of 146,415 pesos.

The following year Atlanta achieved the fifth slot in the final classification of the first division, having played only five games on its own field owing to construction work on the new stadium. That same year three of its players

FIGURE 6.2 "Atlanta al frente."
Source: Front page of El Gráfico, April 4, 1958, Buenos Aires.

TABLE 6.2 Atlanta's rankings, 1959–1970

Year	Clubs	Rank	Division
1959	16	5	First
1960	16	11	First
1961	16	4	First
1962	15	7	First
1963	14	5	First
1964	16	5	First
1965	18	14	First
1966	20	10	First
Metropolitano 1967	11	11	First
Reclasificatorio 1967	10	2	First
Metropolitano 1968	11	9	First
Reclasificatorio 1968	10	2	First
Metropolitano 1969	11	11	First
Reclasificatorio 1969	9	3	First
Metropolitano 1970	21	7	First
Nacional 1970	10	7	First

Source: Author's elaboration.

(Carlos Griguol, Rodolfo Carlos Bettinotti, and Néstor Errea) joined the Argentine national team. In 1961, the team had its best season in professional *fútbol*. The team was ranked fourth, and that year no fewer than five Atlanta players played on the national team: Néstor Errea, Carlos and Mario Guiguol, Luis Artime, and Alberto González. Artime—who would later transfer to River Plate—was the top scorer of the season, scoring twenty-five goals. In 1963 the football team fought for third place on the last day of competition, finally placing fifth in the league table. The 1964 tournament was the culmination of a brilliant run of success that had begun in 1958. In later years the club's soccer seasons would be mediocre and less than exciting. (See Table 6.2.)

A Golden Era

The Kolbowski period was characterized by great advances in both the physical facilities and the social activities of the club. Kolbowski's achievements were particularly notable in light of the fact that these were not glorious years for

Argentine football in general. Ever since its poor performance in the 1958 World Cup games in Sweden, the national team had been far from impressive. The country's hopes of hosting the 1962 World Cup were dashed when FIFA officials decided that its political climate was too unstable to make Argentina a good candidate and awarded the privilege of organizing the international event to neighboring Chile. Other problems afflicting Argentine football included declining attendance at league matches and outbreaks of violence in and around the stadiums (the death of eighteen-year-old Mario Linker in October 1958 following a match between River Plate and Vélez Sársfield marked a low point).[22]

Kolbowski's decade in the presidency saw the construction of dressing rooms, bathrooms, and bocce pitches, and the installation of lighting for the swimming pool, as well as the creation of a credit cooperative, the Cooperativa del Deporte Atlanta de Crédito, Consumo y Vivienda Limitada, in July 1960. The pièce de résistance, however, was, without a doubt, the construction of a sports stadium for thirty-four thousand people, designed by the Jewish Argentine engineer Wainstein and inaugurated on June 5, 1960. The first game held in the new facility, against Argentinos Juniors, was attended by national, municipal, and sports authorities (including Mayor Hernán Giralt and the president of the AFA, Raúl Colombo). This stadium was named after León Kolbowski in 2000.

Fifteen years of starts and stops had passed before the stadium was finally inaugurated in 1960. The idea of building a new field for Atlanta was born shortly after Chacarita dismantled its own stadium in Humboldt Street in 1945. A year later there was talk of a concrete stadium that would bear the name General Juan Domingo Perón, and in the early 1950s the possibility of naming it after Eva Perón was mentioned, but the project remained in limbo for lack of economic resources. A decade later the plan would be revived under the presidency of Alberto Chissotti, but construction did not begin until 1958.

During the La Plata Derby played on May 28, 1959, on the Gimnasia y Esgrima pitch, a section of the stands collapsed, injuring many spectators. As a result, the AFA decided to inspect other stadiums as well. Atlanta's stadium had been suspended four years earlier, but club officers had made temporary repairs so that the team could keep playing. Finally it was decided to put all efforts into building a new stadium, and on June 21, 1959, the last game was played, against Ferrocarril Oeste, on the old field.[23]

During 1958–59, according to the club's 1959 annual report, "all the effort of the people working in the Club is dedicated to a single goal, the construction of the stadium. We must stop wandering among the stadiums of the friendly entities that have taken us into their homes in these difficult times for Atlanta and struggle indefatigably to ready the new field for the beginning of the next tournament."[24]

Twenty months and 15 million pesos after the work began, the new stadium was inaugurated; the *bohemios* were euphoric. The 1960 annual report summarized the construction process in moderate terms:

> When, in the month of August 1958, we decided to begin construction in order to endow the organization with a comfortable stadium, it was considered a real utopia. It was truly impossible to embark on such a work without relying on official support or the proceeds from the sale of some of our real property, or a solid economic foundation.
>
> This last factor was what logic dictated. But we know well that history was never written about anything that did not involve some degree of grit; we decided to take a chance.[25]

This boldness was in fact typical of a visionary like Kolbowski. His battle cry was "create problems in order to resolve them." The daily *La Razón* once quoted him as saying, "I do not understand the calm attitude of those who do not take risks, of those who take refuge in the supposedly 'small' nature of the club they preside over, in order to sit back and do nothing. We have to work, to form managerial teams with selfless people and then some day we can be great."[26] Kolbowski's bold approach would later cost him. (See Figure 6.3.)

To finance this monumental project, four-year subscriptions for stadium seats were sold. Funds were solicited from members, businessmen, industrialists, and local residents. Loans were obtained from credit and banking institutions, endorsed by the members of the board of directors and their associates. As the annual report said, "a typically 'all-out' funding effort was promoted."[27]

However, this effort was insufficient, and in the following years Atlanta expanded the already traditional custom of selling its best players to other clubs. Kolbowski negotiated good prices for these "Bohemian stars," but the authorities, members, and fans were beginning to show a growing discomfort with this policy, which did not allow Atlanta to advance like the major teams. Thus, for example, in 1960 Marcelo Echegaray was transferred to River Plate for the sum of 1.8 million pesos; Cristián Federes was loaned to Excursionistas for a year; Osvaldo Zubeldía was loaned to Bánfield; and a series of players were released as free agents. In 1962, "forced by an accumulation of debts

FIGURE 6.3 Kolbowski supporters celebrating his electoral victory.
Source: Courtesy of Jorge Kolbowski's archive.

resulting from the stadium construction, we found ourselves obliged to get rid of four real assets: Errea, González, Artime, and Griguol"[28]—that is, the stars the club had at the time. The same thing happened in subsequent seasons.

Even these measures—as well as renting the stadium to other teams, such as Deportivo Español to serve as their home turf, or on other occasions to

Argentinos Juniors, Chacarita Juniors, and Ferrocarril Oeste—were not enough to pay off the debts from building the stadium. The club did not manage to pay its bills on time, and the interest inflated the principal. Some creditors became impatient, and according to the 1963 annual report, the board of directors suffered from "a climate of greater difficulty, in view of the fact that some of them obtained from the law courts precautionary measures that, with their resulting costs, interest, and fees, made the situation more difficult, creating a panorama of problems."[29] In the aforementioned interview with *La Razón*, Kolbowski was asked if there were problems in Atlanta. He responded, "You bet. Atlanta is going through a crisis of growth; it is constantly being built and I can assure you that we have not stopped for a single day."[30]

Kolbowski belonged to a small group of powerful club presidents whose authoritarian style of leadership since the 1960s had earned them the appellation "caudillo" presidents. Caudillo was the term used in nineteenth-century Latin America to describe a charismatic leader who used violence and patronage to mobilize support and perpetuate his power. In Argentina the most notorious caudillo was Juan Manuel de Rosas (1793–1877), the Argentine dictator and governor of the province of Buenos Aires known as "the Restorer of the Laws." Other football club presidents included in this group were River Plate's Antonio Liberti, Vélez Sarsfield's José Amalfitani, and Boca's Alberto J. Armando. However, ambitious as he was, Kolbowski did not try to compete with the heads of the major clubs but instead sought to establish himself as the leading voice of the smaller ones.

At that time the five major football clubs (Boca, River, Racing, Independiente, and San Lorenzo) were thinking of organizing a separate championship of their own, excluding the smaller clubs, in order to improve ticket sales. León Kolbowski, together with José Amalfitani from Vélez and the president of Ferrocarril Oeste, fought successfully against this plan. Kolbowski became a central figure in the politics of Argentine football. In most cases it contributed to his popularity among club members—but not always. Some Kolbowski fans, who cherish the memory of the legendary Bohemian leader, told me that the arrangement made in 1967 which contributed to save Chacarita from relegation cost Don León the presidency in the club elections of 1969. Many of his followers never forgave him for that deal.

Beyond football, however, he gave a strong boost to Atlanta's social activities and other sports. The old clubhouse was rebuilt and remodeled, boasting the addition of two swimming pools, dressing rooms, a bocce pitch, a first-aid clinic, covered picnic areas for families, and a subsidized childcare center (the first for any football club). All the local schools—including, obviously, the Jewish ones—began to use the clubhouse at no charge for their physical-education classes. In only six years the member roster grew from two thousand to twenty-two thousand.

Other sports developed considerably during this period. Men's basketball gave the fans of the yellow-and-blue jersey a thrill when they won the second-division championship in 1963, finally allowing them to ascend to the next level after seventeen years of hard labor. And the women's basketball team, which was also promoted to the first division that year, gave Club Atlanta an opportunity to appear in the privileged circle of those ranked first in their region and subsequently to participate in the final round of the tournament of the Asociación Femenina Metropolitana de Básquetbol (the Women's Metropolitan Basketball Association). In 1967 the club enclosed its bocce courts, installing picture windows and the necessary ventilation. "This allowed the administrative entity of this sport to designate our court as the venue for important final games."[31]

In Atlanta's annual reports for those years, the importance of social and cultural activities is clear. For example, the 1958 report notes, "A Steinway and Sons piano was bought, fulfilling the old ambition to have our own piano."[32] The following year the club held in its hall, for the first time, an end-of-the-year banquet for employees, players, and contributors. According to the 1961 annual report, "The kindergarten is becoming a model of its kind; the practice of folklore [music and dances] makes Atlanta one of its bastions."[33] In 1960 the board of directors promoted the foundation of the previously mentioned Cooperativa del Deporte Atlanta. This was the first effort to adapt cooperativist action to the sports field, and it was one more link in the long chain of cooperatives promoted by Don León. In 1966 the Cayetano Di Santo children's playground was inaugurated, and amateur football managed to fulfill the dream of a pitch for children's soccer. The club also began publication of the magazine *Adelante Atlanta*.

When Atlanta celebrated its sixtieth anniversary in 1964, the president of the Republic himself, Arturo Illia, received the club's board of directors—a testimony to the organization's importance. A series of sports events (the main one being a game against the Peñarol club of Montevideo) and social functions (such as a friendship supper and a gala banquet in the social hall) culminated on October 12 with a barbecue attended by close to a thousand guests, including representatives of the political, sports, and economic spheres.

Among Kolbowski's "achievements" should be mentioned the recruitment of Adolfo Mogilevsky as a trainer on Atlanta's professional staff. A free-style wrestling champion in the 1940s and a wrestling coach for the Macabi club, in the 1950s he was already a kinesiologist and a celebrated physical trainer. In the course of his career he was at various times a trainer for Racing, San Lorenzo, Bánfield, and Chacarita, as well as for the Argentine national football team. Mogilevsky belonged to a small group of trainers who sought to change traditional practices and styles of play, as well as the mind-set of Argentine players. They advocated modern tactics and training methods in order to ensure international achievements and recognition. According to Rwany Sibaja, "During his stay at the club, Mogilevsky implemented new [physical] conditioning methods and adopted the defensive tactical schemes from teams like Inter Milan."[34]

Kolbowski managed to persuade him to work for Atlanta, and in the three separate seasons he agreed to do so he revolutionized physical training in the club. In those seasons Atlanta never ended lower than fifth position. Mogilevsky's account sheds additional light on the character of Kolbowski, his views on the club and its professional football team, his patterns of behavior, and the ethnic connection underlying many measures:

> The contact had been [the Jewish Argentine] Bernardo Paley, who had a restaurant next to Don León's business, so he used to see him all the time. Since Bernardo knew that I was not working in football and Atlanta had newly won promotion to the first division, he asked me if I would be willing to work as a physical trainer at Atlanta. It was 1958. I had just come back from Stoke Mandeville, England, where the pre-Olympic trials had been held, and after the games we had taken a research trip to various countries in Europe, ending up at the Fifth Maccabi Games in Israel, where I was the consultant for the Argentine team. . . . I was still doing my jobs at the Escuela de Mecánica, the Colegio Militar, and the Instituto Nacional de Educación Física. . . . And for me, going into it was something that took time. It wasn't just a matter of making them do exercises, run, or maintain discipline. So, at first, I did not accept the proposal.
>
> But Don León did not give up so easily. He insisted, making me an offer that, although interesting, did not meet my aspirations. We were in this tug of-war, when he asked me: How many points do you think you're going to make in a year? I don't remember how many, but apparently he was satisfied with a

point per game. Then he made me an offer worthy of an intelligent leader: "If we win more than that figure, we will pay you whatever you ask." Before the first round was over we had already surpassed that score.

Don León reminded me a lot of my old man. He managed without money, without any problem. He was not frightened by debt. Although he had support from the cooperatives, it was never enough for him. In other words, his plans always required a higher amount than what he had. But he invented a cooperative and paid me with checks drawn on it that never had any backing. You had to wait. The debts always got paid. He had given work to [the football star] Carlos Griguol in his [private] business.

Also he was a sensible leader. Although at games he shouted his head off from the stands, he knew his ground very well. In 1962, among the players transferred to other institutions Atlanta had assets good enough for a national team. In one of our conversations I suggested, Instead of transferring every year, why don't we try to win the championship? In turn, he answered with a question: "How much money will you earn if we end up champions? . . . If in the second round we go first, we'll have to increase the bonuses. If we continue first or second on the last days, we will have to give them the entire box office take. . . . It's worse when we play against the big teams. The fans will wreck the place. . . . We transfer the fourth-division players and we make the same money." That was it.[35]

Another initiative from the Kolbowski period that should be mentioned was the custom of the players throwing flowers to the spectators as the team came out onto the field. Many of my informants mentioned this and emphasized that in this way Atlanta, and football in general, became more attractive for women and encouraged entire families to come to the stadium.

Once Kolbowski took over as club president, an increase in Jewish and Communist club officers was noted. "When my father headed Atlanta," Jorge Kolbowski told us, "there was a Jewish 'epidemic' in the committees and subcommittees."[36] It does appear that in these years ethnic identity trumped ideology.

A Trip to the "Motherland"

The practice of organizing tours inside the country and abroad, which began toward the end of the 1930s with tours to Brazil, Chile, and Colombia, continued in the 1940s with trips to Bolivia and the provinces of Tucumán and Salta,

as well as other places. Although these tours were a tribute to the club's growing prestige, in most cases they represented an effort to earn revenue. In 1963
Kolbowski arranged for Atlanta to make its first tour ever off the continent to
a distant destination: the State of Israel. Atlanta was in fact the first Argentine
team to play a soccer game in the Jewish state, which paid for prizes and all the
expenses of the Atlanta team. This tour in the "motherland" made a great stir in
the local Jewish community, which was largely based in Villa Crespo and rooted
for the neighborhood team. In spite of deteriorating relations between the Soviet Union and Israel, the Atlanta leadership—which included several Communist sympathizers—offered no objection or opposition to the planned trip.

During the tour the team played two games, the first in the national stadium in Ramat Gan against the local team, which won 1–0, with the legendary
Hugo Gatti as Atlanta's goalkeeper. The second game was against Macabi Tel
Aviv, which Atlanta won 3–1.[37] However, if Kolbowski had been hoping that
the trip would also bear economic fruit, he was to be deeply disappointed.[38]
A few weeks after the tour, a combined Israeli team called "Macabi Israel"
returned the visit and appeared in Villa Crespo, where it played the local team
and lost by a narrow margin.

Football was not the only use to which the Atlanta Kolbowski stadium
was put. It was also the scene of other sports and political events, thanks to
its central geographic location and the spaciousness of its facilities. Some of
the more notable sports events included the finals of the metropolitan basketball championship in 1966, the exhibition performance of the former world
heavyweight boxing champion Cassius Clay in 1971, and the appearance of
the winning team of the 1979 FIFA World Youth Championship.[39] Among the
political events staged in the stadium were, memorably, the proclamation of
Héctor Cámpora's candidacy for president of the nation by the Frente Jus-
ticialista de Liberación (FREJULI, Justicialist Liberation Front) in February
1973 and the assembly marking the end of Oscar Alende's presidential campaign on behalf of the Popular Revolutionary Alliance in March of the same
year. In 1973 and 1974, Juventud Peronista (the Peronist youth group) and
Montoneros (a left-wing Peronist guerrilla group) held ceremonies there to
mark the first anniversaries of the Trelew massacre and of FREJULI's victory,
respectively.[40] In the 1980s, the Peronist Party, the CGT, and the Movimiento
al Socialismo (Movement to Socialism) all used Atlanta as the venue for their
political events. Clearly, the club's new stadium was destined to be the scene
of a variety of historical moments and political movements over time.[41]

Building the stadium exacted a high price in many respects, dooming the organization to operate constantly in the red, since its resources were never sufficient to cover its costs. This situation gradually began to affect Kolbowski's image and status. "The decisions made by the executive committee," says the 1965 annual report, "have been questioned by a sector of the membership . . . these facts, which to some extent are disturbing the club atmosphere, are necessarily a source of concern, and naturally have unfavorable outside repercussions for the club."[42] Under these circumstances, President Kolbowski surprised his fellow board members on September 2, 1965, by requesting three months' leave "owing to physical and mental exhaustion."[43] Initially this request was unanimously rejected, but Don León insisted and the board accepted his request, which, according to the annual report, increased "the atmosphere of anxiety."[44] In the following days the Buenos Aires daily papers published stories about unpaid IOUs, delays in paying salaries to the players, and overdue debts.

Kolbowski's leave of absence did nothing to calm this mood. The daily *Crónica* gave ample column space to continuing criticisms of Atlanta's president. Under the title "Formulating Charges Against Kolbowski," it reported a press conference organized by three club members, José Davilman, Ángel Peralta, and Isaac Slinin.[45] The daily explained that in light of the current situation in the club, a group of veteran members, many of whom had collaborated with the president in earlier times, had decided to form a group called the Movimiento de Recuperación de Atlanta to defend the club's patrimony. They agreed on two fundamental goals: to demand that Kolbowski step down, and to petition for the immediate formation of an investigative committee with wide powers to analyze the state of the club's assets.

Harsh words were directed at Kolbowski in this press conference: "The president of the institution must resign his functions definitively because he has ceased to be a uniting figure and, instead, has become the main reason for the disintegration of the Bohemian family." Davilman described Kolbowski's performance as "disastrous," and accused him of ruling in "disorder." Slinin, in turn, asserted that "most of the accomplishments that Kolbowski now takes credit for were achieved in the club before Kolbowski ever dreamed of becoming a member, since he only joined at the end of 1950."[46]

The interim head of the club, Juan José Motta, explained to *El Gráfico*: "I give you my word of honor that no one doubts the honorability, the capability, or the willingness of Don León. He will return to the club because Atlanta needs him."[47] And Kolbowski did return. The club officials called for elections a year earlier than scheduled to prevent the internal struggle from annihilating the club, and the official list, Agrupación Tradicional, was headed by Kolbowski, with Motta running as vice president.

During the electoral campaign Kolbowski assured journalists: "The elections are ours, do or die." He described his opponents as "a bunch of ambitious opportunists" who, if they won, would "return to the first B [division], the little old playing field, the bribery, the AFA's indifference. . . . They will get rid of the kindergarten, the football school that produced so many stars (Artime, Gonzalito, Errea, Gatti, Carone)." He went on to say that "when I came to Atlanta, in 1956, we didn't have even the most basic things. . . . Now we have everything, and they are creating this divisiveness. It's inconceivable. . . . Dear lord, if those people get their hands on the club!"[48]

In 1966 Kolbowski won again, but the turbulent atmosphere persisted in the following months and the same accusations were brandished against him two years later in the next election.[49] According to *Clarín*, "The neighborhood of Villa Crespo is plunged in the tension that is now traditional in the election events of the Club Atlético Atlanta."[50] Things reached the point that physical confrontations were reported—not all that surprising given the growing violence in Argentina at the time—and Kolbowski hurried to explain to the press:

> I always worked at trying to build in Argentine football and in my own organization, without ever resorting to deception or lies. That despicable recourse is repellant to my spirit. Just as I censure with all my strength—if it is true, although I have my doubts—the news I have received of an attack on the headquarters of the opposing group, in the electoral campaign, because there can be no opponents in the Bohemian family. Acts of violence are conceived only by vile, sick beings, accordingly they must deserve the condemnation of everyone and every sector.[51]

On that occasion Kolbowski summarized the investments made since 1958 in acquiring and selling football players. The club had transferred players in exchange for a total of 171,880,000 pesos while spending 55,390,328 pesos, thus gaining a profit of 116,489,372 pesos during those eleven years. These earnings funded the club's building projects (the stadium and the clubhouse) and drove a variety of sports and sociocultural activities.

The beginning of the electoral campaign of the Agrupación Tradicional Lista Amarilla, headed by León Kolbowski and Juan José Motta, appeared promising. When the campaign held its opening event in mid-November 1968, its campaign headquarters at 5500 Corrientes Street turned out to be too small to accommodate the large turnout of members streaming in to endorse the official ticket. Many football stars who at the time were playing in other clubs, such as Juan Carlos "Pichino" ("the Kid") Carone, who was playing in Vélez Sársfield at the time, José Luis Luna, also from Vélez, and Jorge Hugo Fernández, who was playing in Boca Juniors, also came by to show their support for Kolbowski and to thank him for placing Atlanta in a privileged position in Argentine football. He even received the endorsement of Osvaldo Zubeldía, who was managing Estudiantes de La Plata, the club that gave Argentina its second world title among champion clubs. Zubeldía had played in Atlanta and as a coach had managed the club from 1959 to 1963, mentoring players such as Hugo Gatti and Luis Artime.[52]

Nevertheless, as the 1960s drew to a close, Kolbowski found himself ever more marginalized in the club. After twelve years as president, he lost the internal elections held on January 5, 1969, by a few dozen votes, to Amadeo Altamura. According to his friends, the results were falsified. However, he had to step down. His opponents had accused him more than once of mismanaging club funds, among other offenses. Around 1962–63, he also began to lose the support of the Communist Party. During this period, when the revisionist movement led by Nikita Khruschev was ascendant, some of Kolbowski's activist comrades criticized his "Stalinist behavior" and "excessive personalism in managing the club" (in fact, they were projecting the PCA's internal politics in the club); others said that his frequent trips to Mar del Plata did not comply with the code of austerity expected of Communist leaders, and accordingly they transferred their support to another member of the board of directors, also a Communist.[53] According to several of my informants, the 1963 trip to Israel was also used by Communists against Kolbowski. After all, following Israel's occupation of the West Bank and Gaza, the Soviet Union was leading an international propaganda campaign against Zionism. At least one of my sources claimed that at that point Kolbowski withdrew from the Communist Party. In addition, "owing to his intense activity in politics, football, and cooperatives, my father had neglected his business affairs and went bankrupt," Jorge Kolbowski told me bitterly, emphasizing that "the top leaders of the party and of the Instituto Movilizador de Fondos [the coordinating body of Argentine credit unions, which León Kolbowski had helped found], who previously had praised him so highly for his fabulous fund-raising results . . . were conspicuous by their absence. . . . They used him and exploited him."[54]

Despite the less than happy ending of Kolbowski's presidency, he remained enshrined in the collective memory of the Bohemians and neighbors of Villa Crespo as the club's great president: a legendary, almost mythic president who dedicated all his free time to the institution, was obsessed with the search for players, channeled his energy into obtaining resources for the club, and maintained close ties with the AFA, the municipality, and other important bodies. Kolbowski had come into a small club that was fighting for its survival, hampered by a small playing field in danger of being closed down with each city inspection, a meager social structure, and little capital of its own. He managed to transform it into a club of national importance by means of the new stadium it still maintains, the Primera Cooperativa del Deporte Atlanta (1958–68), the acquisition in 1966 of the 6,615 square meters of land in Dorrego Street that had belonged to Ferrocarril, and the best football results in the history of the institution. Kolbowski symbolizes the apogee of the social integration of Jewish immigrants in Argentine society, and the club's Jewish image was forged to a large extent during his presidency.

7

VICTORIES, FANS, AND FIGHT SONGS

After León Kolbowski left the presidency of Atlanta in 1969, the football team suffered one of its worst seasons ever. However, the first half of the 1970s marked the beginning of a new era of sports activity and institutional growth guided by Presidents Amadeo Altamura and José Davilman. Under the shadow of the country's political instability, growing social tension, the return of Perón, and the chaos that opened the door to the brutal military regime of 1976, the club took on additional importance in the life of Villa Crespo.[1]

On the football field, 1973 was the best year of this period and in the history of the club, which finished first in Zone A of the national tournament and third in the final round.[2] A year later a financial conflict over a debt broke out between the players and management; the latter decided to levy sanctions on the players, preventing the professionals from participating in the seasonal games. As a result, Atlanta finished last in Zone D of the 1974 national tournament. The period up to 1979 was characterized by one mediocre performance after another by the team, but none worse than that of the last year of the decade, when the CAA was relegated to Primera B after twenty-four years of playing in the top category of national football. The purgatory of second-division play lasted from 1980 to 1983, when the team was promoted back to Primera A. However, CAA lasted there only one year; by 1985, it was once again playing in Primera B. (See Table 7.1.)

In the institutional sphere, by contrast, the 1970s were the most productive decade in the history of the club, which by then was offering a great variety of activities and sports, including—notably—karate, in which club members won several championship titles during this period. The club's karate division reached its peak in those years, with a total of 150 participants of both sexes. Boxing was another discipline that enjoyed a resurgence of popularity in the 1970s, under the guidance of Antonio Alberto Poggi, who managed to revive the sport by promoting great pugilists such as José Urquiza, Ramón Salvador

TABLE 7.1   Atlanta's rankings, 1971–1985

Year	Clubs	Rank	Division
Metropolitano 1971	19	15	First
Nacional 1971	14	5	First
Metropolitano 1972	18	14	First
Reclasificatorio 1972	6	3	First
Nacional 1972	13	5	First
Metropolitano 1973	17	9	First
Nacional 1973	15 (final round 4 teams)	1 (final round 3rd place)	First
Metropolitano 1974	9	7	First
Nacional 1974	9	9	First
Metropolitano 1975	20	14	First
Nacional 1975	8	6	First
Metropolitano 1976	11	9	First
Reclasificatorio 1976	10	2	First
Nacional 1976	8	5	First
Metropolitano 1977	23	17	First
Nacional 1977	8	4	First
Metropolitano 1978	21	13	First
Nacional 1978	8	4	First
Metropolitano 1979	10	9	First
Reclasificatorio 1979	4	4	First
1980	20	2	Second
1981	22	11	Second
1982	22	2	Second
Torneo Octogonal 1982	8	2	Second
1983	22	1	Second
Nacional 1984	4 (Group H)	3	First
Metropolitano 1984	19	19	First
1985	22	2	Second
Torneo Octogonal 1985	8	2	Second

Source: Author's elaboration.

Franco, and Franco Faiulli, all products of the Atlanta breeding ground. Another contact sport, judo, also gained momentum during this time, affiliating with the Argentine Federation. Indoor soccer, or *fútsal*, emerged as a sport in 1977, when Atlanta formed its first team and hosted the federation for this sport at its facilities.

During these years the club's member roster grew. (See Table 7.2.) By 1975 an increase of 1,846 members had been recorded, 982 of whom were children.[3] In the climate of increasing political violence, many neighborhood parents preferred to send their children to participate in sports activities that were "not dangerous." This period also saw a significant increase in community-center membership, partly in response to the public announcement campaign

TABLE 7.2   Atlanta club members and number of Jews on the Board of Directors, 1970–1996

Year	Total Members	Jews on the Board of Directors	Percentage of Board
1970	9,000 (deduced from the membership dues recorded in the Annual Report)	8 of 27	29
1971	7,628 (deduced from the membership dues recorded in the Annual Report)	7 of 25	28
1972	10,000 (deduced from the membership dues recorded in the Annual Report)	10 of 29	34
1973		10 of 31	32
1974		10 of 30	33
1975–76			
1977	2,720 (according to the 1979 Annual Report)		
1978	3,770 (according to the 1979 Annual Report)		
1979	7,391 (according to the 1979 Annual Report)	3 of 26	11
1980	10,078		
1981	15,224		
1982	16,800	8 of 28	28
1983	18,000	8 of 28	28
1984	18,400	9 of 28	32
1985	9,256	10 of 27	37
1986	7,421	6 of 16	37.5
1987		9 of 28	28.5
1988	8,500	6 of 28	21
1989	800	9 of 28	32
1990		11 of 28	39
1991–95			
1996	253 (deduced from the membership dues recorded in the Annual Report)	8 of 22	36

Source: Ariel Korob, "Procesos identitarios e imaginarios locales. Atlanta: bohemios y judíos" (MA thesis, Universidad de Buenos Aires, 1998).

that asked, "Do you know where your child is now?"[4] Four years later, the number of members had increased fivefold, and in 1980 the club launched a major campaign designed to attract five thousand new members, with the goal of reaching a total membership of fifteen thousand by the end of the year.[5] In 1981–82 the number of members grew despite the country's fragile situation, which included the Malvinas (Falklands) War and deep devaluations of the national currency.[6] As the club's annual report claimed: "The membership, which in the previous years [under the dictatorship], incidentally, had enjoyed a significant rise, not only maintained its level in a year so critical and fateful for the country but increased further by some 10 percent."[7]

During this period Club Atlético Atlanta became more deeply embedded in the local community. It loaned its facilities free of charge to numerous schools in the district, as well as to various public-welfare institutions. The club was filled annually with some four to six thousand schoolchildren who used club facilities for their physical-education activities.[8] Beginning in 1982, the club offered scholarships to more than five hundred local elementary- and secondary-school pupils every year. There was also, it may be remembered, a kindergarten in the club. Atlanta's youth-related activities also extended to organizing summer or holiday camps (although this could not be done in 1975, owing to the country's socioeconomic and security situation).

Activities were not limited to children; the club was also a center for adults. During those years it was the headquarters for one of the branches of the Programa de Atención Médica Integral (PAMI, Comprehensive Medical Attention Program), a public health insurance agency managed by the Ministry of Health, and Atlanta, together with the Ministry of Social Action, the newspaper *Clarín*, and the local Johnson & Johnson affiliate, sponsored a free program called "Sports for Seniors."

A section entitled "The Club and the Community" in the 1979–80 annual report reflects the club's view of neighborhood relations, affirming, "All activities open to the community, in a club open to all," and "In all cases the objective is to place our club permanently at the service of the community to which we belong, as one way to give back some of the many benefits we have received from it."[9] In line with this policy, the club was always organizing cultural activities that would benefit the neighborhood, such as theater productions for adults and children, fashion shows, toy giveaways, film showings, and card tournaments. Since 1959 Atlanta had also housed a folk club called "Urpillay," for fans of the genre. By 1980 there were acting and vocational theater classes, choruses, and painting exhibitions.[10] A year later still other types of events were organized, such as dances, end-of-year parties, and a gastronomy display.[11]

In the second half of the 1970s, the club was enjoying an optimal economic situation, despite the economic and political traumas that were stirring the country. In 1975, despite the crisis produced by the Rodrigazo (the draconian economic policies imposed by Celestino Rodrigo, minister of the economy at the time),[12] the club finished the year with a balanced budget and a significant surplus, thanks to the mass sale of first-division football players—the customary way of resuscitating the club coffers. As the annual report explained, "Unfortunately, halfway through the year, we were unable to avoid the economic disaster that afflicted the whole country, and since desperate times require desperate measures, we had to sacrifice in part the structure of our top team and divest ourselves of some of its good players, which allowed us to reach the end of the financial year unscathed."[13]

Despite these healthy balance sheets, certain activities had to be cancelled—notably, basketball, youth camps, and the plan to publish a magazine.[14] Until the end of the decade, the club continued financially healthy, paying all its debts and again achieving a surplus. As the 1980s began, however, Atlanta began to flounder, ending the year with a deficit.[15]

The clubhouse was undergoing expansion and renovation. The new improvements included a nearly 2,000-square-meter roof for the gym, the installation of eight tennis courts with corresponding locker rooms and lighting, and the chess hall. In 1975 the club considered purchasing a building to house athletes in the city of Merlo, in Buenos Aires province.[16] A few years later construction was completed on the microstadium, a new open-air gymnasium for judo, weightlifting, and gymnastics, as well as an ice-skating rink. An electronic scoreboard for basketball was installed, and in 1984 a new front lobby was built in the clubhouse.[17]

The darkest chapter in the country's history, the so-called Process of National Reorganization, was also characterized by a blatant use and abuse of sports by the military dictatorship. The coup d'état of March 24, 1976, was the sixth military coup in the history of the Argentine Republic—and the bloodiest. In the name of the "doctrine of national security" and the battle against "subversion," tens of thousands of citizens were kidnapped, imprisoned, tortured, and murdered. It was under these circumstances that Argentina hosted the World Cup, an event that the military officers in power seized upon to

show both the world and the local population the image of a developed, orderly country under the guidance of an efficient military government.

The military junta that took power in March 1976 realized immediately
that football was an asset it could put to good use. On the very day of the
coup (March 24), all the radio stations and television channels were placed
under military control; regular programming was suspended and replaced by
military marches and the junta's communiqués. The only program from the
precoup schedule that was broadcast as originally planned was the qualify-
ing football match played in Poland by that country and Argentina. In fact,
all television and radio programs were banned except for that one football
game.[18]

A few months after the military coup, in July 1976, President Jorge Rafael Videla announced that hosting the World Cup was a national duty of the
highest priority and would consequently receive preferential attention from
the government. The military's eagerness to take advantage of the occasion
was clear, particularly since the junta's international image was deteriorating as the foreign media publicized the crimes committed by the Argentine
military. The money the junta invested in construction and services related to
the World Cup was estimated at 10 percent of the national budget, or US$700
million, swelling the already unwieldy foreign debt. By way of comparison,
Argentina's investment in the 1978 World Cup represented 40 percent of its
annual spending on education at that time.[19] The projects planned and carried out included the construction or renovation of three football stadiums
in Mendoza, Córdoba, and Mar del Plata to bring them into accordance with
international standards; infrastructural improvements ranging from roads to
sewers; the renovation of telecommunication networks; and the introduction
of color television. The junta's objective was clear: a perfectly organized World
Cup and the victory of the Argentine team, whatever the cost. And, indeed,
victory was achieved, producing an emotional explosion of ecstasy among
millions of Argentines.

The soccer club in Villa Crespo also felt the impact of the dictatorial re-
gimes in various ways. The club's main link to the military junta was via General Roberto Eduardo Viola, who would briefly serve as the de facto Argentine
president from March to December 1981. Viola's son had played football and
basketball with Atlanta. Thanks to that connection, the club's leadership felt
somewhat protected, and in 1980 Atlanta managed to obtain more than five
hectares of government-owned land in Villa Madero, to build a country house

there called La Bohemia, which was inaugurated in 1984 under the new democratic regime.[20] This land, belonging to the state, was granted to Atlanta by presidential decree issued on March 24, 1981, by the de facto president, Jorge Rafael Videla (the day that he handed the presidency over to Viola), and signed by his minister of the economy, Martínez de Hoz.[21]

Despite this connection, people associated with the club fell victims to state terrorism. One of them was Jorge Toscano, who had grown up in the club as a member of a "Bohemian family," his parents having served on the board of directors in the 1960s and 1970s. Jorge, like his parents, was a very active member, participating in various activities. Ironically, Toscano played on the same basketball team as a son of Viola, a member of the military leadership that caused Toscano's disappearance in 1976 as well as the disappearance of thousands of other Argentines. In another case, Silvia, the daughter of Atlanta's former president Amadeo Altamura, was kidnapped, although that incident had a happy ending, thanks to negotiations with Viola's son and his father which secured her release.[22] By contrast, appeals to General Viola were tragically to no avail in the case of Eduardo Muchnik, nephew of a former vice president of the club.[23] Muchnik was kidnapped in 1980, released, and then went into exile. During a brief stay in Colombia he met several former players of Atlanta. While in Peru, he was kidnapped again, taken back to Argentina, and disappeared.

Decline

In 1985 Atlanta was once more playing in Primera B, only to be relegated further the following year to Primera B Metropolitana, where it would play for almost four years. Thus, Atlanta has gone through divisional ups and downs, but, as of 2014, has never managed to regain the highest level of Argentine football.[24] Teams in the other sports practiced in the club fared similarly, never achieving any significant national success. Institutionally, the club was beginning to collapse, the critical point being its bankruptcy in 1991. Its chaotic state was reflected in the second half of the 1980s by strikes and constant turmoil, and a multitude of lawsuits involving administrators, maintenance staff, instructors, and players. This situation was compounded by the general economic disarray of the country. The year 1989 was characterized by hyperinflation. At one point the annual inflation rate hit 12,000 percent, according to the *New York Times*.[25] Social protests and demonstrations led to food riots, accompanied by episodes of looting in stores and supermarkets during the last part of Raúl Alfonsín's presidency. No wonder that Atlanta's books ended up deeply in the red during the late 1980s.

Despite this institutional disorder, the 1980s saw the beginning of intensive sociocultural activity at the Villa Madero center. These premises provided recreational sports opportunities to more than six hundred local children. The La Bohemia estate was used unrestrictedly and at no charge by many schools in the area. The local population was suffering from severe socioeconomic problems, and the local club headquarters was the only social institution that could provide these kinds of services. The club's influence there was apparently such that in the 1986–87 annual report, Atlanta's leaders expressed some concern over the division between the sympathizers of Villa Crespo and those of Villa Madero.[26]

Because of the near chaos on both the sports and the administrative levels, the Excellens company took over the management of the club in 1989. This company, which belonged to the man who was later president of Boca Juniors, Jorge Ameal, had previously administrated the Club Atlético Defensa y Justicia.[27] Seeking better investments, it decided to divest itself of Defensa and Justicia and take over the management of Atlanta. In that role, it was able to raise the Atlanta team from Primera B Metropolitana to B Nacional. This was an era in which private companies were beginning to involve themselves in all fields of sports administration, including football clubs.[28]

At the end of the 1989–90 season, after the Bohemian team was promoted to B Nacional, Excellens decided to abandon the club, which meant the departure of a large number of players, game losses, and economic and institutional crises. After a period of bad administration in both the institutional and the athletic spheres, which became more marked under the management of Aníbal Diman, Juan Chiarelli, and Bernardo Kravetsky during the years 1987–91, Atlanta went bankrupt when it failed to comply with the payment plan laid out for it at a meeting of its creditors. Its debt had reached two million pesos.[29]

The bankruptcy judgment, handed down by Judge Miguel Bargallo, made Atlanta the first professional football club to declare bankruptcy; it had to close down its facilities and suspend all its activities. However, a support committee was immediately formed under the leadership of Ezequiel Kristal, and in only two months the club was again playing football under the judge's authorization. The most painful part of the bankruptcy for the club was that it forced Atlanta to sell its clubhouse in September 1994.[30] The buyer was Juan Mirena, who at the time was the head of the Cámara de Supermercadistas (an organization of supermarket owners). The new owner never did anything with the lands adjacent to the clubhouse, however; they remained abandoned for many years. That same year, the courts decided to return administration of the club to the managers who had exercised it before the bankruptcy, Pablo Baczynski and Carlos Silver.

Atlanta's tribulations were partly a result of changes in Argentine society that affected the role of clubs. The social boom that had made them grow from the 1950s on had reversed itself. Families were moving away from institutions, and single-sport gyms were becoming increasingly popular. As a result of the fame of the Argentine tennis-player Guillermo Vilas, the city filled up with tennis courts, which had once been found almost solely in sports institutions. Next came gyms, which, in the past had always formed part of larger social and sports institutions with diversified offerings, such as the CAA. The same thing happened to swimming pools and paddle tennis. These changes helped draw members away from Atlanta, as well as from other clubs, such as Vélez, Independiente, Ferrocarril, and River.

The decline of neighborhood clubs has produced nostalgia among many Argentines in recent years, a nostalgia beautifully captured in Juan José Campanella's 2004 film *Luna de Avellaneda*. One of the movie's heroes is Amadeo Grimberg, a Jewish Argentine character played by Eduardo Blanco—yet another testimony in contemporary Argentine popular culture to the importance of Jewish Argentines in the making of modern Argentina.

The 1990s were marred by the high degree of internal violence that Argentina was suffering as a result of socioeconomic problems. The violence spilled over into football, causing concern to the authorities, as was patently clear from a 1999 resolution issued by the interior minister, Carlos Corach. Corach asked all clubs that had video-camera systems in their stadiums to record any acts of hooliganism.[31] The following year, the Government Secretariat of the City of Buenos Aires decreed the creation of the Consejo de Seguridad y Prevención de la Violencia en el Fútbol (Council for Security and Prevention of Violence in Football), which was to supervise security arrangements at all sports events.[32] This was the context for the letter that the president of Atlanta sent in October 2000 to the security committee, requesting that the game between Atlanta and Defensores de Belgrano not take place in the All Boys stadium, for fear of violent conflict between the fans and the local team.[33]

Xenophobia, Racism, and Anti-Semitism

The football-club fans who go to the stadiums are different from the basically passive spectators of the theater or the cinema. Football fans are faithful followers and, as Eduardo Archetti showed in his pioneering research, fundamentally active participants in the football phenomenon. The relationship between the directors of the club and the fans is not one-way. The fan is not merely a customer at a spectacle, nor is he or she simply a consumer of a product or service.[34]

Fans have had to sacrifice a great deal to maintain their loyalty to their favorite team. For a long time—and not only in the 1920s, 1930s, or 1940s—it was no simple matter to buy a ticket, find a place in the stands, gain access to the restroom, or leave the soccer pitch peacefully.[35] Sometimes the fans put up with it all resignedly. At other times they protested, pressured the club authorities, and exploited criticisms in the popular press to create the necessary atmosphere for improvements in the stadium.[36] Moreover, the fans did not limit themselves to insulting the referee, the opposing team, or their mothers and sisters. They might also demand that a poor coach be fired, apply pressure for the acquisition of new players, or prevent the sale of a star. The fact that *socios* actively participated in club elections also gave them a sense of ownership and the feeling that they were entitled to protest whatever they considered acts of injustice.

Analysis of collective identity construction in general and that of football fans, in Argentina and elsewhere, in particular, focuses on the processes of antagonistic elaboration in a bipolar axis of mutual exclusion, especially in concrete spaces such as football fields.[37] While football offers a space for dialogue, it also reveals social and ethnic tensions. Unsurprisingly, racism and anti-Semitism are therefore not uncommon in European and Latin American football stadiums.[38] Writing on British football, Ben Carrington and Ian McDonald pointed to the complex interplay of race, nation, culture, and identity in sport: "In a sense, this is the greatest paradox about sport's relationship to racism. It is an arena where certain forms of racism, particularly cultural racism, have been most effectively challenged. Yet, at the very same time, it has provided a platform for racist sentiments to be most clearly expressed."[39]

Lelia Gándara considers that "the struggle between fans is crossed by the line of an imaginary border that divides the universe into two opposing camps: us and them. On one side of this discursive scene is that which is seen as prestigious and desirable, and on the other, that which deserves disdain." Accordingly,

> it would be a mistake—and terrifying—to suppose that if there are thousands of fans screaming racist, homophobic, or anti-Semitic chants on the football fields, it means that they literally believe, with all that this signifies, what they are saying. In reality, they are putting into practice identity strategies that suppose a categorical contraposition. Insults are words that have been semantically emptied in order to acquire value based on an axiological characteristic, that is, a value judgment.[40]

The choice of an insult depends on repertory already established socially and culturally, and available for the use of the fans. Rarely will football fans contribute some innovation to the existing repertory of insults. In this sense also the terms "Jew" (or "Bolivian," "Paraguayan," "vulgar," "homosexual," and so on) will be used pejoratively on the football field. Moreover, insults depend on the changing sociocultural context. What happens in the stadium is connected with processes and events in "the real world," outside the "football fantasy." Accordingly, even the Middle Eastern conflict in general and the violent relations between Israelis and Palestinians in particular play an important role.

Football discourse constitutes an identity linked to a strong sense of belonging. This phenomenon is reflected in the phrase "an Atlantan since the cradle," in the case of the Bohemians, or "to carry it in the blood/in the heart." The sentence "I belong to Atlanta" means a family identification, by tradition and by neighborhood.[41]

Closely associated with this is the fact that, often, a group's identity may be based on antagonisms and opposition. Moreover, the anonymity an individual feels in large crowds of people opens the door to behaviors that in nearly any other environment would be considered aberrant.[42] As Gaffney notes, stadium rituals tend to "organize and manage the passage of people from one set of rules and normative social positions to another and back again. That is, the nominally transgressive behavior of the stadium is managed and controlled for a brief time in a limited space before returning to 'normalcy.'"[43] "Uncivilized" behavior is tolerated during a specific time period, just as it is at carnivals.

In this antagonism, the "other" is given a status of supposed inferiority: this could be a foreigner from a "poor" country (*boliviano, paraguayo*); a feminized or homosexual male (*puto* [male prostitute]), or someone who plays a passive sexual role;[44] someone who performs socially devalued jobs or roles (*basurero* [garbage collector], *quemero* [trash burner], *tripero* [glutton]), is poor or marginal (*grasa* [common], *villero* [slum-dweller]), or is discriminated against on account of race (*negro* [black]) or religion (*judío* [Jew]).

Physical confrontation between rival fans, especially the confrontations common between neighbors or long-standing rivals, has become the basis for legends of all kinds. This is particularly evident in cities with two competing professional teams: Racing Club and Independiente in Avellaneda, Newells Old Boys and Rosario Central in Rosario, and Gimnasia y Esgrima and Estudiantes in La Plata. In the city of Buenos Aires, with its numerous professional league clubs, the conflicts are diverse. Clubs located in the same neighborhood, now or in the past, can become mortal enemies, as exemplified by the historical rivalry between Huracán and San Lorenzo de Almagro. Violence in Argentine football has a long history, but it has grown worse since the 1960s. In the case of Atlanta, with its Jewish image, anti-Semitic expressions are less a function of racist bigotry than of the club's traditional rivalry with the neighboring football club, Chacarita Juniors, which Atlanta chased out of Villa Crespo in the mid-1940s. Fans of Defensores de Belgrano and All Boys also stand out with their anti-Semitic chants.[45]

The perception of Atlanta as "the Jews' club" is in many respects the result of an identity imposed from outside, by rival fans. Therefore, non-Jewish Atlanta fans are often identified as Jews. One of my informants, E. I., spoke about his own experiences as well as those of his fifteen-year-old son:

> One thing that's happened to me when I'm outside the community is that if you say you're an Atlanta fan, they immediately assume you are of Jewish descent. . . . It still happens to my younger son, L, 15 years old . . . in the club where he's been playing basketball for years, they call him "Russian" because he is an Atlanta fan, or they say he goes to the Hospital Israelita [Jewish Hospital], which is very close to that basketball club (of course L has never set foot in the Hospital Israelita, they're just kidding him).

Most of the people I interviewed referred to anti-Semitic expressions in Atlanta games from the 1960s onward. However, according to at least one of the old fans, racist slogans were heard at Atlanta games in Villa Crespo even back during World War II.

Among the anti-Semitic slogans chanted by fans of rival teams, for example, I once heard the infamous: "Ahí viene Hitler por el callejón, matando judíos para hacer jabón" (Here comes Hitler down the street, killing Jews to make soap). This was accompanied by hissing noises, meant to evoke the sound of the gas chambers. This hateful behavior is not unique to Argentine football fields. In England, Chelsea's fans, the arch rivals of Tottenham, sang "Hitler's gonna gas 'em again/ We can't stop them/ The Yids from Tottenham." Another song urged, "Gas a Jew, Jew, Jew, put him in the oven, cook him through."[46]

In the 1930s, Oswald Mosley's British Union of Fascists marched through London's East End shouting "Down with the Yids," an insulting term equivalent to "nigger" in the United States. Tottenham's fans transform this term into a badge of honor, as many non-Jewish fans have done with the term "ruso." That is, they adopted the term as a kind of defense mechanism; by owning it they deflected the anti-Semitic abuse.

During the Gulf War of the early 1990s, the mantra "Olé, olé, olé, olé, Saddam Hussein" was occasionally heard. The Iraqi leader, considered an enemy of the Jews, was mentioned specifically to provoke Atlanta's fans. And in the mid-1990s, after attacks on the Israeli Embassy and the Jewish community center, Asociación Mutual Israelita Argentina (AMIA),[47] the fans of All Boys sang, " . . . les volamos la embajada, les volamos la mutual, les vamos a quemar la cancha, para que no jodan más . . . " (We blew up the embassy, we blew up the community center, we're going to burn up your field so you don't screw with anyone any more . . .).

In response to questionnaires I distributed among Jewish supporters of Atlanta, most of them remembered either the chant about Hitler coming to kill Jews "to make soap" or episodes of rival fans throwing small pieces of soap onto the pitch as the most offensive insults. The use and abuse of concepts from the Holocaust is surely more powerful than any reference to contemporary events in the Middle East or expressions of hostility toward Zionism.

The fans' chants reflect different uses of the word Jewish—a word that is almost always associated with another, negative, adjective, in case the pejorative use of "Jewish" as an insult is not clear or sufficient. Thus, for example, they would shout, "No se escucha, no se escucha, sos amargo, judío hijo de puta" (Can't hear, can't hear, you're bitter, Jewish son of a bitch). The concepts of "bitter" and "coward" are often used as opposites to the capacity for celebration, vitality, and "*aguante*," understood as persistence and team loyalty.

An incident in 2000, when fans of Defensores de Belgrano pelted the Atlanta team with bits of ham as they came out on the playing field, provoked an interesting reaction on the part of the Delegación de Asociaciones Israelitas Argentinas (DAIA, Delegation of Argentine Jewish Associations), the umbrella organization of Argentina's organized Jewish community. The DAIA asked the AFA to sanction the Defensores de Belgrano club for this act of "discrimination against Atlanta's sympathizers."[48] The AFA accepted the suggestion of organizing workshops on discrimination for the referees. Thus, the DAIA effectively reaffirmed the identification of Atlanta's fans as Jews, just as it accepted the word "Jew" as an insult. Some newspapers resorted to euphemisms such as "anti-Semitic chants that dealt with burning the temples of the Jewish community with which the Bohemian fans are identified," or "insults of an anti-Semitic nature against the Villa Crespo team."[49]

No less interesting was the commentary in *Clarín*, a couple of years later, describing the game between Flandria and Defensores de Belgrano. Flandria lost 3 to 0, and its fans began to shout, "Jews, sons of bitches." According to the *Clarín* correspondent, it was "a song that meant no offense to Defe [Defensores]."[50] In other words, this chant had anti-Semitic significance only when it was used in games against Atlanta.

One example of the complexity and contradictions in the image of Jews in Argentina can be seen in the fact that in the early twenty-first century a bleacher section at the football pitch of the Defensores de Belgrano club bears the name of Marcos Zucker Jr., in homage to the son of the famous Jewish Argentine movie, theater, and television actor. The son, a fan of the club, had been imprisoned by the military authorities for participating in the Montonero counteroffensive in the early 1980s. *Página/12* explained to its readers, "Atlanta, since the time of León Kolbowski—an ex-president of the 1960s—has been associated with the Jewish community and consequently endured all kinds of discriminatory manifestations that almost resulted in sanctions by the AFA. Today the leaders of Defensores feel compelled to reject, once more, that miserable attitude that would have outraged a fan like Marquitos Zucker."[51]

Jorge Rubinska, president of Club Atlanta in those years, tried to differentiate between the chants heard in the Kolbowski period and the more recent ones, and between the meanings of the epithets "Russian" and "Jew."

We cannot isolate discrimination in a football stadium from the times lived by the country. This has to do with the culture of our society. As a boy, when I used to follow Atlanta we would hear the little ditties against "the Russians" which were officialized in the era of León Kolbowski, a former club president. With time, that aggression turned into a common identification. One did not feel discriminated against, because the fact that we were called Russians did not have the weight of that anti-Semitism that society began to adopt in particular in the era of the [1970s National Reorganization] Process. That is where the aggression against Jews in Atlanta took shape. . . . This picture of aggression was gradually exacerbated by socioeconomic problems.[52]

The influence of events in the Middle East on aggression against Atlanta fans has been noted in recent years in comments posted at various Internet sites, particularly www.sentimientobohemio.com.ar, and transcribed by Mauricio Dimant.[53] Two examples will suffice here (I have only corrected the spelling):

. . . no ves que sos pura mierda judío asqueroso, aliado de Bush; ojalá que vengan los árabes y los decapiten a todos los hinchas de Atlanta . . . Viva América Latina libre, igual que Irak y Palestina . . . Aguante San Telmo y la resistencia árabe contra los judíos y los yankee putos . . .

[Don't you see you are pure filthy Jewish shit, you Bush ally; I hope the Arabs come and cut off the heads of all the Atlanta fans . . . Long live a free Latin America, as well as Iraq and Palestine . . . San Telmo rocks and so does the Arab resistance against the Jews and the fucking Yankees . . .]

In the same tone, incorporating a supposed defense of the Palestinians, anti-Semitism, and the identification of Club Atlanta with Jews, another poster writes:

Asco me dan que usurpen un país y tiroteen lugares sagrados, asco me dan de que maten pibitos inocentes, asco me dan las masacres que hacen. . . . Los judíos son un asco, y Atlanta es el club representante de esa colectividad de mierda, rusos de mierda siempre amigos de los poderosos, ojalá algún suicida haga volar Villa Crespo por los aires.

[It makes me sick that they take over a country and shoot up sacred sites, it makes me sick that they kill innocent little kids, the massacres they do make me sick. . . . Jews are nauseating, and Atlanta is the club representing that group of shit, shitty Russians always friends of the powerful, I wish that some suicide (bomber) would blow Villa Crespo to pieces.][54]

To provide some nuance to this picture, it should be stressed that Chacarita Juniors, too, has had a large number of Jewish fans (and at least as many Jewish players as Atlanta);[55] oddly, at least one of them confessed to me that more than once he had chanted anti-Semitic slogans during games between his favorite team and Atlanta. That is, once he entered the stadium his identity as a Chacarita fan carried more weight than his identity as a Jew or as an intellectual. During our conversation he was a little embarrassed to share this confidence with me. This phenomenon should be analyzed in the local context, and the importance of anti-Semitic manifestations in games against Atlanta should not be exaggerated. Korob compared them to the songs sung by fans against Deportivo Armenio about the Turks who killed millions of Armenians during World War I, or the branding of fans of Deportivo Italiano or Deportivo Español as, respectively, "*tano*" (wop) or "*gallego*" (dago) sons of bitches.[56]

Atlanta fans contribute their own share of racist slogans, particularly in games against their arch rival Chacarita Juniors (when they are in the same division):

Qué feo es ser de Chaca y boliviano, en una villa tienen que vivir; tu hermana revolea la cartera, tu vieja chupa pija en San Martín, Che Chaca, che Chaca, che Chaca, che Chaca, no lo pienses más; andate a vivir a Bolivia, toda tu familia está allá.

[How ugly to be a Bolivian from Chaca, in a shanty town they have to live; your sister is a streetwalker, your old lady sucks cock in San Martín, che Chaca, che Chaca, che Chaca, che Chaca, don't think about it any more; go live in Bolivia, your whole family is out there.]

Obviously, the confrontational nature of team sports and the strong identities and emotions associated with football teams at times contribute to the use of racist and anti-Semitic slogans (even in teams associated with Communists and Socialists, who preach the brotherhood of nations).

There is a gender issue here as well. One of the most significant aspects of Latin American fan culture is the ferocity with which fans defend the masculinity of their own club and question that of rival teams. Ultimately, football is often conceived as a war in which "the strongest" wins, and the songs sung in the stands, as Archetti has shown, "are part of the dramatic element associated with masculinity and the boundaries between the genders."[57] According to Parrish and Nauright, "While *cantitos* [chants] are reminiscent of football songs heard at stadiums across Europe, there is a key difference between Argentine *cantitos* and the majority of English chants in that the Argentine chants place sexual domination and infantilization at the core of expression."[58] Thus, characterizing the Atlanta team as Jewish is a way of challenging its masculinity, since the stereotype of Jews as feminine is common. Likewise, Jewish circumcision is evoked in an effort to characterize Atlanta players as impotent. Underlying insults of this sort is the attempt to equate the size of the penis with its effectiveness. Many of the chants of the fans of rival teams focus on this: "oh, la pija cortada no les sirve para nada" (oh, a cut-off prick doesn't do you any good"). To this, the Bohemians usually retaliate with "El ruso te la puso" (You've been screwed by the Russian [that is, Jew]). This last chant is probably one of the favorites among both Jewish and non-Jewish fans of Atlanta that I have interviewed.

Fans adopted this chant as a way of appropriating the term to deflect anti-Semitism. Again, Tottenham's fans have had a somewhat similar experience. In a game against Manchester City in the early 1980s, Manchester's supporters started singing:

> We'll be running around Tottenham with our pricks hanging out tonight.
> We'll be running around Tottenham with our pricks hanging out tonight.
> Singing I've got a foreskin, I've got a foreskin, I've got a foreskin, and you ain't
> We've got a foreskin, we've got a foreskin, you ain't.

Tottenham, in response, rounded up some of its Jewish fans and encouraged them to drop their pants and wave their circumcised members in defiance.[59]

As we can see, masculinity and an active sexual role, being white and not poor, as well as professing love and loyalty to one's own team, are all values emphasized by the fans, who in fact all share the same socioeconomic, ethnic, and religious heterogeneity. "Canten, rusos!" (Sing, Russians [Jews]!) is not meant to describe Atlanta so much as it is a war cry that the members of the *barra brava* (fan group) use to intimidate the fans and make them sing. It is one more indication that Atlanta's status as Jewish often comes out in the anger or mockery expressed against the other team.

At the same time, not all Bohemians feel comfortable with this identification. The idea of a large Jewish fan-base has been unsettling at times for some non-Jewish supporters of Atlanta. One sector of fans, a *barra brava* known as La Loza, used to try to establish differences and distance with respect to the fans of Jewish origin in their club. On several occasions these fans put up a flag with a swastika on the playing field. In this way some of the fans were trying, in vain, to protest against the identification of the club, and therefore themselves, as "Jews"—thus acknowledging that they saw being "Jewish" as an insult.[60]

Analysis of these semantics should not be limited to playing-field chants; it should be extended to the streets and, specifically, the graffiti on the walls of Villa Crespo. (See Figure 7.1.) Those markings also reflect the argot that constitutes the collective identity of Atlanta fans, on one hand, and that of the fans of rival teams, on the other. After all, these identities are linked to territorial values, in the neighborhood as well as the stadium. Graffiti reflects both a dialog between the fans and the competition for space on the wall, which parallels the competition on the football pitch, through crossings-out

FIGURE 7.1 Graffiti on a neighborhood wall.
Source: Courtesy of Lelia Gándara.

and superimposed slogans. Atlanta's emblem, colors, and name figure prominently in some graffiti, at times accompanied by slogans such as "VILLA CRESPO RULES," "VILLA CRESPO IS THE KING," or "ATLANTA IS TOP." Occasionally negative mentions ("the motherfuckers of the B") of one of the rival teams (such as Chacarita, Argentinos Juniors, or All Boys) are added at the side. Often messages of all kinds are appended, running the gamut from a swastika to simply "sons of bitches," painted or written in a different hand.[61]

Family, Food, and Language

The Jewish American author Philip Roth referred once to his youthful enthusiasm for baseball, a sport he described as "a kind of secular church that reached into every class and region of the nation and bound millions upon millions of us together in common concerns, loyalties, rituals, enthusiasms, and antagonisms."[62] The same holds true for football and Jewish Argentines, especially for those *porteño* Jews who turned the Atlanta soccer field into a temple where they expressed their Jewish Argentine identity. An anecdote that points to the stadium as an alternative temple is the story told by journalist Alejandro Melincovsky. He remembers meeting several Jewish Argentines who, like himself, fasted on Yom Kippur, left the neighborhood synagogue to walk to the León Kolbowski Stadium to watch the match and then went back to the synagogue. In the mid-1990s, precisely on Yom Kippur, Atlanta had a crucial game to play against Tigre. "We drove to the Tigre field to watch the game," Melincovsky explains half-apologetically. "It was a matter of life or death. After the game, we drove back to the synagogue."[63]

In all the interviews I have conducted, it is clear that Atlanta has played a central role in family rituals and the daily lives of Jewish Argentines in general and those living in Villa Crespo in particular. A couple of examples should suffice here for a glimpse of Jewish Argentine family rituals involving football. When I asked Bernardo Lichtensztajn, born in 1947, for his favorite anecdote about his long-term loyalty to Atlanta he recounted:

> On Sundays when Atlanta was playing a home game, I would meet my uncle
> on the corner of Corrientes and Malabia, where he lived. I would take the bus
> and the subway from my house, or my father would drop me off. This "ritual"
> began when I was ten years old. Usually I met him at ten in the morning. We
> would go to the café at the corner of Vera and Malabia, where my uncle hung

out every day, but especially Saturdays and Sundays. There we would meet the guys from the café, my uncle's friends, all of them bachelors (the group kept getting smaller each time one of them got married). All the guys were Jewish. I think the only *goys* were the "Spaniard" who owned the bar, and the two waiters. There weren't any women at all, of course. I would watch them and learn to play dice (*generala*) or cards (*truco, tute cabrero,* and *chinchón*), while they were enjoying a glass of vermouth. THAT was my great pleasure. I did not drink alcohol, I was a child, but I did drink coca cola or Fanta or Crush or *bidú* [an Argentine soft drink], and I ate everything that accompanied the vermouth. There were many little dishes, all with tasty snacks . . . all delicious.

At 12:30 "it's lunchtime," so I'd eat a plate of ravioli or noodles with pesto and tomato sauce. Delicacies. At two o'clock the guys from the café (about twenty-five men) split in two. The smaller group would get up and leave. Those were the fans of other clubs (River, Boca, Ferro, Racing, San Lorenzo, Independiente), who had to get to more remote football fields. The games began at exactly 3:30 p.m. The rest, the vast majority, would stay in the bar, drinking coffee, until 2:30, and at that time we would all go to the pitch together, strolling along leisurely for about ten minutes and chatting. I walked holding my uncle's hand, listening without talking, but very excited and happy and eager to get to the stands. Entering the field and settling in the stands made my heart beat faster and filled me with joy.[64]

When and how does one become a football fan? Nick Hornby, in his *Fever Pitch*, shares with the readers a typical socialization process:

I fell in love with football as I was later to fall in love with women: suddenly, inexplicably, uncritically, giving no thought to the pain or disruption it would bring with it. In May '68, just after my eleventh birthday, my father asked me if I'd like to go with him to the FA Cup Final between West Brom and Everton. . . . I told him that I wasn't interested in football, not even in the Cup Final—true, as far as I was aware, but perversely I watched the whole match on television anyway. A few weeks later I watched the Man Utd-Benfica game, enthralled, with my mum . . . with a passion that had taken me completely by surprise; it lasted three weeks, until my dad took me to Highbury for the first time.[65]

Indeed, most of the people I interviewed became Atlanta fans at a young age, with the family—especially fathers and/or brothers—playing a special role in this socialization process.[66] "Paternal influence" was Carlos Storz's succinct explanation of his lifelong loyalty to Atlanta, unwittingly repeating the exact words of the much older Nujem Guernik, born in 1923 in Villa Crespo. Guillermo Estiz claims, "I've been rooting for Atlanta since I was in the crib, as a member and a fan; before taking me to the civil registry [as a baby], my father made me a member of Atlanta." When I asked Clody Plotinky, a fanatic Atlanta supporter born in Villa Crespo in 1959, whether his family members were also club members or supporters, he said, "Father, mother, sister, uncles, cousins."[67] Often it was not the football but the club that attracted children to Atlanta and turned them into football fans. After all, from its early days Atlanta had organized various social and cultural activities for its members, and once it settled in Villa Crespo, it became a pillar of social life in the neighborhood. Weekend dancing parties and barbecues, patriotic commemorations and anniversary ceremonies, a variety of athletic activities for men, women, and children, music festivals or lectures—at certain points in its history even a kindergarten, library, and café—all have contributed to transform the club into a social forum, establishing it as an axis of the collective imaginary. "My family went to the club's social center for recreation," recalls Felipe Leibovich. Pablo Waisberg was eight years old when he was invited "to a birthday at the club headquarters, and from that day, November 20, 1973, and for a very long time, it became my second home."

When it was not a family member, it was usually the influence of a friend and a form of male bonding that brought youngsters into the club:

> I was a member as a child for a short time, in 1980 and 1981. At that time I went mostly to summer camp and basketball practice. Years later, in 1994, I met a guy—also Jewish—in the Faculty of Humanities, who started to go to Atlanta games. He, in turn, went because of another friend—Jewish as well—who was a fan and had played in their junior leagues. We became friends and he convinced me to go the Atlanta stadium. What's more, I lived only eight blocks away from the field most of my life, so I identified with the neighborhood.[68]

But Atlanta and its football team were important not only to the boys, their fathers and their male friends. As Silvio Melincovsky told me, "My father was a supporter, my brother a fan, and my sister a fan. My mother, in solidarity with us, [was] also [a fan]. Then my two sons became fans and my wife as well." When asked about his favorite anecdote, Víctor Zamenfeld responded immediately, "My *bobe* [grandmother] praying and suffering for Atlanta (and for all the relatives going to the football pitch, especially my uncle

Enrique). My grandmother was very *gringa* [foreign], she spoke Yiddish and bad Spanish in a way that was very endearing to us, especially when she talked about Atlanta, whose most famous players or scorers she knew well."[69]

As Jennifer Schafer demonstrated in her discussion of the 1978 soccer World Cup games held in Argentina, participation at the stadium, consumption of news about the games, and the fervor that accompanied the national team were not exclusively masculine.[70] An article in the daily *Clarín* stated, just six days before the final game:

> The World Cup of '78 created a surprise mutation: the women—usually detractors of soccer, which every Sunday robs them of their husbands—have fallen into the trap of the eleven against eleven. And this is not mere tolerance, condescension or kindness, but rather something summarily similar to the passion of the masses, until now almost exclusively masculine. Girls, older women, up to grandmothers, in the fair, the street or the hair salon, are proving to be as obsessed as men.

This "surprise mutation" in fact took place decades before the 1978 games that the brutal military dictatorship cynically used and abused for political purposes.[71] During the years of León Kolbowski's presidency, Atlanta became known for players throwing flowers to the spectators as they came out on the field. This made Atlanta and football in general more attractive to women and encouraged entire families to come to the stadium. For Julio Bichman this was a decisive moment in his life as a fan:

> I had that experience at an Atlanta friendly in Mar del Plata in the 60s. The team used to come into the field with flowers for the ladies, and in that particular game, a legend of Argentinean football, Carlos Timoteo Griguol, handed my mother a flower and [her friend] Berta the other. The emotion was such that I felt that I had fallen in love with Atlanta, its colors and everything related to the club.[72]

During that period Cecilio Barak was called by Adolfo Mogilevsky, Atlanta's much admired physical therapist, to serve as the team's physician. Barak remembers "my trips to the countryside with them. Even my wife came on those trips; she would walk onto the pitch with the team's ball."[73]

As a kid in the late 1930s and early 1940s, Esther Rollansky was sometimes locked in her room by her brother Rubén and not allowed out until she was able to "sing" the names of all Atlanta players.[74] Novelist Manuela Fingueret was born in 1945 near the Atlanta stadium and lived there until she was fourteen years old. The Atlanta football club was a prominent part of her childhood and made her an enthusiastic fan of Atlanta all through her life; in 2006, she, together with poet Juan Gelman, was given an honorary life membership in the club.[75] Fingueret is one of several Jewish Argentine writers whose work includes clear references to the presence of football in the main characters' lives.[76] Liliana Heker's short story "La música de los domingos" (Sunday music) evokes childhood memories of weekends filled with the sound of soccer games on radio and television.

Another example of family rituals, similar in nature but from a younger generation, is taken from the testimony of Guido Martín Nejamkis, born in 1969:

> We lived in Villa Crespo, and we used to walk to the football field. On our way to the stadium—now called León Kolbowski—which was about eight blocks, we used to pass synagogues and Jewish schools. However, what I noticed was the businesses, some with Hebrew names, like the Kolbo chain of perfume shops and cleaning goods. Of course, the local bakeries sold, and still do today, delicious *pletzalach* [onion buns] with cucumber and pastrami, and sometimes we would have one after the game.[77]

Yiddish was spoken in the stadium on Humboldt Street for many years, marking it as a Latin American language.[78] Architect Benjamín Fryd remembers nostalgically, "It was fun watching the neighborhood's quirky characters in the cheap seats: classic Jews with their insults in Yiddish, or in Spanish with a Yiddish accent." Psychologist Jaime Mandelman recalls how back in the 1960s "during one of the games, in the cheap seats, there was a ten- or twelve-year-old boy who would keep getting up, blocking our view. At some point I said, "Sit down, *yingle*." The boy turned, surprised, and then asked his father, "Dad, where does this guy know me from?"[79]

Jewish businesses sponsored the broadcasting of Atlanta games on the radio. According to Nejamkis:

> Often I listened to games on the radio [Internet]. One of the sponsors of these broadcasts was a restaurant that sold *kreplach*, *varenikes*, *knishes*, and *pletzalach*. It was called El Sabor de la Niñez [The Taste of Childhood]. The advertisement said:
>
> > Thank you, *Zeide* [Grandfather], thank you, Papa!!!
> > The Taste of Childhood. Kreplach–Varenikes–Knishes.[80]

The Last Tango

Almost a decade after Atlanta's bankruptcy, in the year 2000, fans and club members who were dismayed by the neglect of the property that Atlanta had sold decided to organize and lobby the Buenos Aires legislature asking that the clubhouse be declared a historical city landmark and a site of cultural interest. These efforts bore no fruit, but three years later the struggle to win back the clubhouse was revived, with the result that on December 9, 2003, the Buenos Aires legislature approved Deputy Jorge Giorno's draft law declaring the property to be of public utility.[81] In March 2004 the head of the municipal government, Aníbal Ibarra, approved a law expropriating this land, which became the property of the city of Buenos Aires. Two years later, the head of government at that time, Jorge Telerman (a Jewish Argentine who was reportedly a supporter of Club Atlanta), decided to divide the land up, giving part of it to Atlanta to use for a sports center and clubhouse, with the other part to be used for a school, a cultural center, and a green space.

The joy over recovering Atlanta's clubhouse had scarcely subsided when the tragedy of the República Cromañón nightclub fire prompted a series of very strict municipal inspections, and in February 2005 the Don León Kolbowski Stadium was closed for inadequate sanitation and security. This was the beginning of a series of reopenings and closures. The latest prohibition against play in Humboldt Street continued for several years by court order because of some acts of violence and indiscipline by Atlanta's fans. The club newsletters for 2005 reveal that institutional and cultural activity continued. A department was created specifically to recruit new members and to rehabilitate those who owed dues; the club's subcommittees organized a tango show with the participation of Alberto "Toto" Fontan and Juan Carlos de María, and a course for institutional management was inaugurated. The club even embarked on a new financial venture, reaching an agreement with the Credicoop Bank to launch an Atlanta credit card. This initiative was backed by the Villa Crespo Chamber of Commerce, which offered discounts to anyone who used the card for purchases. Thus, the club continued to play an active part in the neighborhood.

Around 2007 the closures and disqualifications were lifted, and the board of directors decided to build new concrete stands in the stadium to replace the wooden ones that still stood there (Atlanta's branch in Israel contributed to this project),[82] unveiling them on March 29, 2009, on the occasion of a game against Deportivo Español, which it won handily 3–1 to the cheers of six thousand supporters in the new concrete grandstands.[83] After more than a decade of hardship, Atlanta had been granted a new lease on life thanks to the recovery of its clubhouse, the renovation of its stadium, and the team's promotion to the National B division in 2011. Whether Atlanta's resurgence as a football club and especially as a social entity endures will depend on its management, its members, and its fans. As I was completing this manuscript, during the 2012–13 football season, Atlanta was again playing in the third division, the B Metropolitana, but it was in first place, with a good chance of moving back to the B Nacional.

Oddly enough, despite the ever-diminishing Jewish presence in Villa Crespo, Atlanta's image as a "Jewish club" and of its fans as "Russians" seems more deeply engrained than ever in the world of Argentine football. Stereotypes and fantasies have a life of their own, and their relation to any social reality is tenuous. Sports commentators would say that in Atlanta's case its nicknames (such as "Bohemian") express the marginal status of the club throughout its history relative to the more popular clubs among which it always felt it belonged. Moreover, they would say that the sale of players, which has been a norm in Atlanta's history and even a source of pride for the club as an "exporter" of players, in fact confirms "the subsidiary role that Atlanta assumed in the market of the football spectacle": an exporter of protagonists, never a protagonist itself. However, for those of us who are interested in the history of Argentina and who know that a major key to understanding its society lies in its role as an immigrant melting pot, Atlanta serves as a worthy example for the study of a topic seldom or never explored before: the alternative ways that immigrants (Semitic or otherwise) and their Argentine-born descendants have integrated socially into the urban life of Buenos Aires.

EPILOGUE

Cao Hamburger's moving 2007 film *O Ano em que Meus Pais Saíram de Férias* (The Year that My Parents Went on Vacation) makes a good starting point for a discussion about football and ethnicity.[1] The movie takes place in Brazil in 1970, under the military dictatorship. At the time, the national football team, starring Pelé and Jeorjinho, was playing in the World Cup in Mexico. The protagonist, Mauro, is the child of a Jewish father and a non-Jewish mother who are opponents of the regime (parts of the script are based on Hamburger's own childhood). They tell their son that they have to go on vacation without him. Fearing for their lives, they flee their home, leaving Mauro at the entrance of his Jewish grandfather's building in São Paulo's Bom Retiro neighborhood. However, the grandfather has just passed away, and Mauro is adopted by the Jewish elders of the neighborhood.[2] The film's portrayal of these elderly Jews cheering in support of Brazil's national football team, and their enthusiasm for the local football club, points to the need to look at various ethnic groups in South America and the importance of this sports activity to their identities.

Chilean football offers a no less fascinating example for the exploration of football's ethnic dimension. Two flags waving in the breeze greet those entering Santiago's La Cisterna Stadium on game days—the Chilean and the Palestinian. Club Deportivo Palestino (Palestine Football Club) claims to represent Chile's more than three hundred thousand Palestinian descendants, the largest concentration of Palestinians outside the Middle East. Some of the club's fans arrive at matches sporting the black-and-white keffyeh that reflects their place of origin. They call themselves "*baisanos*" (*paisanos* spelled with a "b" to emphasize the mother tongue associated with their Arab origins), and their website reads, "si eres un baisano de corazón, abonate al club" (if you are a *baisano* at heart, join the club). On that fan website supporters have posted expressions of solidarity with the Palestinian people and condemnations of the Israeli occupation of the West Bank and the blockade of Gaza.[3]

On the other side of the world the Palestinian National Team, which has for a decade competed in World Cup elimination rounds (though Palestine is not yet an independent state), boasts several Deportivo Palestino players.[4] According to FIFA rules the grandchild of an immigrant can play on the national team of his place of residence, or on that of his grandparent's place of birth. In most cases, the grandparents in question were post-World War I Christian Palestinian immigrants looking for a new life in Chile.[5]

In broad strokes, the story of Club Deportivo Palestino is the story of immigrant sport clubs in hundreds of cities and towns in the Americas. It was founded by Palestinian Chileans in August 1920 in the southern city of Osorno. Led by the wealthy Yarur family, owners of an important textile factory, the club was sponsored by community leaders.[6] For three decades Club Deportivo Palestino played as amateurs, going professional in 1952. Competing at first in the second division, within a year it won the championship and graduated to the premier league where it has played ever since. In parallel to the ascent of the team—perhaps serving as a metaphor for the ascent of the Palestinian Chilean community itself—members of the Yarur family became key figures in the Chilean Football Federation.[7]

Deportivo Palestino serves as a useful lens through which to consider ethnic identity in Latin America, the relations between Diaspora and homeland (real and imagined), and football as a channel both for the integration of ethnic communities into larger Latin American societies, and for the preservation of those same ethnic communities as distinct.

This book aims at encouraging a scholarly discussion devoted to sports and ethnicity in South America. While it focuses on the Club Atlético Atlanta of Buenos Aires, identified with the local Jewish community, it is relevant to other cases, such as the Club Deportivo Palestino of Chile, the Club Deportivo Armenio of Buenos Aires, or the Club Palmeiras of São Paulo, established by the local Italian community of São Paulo.

Studies of ethnicity in Latin America and the Caribbean often focus on discrete groups in transnational settings. We study German Brazilians and their differences and similarities vis-à-vis German Argentines and German Mexicans. We examine Chinese Panamanian experiences by contextualizing them within Chinese Peruvian ones. Such an approach rests on the assumption (usually untested) that ethnicity is derived solely from the Diaspora rather than constituted in the nation. What the historiography of Latin America and the Caribbean often lacks is comparison across groups.

My own research in recent years takes a different approach to ethnicity.[8] It asks how Arabs and Jews, for example, two groups generally marked as different, operate not only in relation to some supposed point of origin elsewhere, but also within the national or regional settings.[9] The insights that can be gained with this different focus are significant. Take, for instance, the ways that Arab and Jewish identities are played out in *fútbol.*

In 2008 Deportivo Palestino needed two million dollars to buy new players and remodel their rented stadium in Santiago. The ethnic-national identity of the team and its fans led the directors to make a fascinating decision about how to raise the money: they would attempt to sell shares on the Santiago and Nablus (West Bank) stock exchanges. The club's general manager, Francisco Riveros, linked ethnicity and nation to the business of football in an interview with Reuters: "We chose Palestine because of the emotional bond and our board's interest in sharing their pride in this club with the Palestinians and Arabs in the motherland, and we are looking for people seeking investment opportunities." Although the Bank of Palestine does not operate in Chile, it became a team sponsor in June 2009.[10] Deportivo Palestino's decision can be viewed as an expression of transnational identity, but I would like to insist on its national dimension as well. The funds from a Palestinian business are used to further two national goals: to better integrate Palestinians into Chilean society via football, and to win Chile's national championship.

Not all ethnic relations in Chile mirror those we see in the Deportivo Palestino case. Jewish Chileans, for example, do not claim allegiance to a professional football club, and they often seek to minimize their public presence (I do not refer here to sports activities within the framework of community institutions, like the basketball team of the Club Israelita or activities in the Gimnasio Macabbi). Yet it would be a mistake to understand the Jewish lack of visibility as the result of anti-Semitism, or the Palestinian visibility as a function of contemporary politics alone. The problem of making broad claims from single experiences becomes clear when we look at Arab and Jewish football in Argentina. Some may construe the country as being both anti-Semitic and pro-Arab. The 1989 election of Carlos Menem, a Syrian Argentine, as president and the 1994 bombing of the Jewish community center, the Asociación Mutual Israelita Argentina (AMIA), are often invoked as evidence. Yet when we look at football the Chilean case is reversed. In Argentina no Arab group has a professional soccer team, but since the 1920s, Jews have been claiming the Club Atlético Atlanta of Buenos Aires as their own. Fans of rival teams chant anti-Semitic slogans during matches (the most recent example is the Chacarita-Atlanta game of Sunday, March 11, 2012),[11] and when CAA first played outside of Latin America, in 1963, the location was Tel Aviv, Israel. Atlanta's fans are active in Israel just as Deportivo Palestino's are in Palestine. The two sides of the coin are present here: the national and the transnational. At the same time, looking at Jews and Arabs together reveals how the nation and the state play important roles in making national ethnicity. Similarities, in this new kind of comparative framework, become as important as differences.

The image of Atlanta as a "Jewish club" is very much rooted in Buenos Aires. The most popular *telenovela* in 2012 Argentina was *Los Graduados*.[12] This TV series centers on the Falsini and Goddzer families. The Goddzers are a caricature that brings together all the stereotypes of a supposedly typical Jewish Argentine family. How do we know that they are Jewish? Because of the Yiddish words they sometimes use in their conversations (from "*mishpuche*" to "*tuches*"), because of some of the foods that they serve (the mother, Dana Blatt de Goddzer, offers her "*knishes*" or "*geufiltefish*" to all visitors in her house), and because of the father's (Elías Goddzer) passion for football. And what is the father's favorite team? Obviously, the Club Atlético Atlanta. In one of the episodes, which aired in May 2012, the Goddzers' neighbor, Tano Pasman—probably the most famous football fan in Argentina that year—comes over to watch the Atlanta–River Plate game on TV with Elías.

Indeed, for many Argentines, the big news of Sunday, April 8, 2012, was the defeat of Club Atlético River Plate. Playing in the B Nacional, the legendary "millionaires" of Núñez lost 1–0 to the humble Club Atlético Atlanta of Villa Crespo. Atlanta's fans enjoyed an unforgettable moment, and the social media began to buzz with the inevitable jibes and jokes at River's expense. Some of the messages posted online alluded to the "Jewish" image of Atlanta, a football club rooted in a Buenos Aires neighborhood with a notable Jewish presence. For example, one caricature linked the victory of the Villa Crespo team with the Jewish Passover holiday being celebrated that same weekend.[13] The fan site La Taberna del Siome published the cover of a recipe book entitled *Empire Kosher Chicken Cookbook*, showing a plate of chicken, a clear allusion to River. A photo was posted on Facebook of River fans in Jerusalem at the Wailing Wall with the caption, "They did not realize that the wall was playing for us."

In his book *Does Your Rabbi Know You're Here?* Anthony Clavane tells a story from his days as a student in Selig Brodetsky Jewish Day School in Leeds, England.[14] It was the late 1960s and the head teacher, Mr. Abrahamson, strongly believed that "football is not for a *Yiddisher* boy!" Abrahamson was worried by the growing popularity of "the English game" among Jewish youngsters and the fact that the football team of Leeds United was drawing a bigger Jewish crowd on Saturday than the local synagogue. Therefore, he confiscated Clavane's ball and told him and his friends that Jews were people of the book, not the penalty kick. But you don't need a real leather ball to play soccer, and the boys found an alternative in order to continue playing.

Jews have inserted themselves into the modern urban fabric of Buenos Aires via different channels. One of them clearly has been through the participation in sports activities in general and in football in particular. This involvement has given them a significant sense of identity and belonging. After all, no other event or performance in twentieth-century Argentina has brought as many Argentines into close contact—physical or imagined—as *fútbol*. Accordingly, this book uses soccer as an additional lens to gain insight into certain aspects of Argentine history.

The Club Atlético Atlanta, without doubt, has become a central element in the lives of very many Jews both in Villa Crespo and outside its borders. In such a dense urban society segmented by social class, ethnicity, and gender, Atlanta and its stadium have provided a gathering place for tens of thousands of people, Jews and non-Jews alike, bound together by their loyalty to their sport club. Thus, Atlanta has functioned as an integrative public space and its stadium as a site of neighborhood identification.

One of the basic characteristics of Atlanta fan culture is the dramatization of the persevering struggle by the relatively weak against the mighty, a combination of the Jewish myth of David and Goliath, and Argentine nationalism challenging external forces such as Anglo-Saxon imperialism. If one of the attractions of football has been that the poor could compete with the rich and win, in the case of Atlanta, many Jews have felt proud that "their" team could challenge leading "gentile" teams and sometimes win.

This holds true for Jewish Argentine fans of other football clubs as well. In his novel *Mestizo*, Ricardo Feirestein tells the story of David and his son Eduardo, both San Lorenzo fans who go to a soccer match together and enjoy their team's victory over Tigre:

"Dad," Eduardo reflects. "It's something very strange."

"What do you find strange?"

"To be part of San Lorenzo, here and now. To have won."

"And what's strange about that?"

"To be in the majority, Dad. It's the first time that's happened to me. We could have done anything we wanted with the Tigre fans. Did you realize that? Take away their flags, hit them, allow them to live, kill them, quiet their songs with our shouting, crush them . . . Didn't you feel good?"

Images overcome David: Jew, intellectual, sociologist, immigrant in Israel, unemployed, social bastard wherever he might remember, always condemned to be a minority. Now, for once—and his son was right—it was like a bit of heat in winter, when a liquor circulates inside and warms the innards. To be one of those who win, of the majority, of those who decide. For the first time.[15]

I started this book with the following question, posed in the Introduction: "If we cannot write the history of Argentine Jews without including the history of the Jews of Buenos Aires, and if we cannot write the history of Buenos Aires Jews without including the history of the Jews of Villa Crespo, can we write the history of Argentine Jews without mentioning the Atlanta football club?" I hope that this study and the testimonies I have gathered within it offer a clear answer to this question.

REFERENCE MATTER

NOTES

INTRODUCTION

1. For a general overview of the importance of sports in Latin America, see, for example, Joseph L. Arbena, ed., *Sport and Society in Latin America: Diffusion, Dependency, and the Rise of Mass Culture* (New York: Greenwood, 1988); Rory M. Miller and Liz Crolley, eds., *Football in the Americas: Fútbol, Futebol, Soccer* (London: Institute for the Study of the Americas, 2007); Tony Mason, *Passion of the People? Football in South America* (London: Verso, 1995); Pablo Alabarces, ed., *Peligro de gol: estudios sobre deporte y sociedad en América Latina* (Buenos Aires: CLACSO, 2000); Joshua H. Nadel, *Fútbol: Why Soccer Matters in Latin America* (Gainesville: University Press of Florida, 2014).

2. Adriana Brodsky and Raanan Rein, eds., *The New Jewish Argentina: Facets of Jewish Experiences in the Southern Cone* (Boston: Brill, 2013).

3. Jeremy MacClancy, "Preface," in *Sport, Identity and Ethnicity*, ed. J. MacClancy (Oxford: Berg, 1996), 3.

4. Rory M. Miller, "Introduction," in *Football in the Americas*, ed. Rory M. Miller and Liz Crolley, 23.

5. John Goldhurst, *Playing for Keeps. Sport, the Media and Society* (Melbourne: Longman Cheshire, 1987), ix.

6. See, for example, Eduardo P. Archetti, *Masculinities: Football, Polo and Tango in Argentina* (Oxford: Berg, 1999); Pablo Alabarces, *Fútbol y patria: el fútbol y las narrativas de la nación en la Argentina* (Buenos Aires: Prometeo, 2002); Julio D. Frydenberg, *Historia social del fútbol: del amateurismo a la profesionalización* (Buenos Aires: Siglo Veintiuno, 2011).

7. "Atlanta: Alma de Bohemios," http://galeon.com/villacrespo/deportes/atlanta .html. Accessed on May 26, 2014.

8. Cayetano Francavilla, *Historia de Villa Crespo* (Buenos Aires: Ediciones Argentinas, 1978), 59.

9. "Rapsodia Bohemia," *Página/12*, 30 Mar. 2009.

10. See, for example, "Atlanta corazón de campeón" (special supplement), *Clarín*, 8 May 2011; "Atlanta le dio un título a su propio renacer," *Perfil*, 8 May 2011.

11. Esther Rollansky, interview by author, Tel Aviv, July 2010.

12. See, for example, Michael Brenner and Gideon Reuveni, eds., *Emancipation Through Muscles: Jews and Sports in Europe* (Lincoln: University of Nebraska Press, 2006).

13. On Zionism and the cult of the new Jewish body, see George Eisen, "Jewish Sport History and the Ideology of Modern Sport: Approaches and Interpretations," *Journal of Sport History* 25 (1998): 482–531. On sports history in Palestine/Israel, see Haim Kaufman, "Jewish Sports in the Diaspora, Yishuv, and Israel: Between Nationalism and Politics," *Israel Studies* 10, no. 2 (2005): 147–67.

14. Peter Levine, *Ellis Island to Ebbets Field: Sport and the American Jewish Experience* (New York: Oxford University Press, 1992), 9.

15. For a list of Jewish-Argentine athletes, see Ricardo Feierstein, *Historia de los judíos argentinos* (Buenos Aires: Planeta, 1993), 345–47.

16. Matthew B. Karush, "National Identity in the Sports Pages: Football and the Mass Media in the 1920s Buenos Aires," *The Americas* 60, no. 1 (July 2003): 11–32

17. For similar arguments, see Peter Levine's analysis of Jews and sports in the United States in his classic *Ellis Island to Ebbets Field*.

18. On stadiums and their social significance in South America, see Christopher Thomas Gaffney, *Temples of the Earthbound Gods: Stadiums in the Cultural Landscape of Rio de Janeiro and Buenos Aires* (Austin: University of Texas Press, 2008).

19. Samuel Glusberg, "Mate Amargo," in *La levita gris: cuentos judíos de ambiente porteño* (Buenos Aires: Editorial Babel, 1924).

20. Tomás Sánz and Roberto Fontanarrosa, *El fútbol argentino: pequeño diccionario ilustrado* (Buenos Aires: Clarín/Aguilar U.T.E., 1994).

21. Alberto Vaccarezza, *El barrio de los judíos: sainete en un acto y tres cuadros y en verso* (Buenos Aires: El Teatro Nacional, 1919).

22. For a popular image of Watson Hutton, presented as the apostle of Argentine football, see the movie *Escuela de campeones*, dir. Ralph Pappier (Argentina, 1950).

23. Diego Armus, *The Ailing City: Health, Tuberculosis, and Culture in Buenos Aires, 1870–1950* (Durham, NC: Duke University Press, 2011), ch. 9.

24. On Ajax and its Jewish image, see Simon Kuper, *Ajax, the Dutch, the War: Football in Europe During the Second World War* (London: Orion, 2003). On Tottenham, see John Efron, "When Is a Yid Not a Jew? The Strange Case of Supporter Identity at Tottenham Hotspur," in *Emancipation Through Muscles*, 235–56.

25. Similarly offensive songs have been directed at Tottenham fans in London, such as "The Spurs are on their way to Auschwitz."

26. On the Palmeiras club, see Gregg P. Bocketti, "Italian Immigrants, Brazilian Football, and the Dilemma of National Identity," *Journal of Latin American Studies* 40 (2008): 275–302; José Renato de Campos Araújo, *Imigracao e futebol. O caso Palestra Itália* (São Paulo: Editora Sumaré, 2000).

27. L. Millones, A. Panfichi, and V. Vich, eds., *En el corazón del pueblo: pasión y gloria de Alianza Lima, 1901–2001* (Lima: Fondo Editorial del Congreso del Peru, 2002); Raanan Rein, "Deporte y etnicidad: Club Deportivo Palestino (Chile) y Club Atlético Atlanta (Argentina)," in *Más allá del Medio Oriente: las diásporas judía y árabe en América Latina*, ed. Raanan Rein (Granda: Editorial de la Universidad de Granada, 2012), 117–40.

CHAPTER 1

1. Roberto Arlt, "Un simulacro de ghetto"; originally published in the Buenos Aires daily *El Mundo* (28 July 1928) in a series of his articles entitled "Aguafuertes."

2. James Scobie, *Buenos Aires: Plaza to Suburb, 1870–1910* (New York: Oxford University Press, 1974); Richard Walter, *Politics and Urban Growth in Buenos Aires, 1910–1943* (New York: Cambridge University Press, 1994); Adrián Gorelik, *La grilla y el parque: espacio público y cultura urbana en Buenos Aires, 1887–1936* (Buenos Aires: Universidad Nacional de Quilmes, 2010).

3. On Alberdi's views, see his *Bases y puntos de partida para la organización de la República Argentina* (Buenos Aires: Centro Editor de América Latina, 1979), an essay originally sent to the delegates of the Constitutional Assembly who shaped the 1853 Argentine constitution.

4. For a general overview of immigration to Argentina, see Carl Solberg, *Immigration and Nationalism, Argentina and Chile, 1890–1914* (Austin: University of Texas Press, 1970); José Moya, *Cousins and Strangers: Spanish Immigrants in Buenos Aires, 1850–1930* (Berkeley: University of California Press, 1998); Samuel Baily, *Immigrants in the Land of Promise: Italians in Buenos Aires and New York City, 1870–1914* (Ithaca, NY: Cornell University Press, 1999).

5. For a general overview on Jewish immigration to Argentina, see Haim Avni, *Argentina and the Jews: A History of Jewish Immigration* (Tuscaloosa: University of Alabama Press, 1991); Victor A. Mirelman, *Jewish Buenos Aires, 1890–1930: In Search of an Identity* (Detroit, MI: Wayne State University Press, 1990).

6. See, for example, Albert Hourani and Nadim Shehadi, eds., *The Lebanese in the World: A Century of Emigration* (London: I. B. Tauris, 1992). Raymundo Kabchi, ed., *El mundo árabe y América Latina* (Madrid: UNESCO, Prodhufi, 1997); Raanan Rein, ed., *Árabes y judíos en Iberoamérica: similitudes, diferencia y tensiones* (Seville: Fundación Tres Culturas, 2008); Raanan Rein, ed., *Más allá del Medio Oriente: las diásporas judía y árabe en América Latina* (Granada: Editorial de la Universidad de Granada, 2012).

7. Alberto Gerchunoff, *Los Gauchos judíos* (La Plata, Argentina: Talleres Gráficos Joaquín Sesé, 1910). For an English translation, see Alberto Gerchunoff, *The Jewish Gauchos of the Pampa*, trans. Prudencio de Pereda (Albuquerque: University of New Mexico Press, 1998).

8. Ricardo Feierstein, ed., *Los mejores relatos con gauchos judíos* (Buenos Aires: Ameghino Editora, 1998). On the symbolic importance of the colonies as reflected in Argentine cinema, see Tzvi Tal, "The Other Becomes Mainstream: Jews in Contemporary Argentine Cinema," in *The New Jewish Argentina: Facets of Jewish Experiences in the Southern Cone*, ed. Adriana Brodsky and Raanan Rein (Boston: Brill, 2013), 365–91.

9. These agricultural settlements have received much scholarly attention. The most comprehensive account is still Haim Avni, *Argentina, "The Promised Land": Baron de Hirsch's Colonization Project in the Argentine Republic* [Hebrew] (Jerusalem: Magnes, 1973). For a recent contribution, see Iván Cherjovsky, "La faz ideológica del conflicto colonos/JCA: el discurso del ideal agrario en las memorias de Colonia Mauricio,"

in *Marginados y consagrados: nuevos estudios sobre la vida judía en la Argentina*, ed. Emmanuel Kahan et al. (Buenos Aires: Lumiere, 2011), 47–66. Many memoirs of life in the colonies have been written. See, for example, Raquel Zimerman de Faingold, *Memorias* (Buenos Aires: n.p., 1987); Helene Gutkowski, *Rescate de la herencia cultural. Vidas… en las colonias* (Buenos Aires: Editorial Contexto, 1991); Haim Avni and Leonardo Senkman, eds., *Del campo al campo: colonos de Argentina en Israel* (Buenos Aires: Milá-AMIA, 1993).

10. In the colonial period, Latin America had experienced the effects of the Inquisition, which tried to eradicate any vestige of Jewish faith, persecuting and prosecuting new Christians suspected of being crypto-Jews, or *marranos*. In contrast to that rejection, by the late nineteenth and early twentieth centuries the entire region, including Argentina, was opening its doors to Jews.

11. Haim Avni, *Argentine Jewry: Social Status and Organizational Profile* [Hebrew] (Jerusalem: Ministry of Education and Culture, 1972); Robert Weisbrot, *The Jews of Argentina: From Inquisition to Perón* (Philadelphia, PA: Jewish Publication Society of America, 1979); Efraim Zadoff, *A Century of Argentinean Jewry: In Search of a New Model of National Identity* (Jerusalem: Institute of the World Jewish Congress, 2000); Brodsky and Rein, eds., *New Jewish Argentina*.

12. Quoted in Ignacio Klich, "Criollos and Arabic Speakers in Argentina: An Uneasy Pas de Deux, 1888–1814," in *The Lebanese in the World*, ed. Hourani and Shehadi, 266.

13. Quoted in Solberg, *Immigration and Nationalism*, 88–89.

14. Ernesto M. Aráoz, *La inmigración en la Argentina y sus vinculaciones con la cuestión social* (Salta, Argentina: Imprenta de las Llanas, 1919), 48.

15. On anti-Semitism in Argentina, see, among others, Haim Avni, "Antisemitism in Argentina: The Dimensions of Danger," in *Approaches to Antisemitism: Context and Curriculum*, ed. Michael Brown (New York: American Jewish Committee, 1994), 57–77; Daniel Lvovich, *Nacionalism y antisemitismo en la Argentina* (Buenos Aires: Vergara, 2003); Leonardo Senkman, ed., *El antisemitismo en la Argentina*, 2d ed. (Buenos Aires: CEAL, 1989).

16. For recent studies, see Adrián Jmelnizky and Ezequiel Erdei, *La población judía de Buenos Aires: estudio sociodemográfico* (Buenos Aires: AMIA, Centro de Documentacion e Informacion sobre Judaismo Argentino Marc Turkow, 2005); Yaacov Rubel, *La población judía de la Ciudad de Buenos Aires. Perfil sociodemográfico* (Buenos Aires: Agencia Judía para Israel, Iniciativa de Demografía Judía, 2005); Sergio DellaPergola, "Jewish Autonomy and Dependency: Latin America in Global Perspective," in *Identities in an Era of Globalization and Multiculturalism: Latin America in the Jewish World*, ed. Judit Bokser Liweran, Eliezer Ben-Rafael, Yossi Gorny, and Raanan Rein (Leiden and Boston: Brill, 2008), 47–80.

17. Ezequiel Erdei, "Demografía e identidad: A propósito del studio de la población judía en Buenos Aires," in *Pertenencia y alteridad. Judios en/de America Latina: cuarenta años de cambios*, ed. Haim Avni et al. (Madrid: Iberoamericana, 2011), 341–63.

18. Avni, *Argentina, "Promised Land,"* ch. 3; Judith Noemi Freidenberg, *The Invention of the Jewish Gaucho: Villa Clara and the Construction of Argentine Identity* (Austin:

University of Texas Press, 2009); Daniel Fernando Bargman, "Un ámbito para las relaciones interétnicas: las colonias agrícolas judías en Argentina," *Revista de Antropología* 11 (1992): 50–58; Lea Literat-Golombek, *Moisés Ville: crónica de un shtetl argentino* (Jerusalem: La Semana Publicaciones, 1982).

19. Ira Rosenswaike, "The Jewish Population of Argentina: Census and Estimate, 1887–1947," *Jewish Social Studies* XXII, no. 4 (Oct. 1960): 205.

20. On Jewish social life in contemporary Buenos Aires, see Eugene F. Sofer, *From Pale to Pampa: A Social History of the Jews of Buenos Aires* (New York: Holmes & Meier, 1982); Mollie Lewis Nouwen, *"Oy, My Buenos Aires": Jewish Immigrants and the Creation of Argentine National Identity, 1905–1930* (Albuquerque: University of New Mexico Press, 2013).

21. See the important works by Federico Finchelstein, *La Argentina fascista: los orígenes de la dictadura* (Buenos Aires: Sudamericana, 2008), and "The Anti-Freudian Politics of Argentine Fascism: Antisemitism, Catholicism and the Internal Enemy, 1932–1945," *Hispanic American Historical Review* 87, no 1 (2007): 77–110.

22. Leonardo Senkman, *Argentina, la segunda guerra mundial y los refugiados indeseables, 1933–1945* (Buenos Aires: Grupo Editor Latinoamericano, 1991).

23. The Argentine nationalists' discourse echoed, at least in part, the religious component of traditional Catholic anti-Semitism. See Graciela Ben-Dror, *The Catholic Church and the Jews: Argentina, 1933–1945* (Lincoln: University of Nebraska Press, 2009).

24. On this measure, see Leonardo Senkman, "Ethnicidad e inmigración durante el primer peronismo," *Estudios interdisciplinarios de América Latina y el Caribe* 3, no.2 (1992): 5–38; Susane M. Sassone, "Migraciones ilegales y amnistías en la República Argentina," *Estudios Migratorios Latinoamericanos* 6–7 (1987): 249–89.

25. Debate continues on the admission of Nazis into Argentina and the complicity of the Argentine authorities. For two opposing views, see Uki Goñi, *The Real Odessa: How Perón Brought the Nazi War Criminals to Argentina* (London: Granta, 2002); and also Ronald C. Newton, *The "Nazi Menace" in Argentina, 1931–1947* (Stanford, CA: Stanford University Press, 1992).

26. Michael M. Laskier, *The Jews of Egypt, 1920–1970: In the Midst of Zionism, Anti-Semitism, and the Middle East Conflict* (New York: New York University Press, 1992), 252–64; Raanan Rein, "Diplomacy, Propaganda, and Humanitarian Gestures: Francoist Spain and Egyptian Jews, 1956–1968," *Ibero-Americana* 23 (2006): 21–33.

27. Eduardo Wilde, *Obras completas* (Buenos Aires: Talleres Peuser, 1917), 2: 29–30.

28. Sofer, *From Pale to Pampa.*

29. On Jewish prostitution in Argentina, see, among others, Mir Yarfitz, "Uprooting the Seeds of Evil," in *The New Jewish Argentina*, ed. Brodsky and Rein, 55–79; Haim Avni, *"Clients," Prostitutes and White Slavers in Argentina and Israel* [Hebrew] (Tel Aviv: Yedioth Ahronoth, 2009); E. J. Bristow, *Prostitution and Prejudice: The Jewish Fight Against White Slavery, 1870–1939* (New York: Schocken Books, 1983). A recent study argued that Buenos Aires had "the world's largest, best organized community of East European criminals." See Charles Van Onselen, *The Fox and the Flies: The Secret Life of a Grotesque Master Criminal* (New York: Walker Publishing Company, 2007), 346.

30. On the importance of Yiddish in twentieth-century Jewish Argentine culture, see Eliahú Toker, *El ídish es también Latinoamérica* (Buenos Aires: Instituto Moviliza-dor de Fondos Cooperativos, 2003); Perla Sneh, ed., *Buenos Aires ídish* (Buenos Aires: CPPHC, 2006); Perla Sneh, "Ídish al sur, una rama en sombras," in *Pertenencia y alteri-dad. Judíos en/de America Latina*, ed. Avni et al., 657–76.

31. José C. Moya, "The Jewish Experience in Argentina in a Diasporic Comparative Perspective," in *The New Jewish Argentina*, ed. Brodsky and Rein, 7–29, 17.

32. On the Tragic Week, see John Dizgun, "Immigrants of a Different Religion: Jew-ish Argentines and the Boundaries of Argentinidad, 1919–2009" (PhD diss., Rutgers University, 2010), ch. 1; Marcelo Dimenstein, "En busca de un pogrom perdido: memo-ria en torno de la semana trágica de 1919," in *Marginados y consagrados*, ed. Kahan et al., 121–41; David Rock, *Politics in Argentina, 1890–1930: The Rise and Fall of Radicalism* (London: Cambridge University Press, 1975), 157–79; Edgardo Bilsky, *La semana trágica* (Buenos Aires: Centro Editor de América Latina, 1984); Julio Godio, *La semana trágica de enero de 1919* (Buenos Aires: Granica, 1985).

33. Alberto Vaccarezza, *El Conventillo de La Paloma* (Buenos Aires: Ediciones del Carro de Tespis, 1965).

34. Nerina Visacovsky, "Los judíos textiles de Villa Lynch y el I. L. Peretz" (paper presented at the seminar "Democracia, Estado y Sociedad en la Argentina Contem-poránea," University of Buenos Aires, 2005).

CHAPTER 2

1. On the history of Villa Crespo, see Diego A. del Pino, *El barrio de Villa Crespo* (Buenos Aires: Municipalidad de Buenos Aires, 1974); Diego A. del Pino, *Villa Crespo: sencilla historia* (Buenos Aires: Librerías Turísticas, 1997); Vicente Osvaldo Cutolo, *His-toria de los barrios de Buenos Aires*, 2d ed. (Buenos Aires, Editorial Elche, 1998), II: ch. 21; Cayetano Francavilla and Miguel Angel Lafuente, *Villa Crespo* (Buenos Aires: Fun-dación Banco de Boston, 1993); and Cayetano Francavilla, *Historia de Villa Crespo* (Bue-nos Aires: n.p., 1978).

2. On early industrialization in Argentina, see Fernando Rocchi, *Chimneys in the Desert: Argentina During the Export Boom Years, 1870–1930* (Stanford, CA: Stanford University Press, 2006).

3. For information on the Fábrica Nacional de Calzado, see Dr. Moorne, *Las indus-trias fabriles en Buenos Aires* (Buenos Aires: Librairie Francaise, 1893); Francesco Scar-din, *La Argentina y el trabajo* (Buenos Aires: Peuser, 1906); Florentino N. Torello, "La industria del calzado en la República Argentina," *Revista de Ciencias Económicas* 3 (May 1928).

4. James Scobie, *Buenos Aires: Plaza to Suburb, 1870–1910* (New York: Oxford Uni-versity Press, 1974), 169.

5. María Marta Lupano, "Villa Crespo: una villa obrera entre el modelo higienista y el paternalismo obrero," *Anales del Instituto de Arte Americano e Investigaciones Estéticas Mario J. Buschiazzo* 27–28 (1989–91): 127–37.

6. James R. Scobie, *Argentina, A City and a Nation* (New York: Oxford University Press, 1971), ch. 7; James R. Scobie, *Buenos Aires Plaza to Suburb, 1870–1910*; Richard Walter, *Politics and Urban Growth in Buenos Aires, 1910–1942* (New York: Cambridge University Press, 1993).

7. On economic policies during the last quarter of the twentieth century, see Mario Rapoport et al., *Historia económica, política y social de la Argentina* (Buenos Aires: Editores Macchi, 2000), chs. 7–8.

8. Leopoldo Marechal, *Adán Buenosayres*, 14th ed. (Buenos Aires: Sudamericana, 1992). On Marechal in Villa Crespo, see Graciela Maturo, *Marechal, el camino de la belleza* (Buenos Aires: Biblos, 1999), ch. 2.

9. On Sephardic Jews in Buenos Aires, see Margalit Bejarano, "The Sephardic Communities of Latin America," and Susana Brauner, "Syrian Jews in Buenos Aires," both in *Contemporary Sephardic Identity in the Americas*, ed. Margalit Bejarano and Edna Aizenberg (Syracuse, NY: Syracuse University Press, 2012); Adriana Mariel Brodsky, "Re-configurando comunidades: judíos sefardíes/árabes en Argentina, 1900–1950," in *Árabes y judíos en Iberoamerica*, ed. Raanan Rein (Seville: Fundación Tres Culturas, 2008): 117–34; Victor Mirelman, "Sephardim in Latin America after Independence," in *Sephardim in the Americas*, ed. Martin A. Cohen and Abraham J. Peck (Tuscaloosa, AL: American Jewish Archives, 1993), 235–65. On cafés in the neighborhood, see Diego A. Del Pino, *Los cafés de Villa Crespo* (Buenos Aires: InterJuntas, 1992).

10. See Dizgun, "Immigrants of a Different Religion," ch. 1; Dimenstein, "En busca de un pogrom perdido"; Bilsky, *La semana trágica*; Godio, *La semana trágica de enero de 1919*.

11. Carlos Waisman, "La ideología del nacionalismo de derecha en Argentina: el capitalismo, el socialismo y los judíos," in *El antisemitismo en la Argentina*, ed. Leonardo Senkman, 2d ed. (Buenos Aires: CEAL, 1989).

12. On Jewish education in Buenos Aires, see Efraim Zadoff, *Historia de la educación judía en Buenos Aires (1935–1957)* (Buenos Aires: Milá, 1994).

13. Iaacov Rubel, *Los judíos de Villa Crespo y Almagro: perfil socio-demográfico* (Buenos Aires: AMIA, 1989); *Los tres berretines*, dir. Enrique Telémaco Susini (Argentina, 1933).

14. On Gleizer, see Ana Ojeda Bär, "Manuel Gleizer: el último de los editores románticos," *La Nación*, 2 Apr. 2006; Verónica Delgado and Fabio Espósito, "La emergencia del editor moderno," in *Editores y políticas editoriales en Argentina, 1880–2000*, ed. José Luis de Diego (Buenos Aires: Fondo e Cultura Económica, 2006), 59–88, esp. 76–78; Domingo Buonocore, *Libreros, editores e impresores de Buenos Aires* (Buenos Aires: Bowker, 1974), 87–111, esp. 102–5.

15. Del Pino, *Villa Crespo: sencilla historia*, 273.

16. On César Tiempo, see Leonardo Senkman, *La identidad judía en la literatura argentina* (Buenos Aires: Pardes, 1983), 153–95; Raanan Rein, "Politically Incorrect: César Tiempo and the Editorial Staff of the Cultural Supplement of La Prensa," in *The New Jewish Argentina*, 213–33.

17. Eliahu Toker, ed., *Buenos Aires esquina Sábado. Antología de César Tiempo* (Buenos Aires: Archvio General de la Nación, 1997), 9.

18. César Tiempo, "Sol semita," as quoted in Del Pino, *Villa Crespo: sencilla historia,* 287.

19. As film scholars have correctly remarked with respect to Hollywood, people with "non-Jewish" names are not necessarily non-Jews. In Argentina, many Jews prominent in popular culture have adopted non-Jewish names. Apart from Molar and Tiempo, other notable examples are the tango singers Roberto Beltrán (Marcos Zucker), Juan Pueblito (Noiej Scolnic), and Julio Jorge Nelson (Isaac Rosofsky), as well as the sports journalist Elías Sojit (Elías Shoijet).

20. Ben Molar, "Prólogo," in *El Tango, una historia con judíos,* by José Judkovsky (Buenos Aires: IWO, 1998), 13.

21. On the history of tango, see, among others, Julie M. Taylor, "Tango: Themes of Class and Nation," *Ethnomusicology* 20, no. 2 (1976): 273–91; Simon Collier, *The Life, Music and Times of Carlos Gardel* (Pittsburgh, PA: University of Pittsburgh Press, 1986); Simon Collier, "The Popular Roots of the Argentine Tango," *History Workshop Journal* 34 (1992): 92–100; Maria Susana Azzi and Simon Collier, *Le Grand Tango: The Life and Music of Astor Piazzola* (New York: Oxford University Press, 2000); Ricardo Horvath, *Esos malditos tangos: apuntes para la otra historia* (Buenos Aires: Biblos, 2006).

22. Del Pino, *Villa Crespo: sencilla historia,* 241.

23. Enrique D. Cadícamo, "Salón Peracca," in *Poemas del bajo fondo—Viento que lleva y trae* (Buenos Aires: Editorial Fermata, 1945), 69–70.

24. Julio Cortázar, "Adán Buenosayres, de Leopoldo Marechal," *Realidad. Revista de Ideas* [Buenos Aires] V, no. 14 (Mar.–Apr. 1949): 232–38.

25. Sara Gabriela Minaberrigaray and Silvia Ester Oviedo, "Club Social y Deportivo Villa Malcolm," *Todo es Historia* [Buenos Aires], no. 448 (Nov. 2004).

26. On Jewish workers in Villa Crespo, see Edgardo J. Bilsky, Gabriel Trajtenberg, and Ana Epelbaun Weinstein, *El movimiento obrero judío en la Argentina* (Buenos Aires: Centro de Documentación e Información sobre Judaismo Argentino Marc Turkow, 1987).

27. Leopoldo Marechal, *Historia de la calle Corrientes* (Buenos Aires: Municipalidad de la Ciudad, 1937); Valeria Gruschetsky, "'El espíritu de la calle Corrientes no cambiará con el ensanche.' La transformación de la calle Corrientes en avenida. Debates y representaciones. Buenos Aires 1927–1936" (thesis, Universidad de Buenos Aires, 2008).

28. Julio Frydenberg, *Historia social del fútbol: del amateurismo a la profesionalización* (Buenos Aires: Siglo XXI, 2011), ch. 4.

29. Diego Armus, *The Ailing City: Health, Tuberculosis, and Culture in Buenos Aires, 1870–1950* (Durham, NC: Duke University Press, 2011), ch. 9.

30. Jeffrey William Richey, "Playing at Nation: Soccer Institutions, Racial Ideology, and National Integration in Argentina, 1912–1931" (PhD diss., University of North Carolina at Chapel Hill, 2013), iii–iv.

31. Asociación Atlética Argentinos Juniors, official website: http://www.argentinos juniors.com.ar/club/historia/historia/1900-1920. Accessed on May 26, 2014.

32. La Gloriosa Tricolor, Atlético Chacarita Juniors website: http://www.laglorio satricolor.com.ar/p/historia.html. Accessed on May 26, 2014.

33. Ibid.

34. *La Cancha* 879 (28 Mar. 1945).

35. Alejandro Fabbri, *El nacimiento de una pasión: historia de los clubes de fútbol* (Buenos Aires: Capital Intelectual, 2006), ch. 1.

CHAPTER 3

1. On early associationism in Buenos Aires, see Leandro Gutiérrez and Luis Alberto Romero, *Sectores populares, cultura y política. Buenos Aires en la entreguerra* (Buenos Aires: Sudamericana, 1995); Luciano de Privitellio and Luis Alberto Romero, "Organizaciones de la sociedad civil, tradiciones cívicas y cultura política democrática: el caso de Buenos Aires, 1912–1976," *Revista de Historia* 1 (2005); Hilda Sábato, Luis Alberto Romero, and José Luis Moreno, *De las cofardías a las organizaciones de la sociedad civil: Historia de la iniciativa asociativa en la Argentina, 1776–1990* (Buenos Aires: Gadis, 2002).

2. Víctor Raffo, *El origen británico del deporte argentino* (Buenos Aires: Prendergast, 2004).

3. On the early history of River Plate, see Rodrigo Daskal and Mariano Gruschetsky, "Clubes de fútbol: su dimensión social. El Club Atlético River Plate a comienzos del siglo XX," *EFDeportes.com, Revista Digital* [Buenos Aires] 176 (Jan. 2013), http://www .efdeportes.com/. Accessed on May 26, 2014.

4. Julio D. Frydenberg, "Los clubes de fútbol de Buenos Aires en los años veinte," in *Fútbol, historia y política*, ed. Julio Frydenberg and Rodrigo Daskal (Buenos Aires: Aurelia Libros, 2010), 23–81.

5. Jorge Iwanczuk, *Historia del futbol amateur en la Argentina* (Buenos Aires: Autores Editores, 1992).

6. Armus, *Ailing City*.

7. Domingo Faustino Sarmiento, *Obras completas* (Buenos Aires: Luz del Día, 1951), 22: 268–69.

8. Julio Frydenberg, "Los nombres de los clubes de fútbol, Buenos Aires, 1880–1930," *EFDeportes.com, Revista Digital* 2 (Sept. 1996), http://www.efdeportes.com/. Accessed on May 26, 2014.

9. Rodrigo Daskal, "Clubes, deporte y política en el Honorable Concejo Deliberante de la Ciudad de Buenos Aires (1895–1920)," in *Fútbol, historia y política*, ed. Frydenberg and Daskal, 203–39.

10. *El Gráfico*, 25 Aug. 1928, 17.

11. *La Cancha*, 4 June 1932.

12. Frydenberg, "Los clubes de fútbol de Buenos Aires en los años veinte," 33; "La popularidad del football: pequeña estadística de La República", *La República*, 25 May 1919.

13. Ernesto Escobar Bavio, *El football en el Río de la Plata (desde 1893)* (Buenos Aires: Editorial Sports, 1923), 8–10. On physical education in Argentine schools, see Angela Aisenstein and Pablo Scharagrodsky, *Tras las huellas de la educación física escolar argentina. Cuerpo, género y pedagogía* (Buenos Aires: Prometeo, 2006).

14. Adrián Beccar Varela, "El football: elemento sociológico", *La Nación*, 8 Aug. 1920, 8.

15. See Sylvia Saítta, *Regueros de tinta. El diario Crítica en la década de 1920* (Buenos Aires: Sudamericana, 1998); Sylvia Saítta, "Fútbol y prensa en los años veinte: Natalio Botana, presidente de la Asociación Argentina de Fútbol," *EFDeportes.com, Revista Digital* 50 (July 2002), http://www.efdeportes.com/. Accessed on May 26, 2014.

16. Eduardo P. Archetti, "Estilos y virtudes masculinos en *El Gráfico*: La creación del imaginario del fútbol argentino," *Desarrollo Económico* 35, no. 139 (1995); Martín Bergel and Pablo Palomino, "La revista *El Gráfico* en sus inicios: una pedagogía deportiva para la ciudad moderna," *EFDeportes.com, Revista Digital* 17 (Dec. 1999). http://www.efdeportes .com/. Accessed on May 26, 2014.

17. On the early history of the radio in Argentina, see Carlos Ulanovsky, Marta Merkin, and Juan José Panno, *Días de radio: 1920–1959* (Buenos Aires: Emecé, 2004); Robert H. Claxton, *From Parsifal to Perón: Early Radio in Argentina, 1920–1944* (Gainesville: University Press of Florida, 2007); Matthew B. Karush, *Culture of Class: Radio and Cinema in the Making of a Divided Argentina, 1920–1946* (Durham, NC: Duke University Press: 2012).

18. For an interesting study on the Mataderos neighborhood and the role of the football club there, Nueva Chicago, see María Teresa Sirvent, *Cultura popular y participación social: una investigación en el barrio de Mataderos* (Buenos Aires : Miño y Dávila, 1999).

19. Alejandro Domínguez, *La historia de Atlanta* (Buenos Aires: Bemase Artes Gráficas, 1998), 17–18.

20. Carlos Stortz, "Historia de Atlanta, fundación y amateurismo," Planeta Bohemio, http://www.planetabohemio.com.ar/historia/amateurismo.htm. Accessed on Feb. 6, 2013.

21. Raanan Rein, *The Franco-Perón Alliance: Relations between Spain & Argentina, 1946–1955* (Pittsburgh, PA: University of Pittsburgh Press, 1993), 282.

22. Domínguez, *La historia de Atlanta*, 18.

23. "Atlanta," *Dictionary of American Naval Fighting Ships*, http://www.history.navy .mil/danfs/a13/atlanta-ii.htm. Accessed on Jan. 26, 2014.

24. Lucas Fiszman et al., "Fundación," *Club Atlético Atlanta.Sitio Oficial*, 2009, http://www.caatlanta.com.ar/atlanta/institucional/historia.htm. Accessed on Feb. 6, 2013.

25. Edgardo Imas, "Cuando 'Atlanta' jugaba el béisbol," *Sentimiento Bohemio*, 28 Nov. 2012, http://sentimientobohemio.info/?p=12049. Accessed on Feb. 6, 2013.

26. Fiszman et al., "Fundación."

27. Stortz, "Historia de Atlanta, fundación y amateurismo."

28. Diego A. Del Pino, *Villa Crespo: sencilla historia* (Buenos Aires: Librerías Turísticas, 1997).

29. Eduardo Aruj, "Villa Crespo," in *Historia de Villa Crespo* (Buenos Aires: Ediciones Argentinas, 1978), 60.

30. Del Pino, *Villa Crespo*, 197.

31. *La Cancha*, 13 Jan. 1934, 21.

32. Fiszman et al., "Fundación."

33. "Atlanta Pasión, Historia," Parte I, http://www.atlantapasion.com.ar/historia. php; "Argentine Football Association 1906," http://futsandokan76.blogspot.co.il/2012/01/argentine-association-football-league.html. Accessed on Feb. 6, 2013.

34. "Cien años de una histórica goleada," *Sentimiento Bohemio* VI, no. 190 (30 Apr. 2007), http://www.sentimientobohemio.com.ar/ATLANTA21_CAI1.htm. Accessed on May 26, 2014.

35. Domínguez, *La historia de Atlanta*, 25.

36. Club Atlético Atlanta, *Libro de Actas de Asambleas, 1918–1934.*

37. On Bard, see Rodrigo Daskal, "Leopoldo Bard y la vida como compromiso," *EFDeportes.com, Revista Digital* 108 (May 2007), http://www.efdeportes.com, accessed on May 26, 2014; and Bard's autobiography, *Estampas de una vida. La fe puesta en un ideal. "Llegar a ser algo"* (Buenos Aires: Juan Perrotti, 1957). Well-known Jewish footballers of River Plate include Felipe Steimberg, "Semilla" Merenstein, Guillermo Fain, and Roberto Jaime Zywica, among others.

38. Juan Carlos Tissoni, *Los 75 años de Atlanta* (Buenos Aires, 1979), 12.

39. Stortz, "Historia de Atlanta, fundación y amateurismo."

40. Domínguez, *La historia de Atlanta*, 23–24.

41. Alejandro Fabbri, *El nacimiento de una pasión: historia de los clubes de fútbol* (Buenos Aires: Capital Intelectual, 2009), 30.

42. Stortz, "Historia de Atlanta, fundación y amateurismo."

43. Domínguez, *La historia de Atlanta*, 29.

44. *El Día*, 15 July 1912; *El Argentino*, 15 July 1912; Fiszman et al., "Fundación."

45. Domínguez, *La historia de Atlanta*, 29.

46. *La Mañana*, 3 Apr. 1916, 11.

47. Fabbri, *El nacimiento de una pasión*, 31.

48. Ariel Korob, "Procesos identitarios e imaginarios locales. Atlanta: bohemios y judíos" (master's thesis, Universidad de Buenos Aires, 1998), 38.

49. Quoted in "Aquellos años '20," *Planeta Bohemio*, http://www.planetabohemio .com.ar/historia/ladecada20.htm. Accessed on Feb. 6, 2013.

50. Richey, "Playing at Nation," 67.

51. Club Atlético Atlanta, *Libro de Actas para Asambleas 1918–1934, Memoria de 1920.*

52. Stortz, "Historia de Atlanta, fundación y amateurismo."

53. Club Atlético Atlanta, *Libro de Actas para Asambleas 1918–1934, Memoria de 1920.*

54. Domínguez, *La historia de Atlanta*, 33–34.

55. See also *El Gráfico*, 1 Aug. 1931, 42.

56. Korob, "Procesos identitarios e imaginarios locales. Atlanta: bohemios y judíos," 23.

57. Domínguez, *La historia de Atlanta*, 39–42.

58. Daskal, "Clubes, deporte y política en el Honorable Concejo Deliberante de la Ciudad de Buenos Aires (1895–1920)."

59. *Crítica*, 9 June 1925.

60. Domínguez, *La historia de Atlanta*, 43.

61. *La Cancha* 248, 25 Feb. 1933; *La Cancha* 265, 24 June 1933; *Alumni* 54, 1933.

62. *La Cancha* 281, 14 Oct. 1933.

63. On the history of Argentinos Juniors, see Hugo Frasso, *Argentinos Juniors. Historia de un sentimiento* (Buenos Aires: Aguafuertes Libros, 2003). On the club's difficulties in the early 1930s, see *La Cancha* 231, 5 Nov. 1932 and *La Cancha* 248, 25 Feb. 1933.

64. *El Gráfico*, 3 Feb. 1934, 9.

65. *La Cancha*, 23 July 1932.

66. Fabbri, *El nacimiento de una pasión*, 34.

67. Nestor Straimel, "Los judeoargentinos del deporte," *Piedra Libre*, 12 Jan. 2010.

68. Club Atlético Atlanta, *Memoria y Balance (20 de septiembre al 20 de noviembre)* (Buenos Aires: n.p., 1934), 3.

69. Ibid.

70. *La Cancha*, 29 Sept. 1934, 17.

71. Club Atlético Atlanta, *Memoria y Balance (20 de septiembre al 20 de noviembre)*, 7.

72. Ibid.

73. Club Atlético Atlanta, *Memoria y Balance (20 de septiembre al 20 de noviembre)*, 15.

74. Domínguez, *La historia de Atlanta*, 58.

75. Club Atlético Atlanta, *Memoria y Balance General correspondiente al 31° ejercicio administrativo (20 de septiembre 1934 al 31 de diciembre 1935)* (Buenos Aires: n.p., 1936), 9.

76. Ibid., 10.

77. Ibid.

78. Ibid., 10–11.

79. Ibid., 14.

80. This calls to mind the use of ethnic nicknames discussed in Jeffrey Lesser's *A Discontented Diaspora: Japanese Brazilians and the Meaning of Ethnic Militancy* (Durham, NC: Duke University Press, 2007).

81. Edgardo Imas, "Los hermanos sean bohemios," *Sentimiento Bohemio X* 346 (21 June 2010), http://www.sentimientobohemio.com.ar/prod_hermanosbohemios.htm. Accessed on May 26, 2014.

CHAPTER 4

1. Frydenberg, "Los clubes de fútbol de Buenos Aires en los años veinte," 32.

2. *Historia de los cinco grandes del fútbol argentino* (Buenos Aires: Castroman Hnos., n.d.).

3. Club Atlético Atlanta, *Memoria y Balance General correspondiente al 32° ejercicio administrativo (1° de enero 1936 al 31 de diciembre 1936)* (Buenos Aires: n.p., 1937), 11.

4. Próspero Alemandri, *Moral y deporte* (Buenos Aires: Librería del Colegio, 1937), 33.

5. On the popularity of boxing in Argentina, see Eduardo P. Archetti, *El potrero, la pista y el ring: las patrias del deporte argentino* (Buenos Aires: Fondo de Cultura Económia, 2001); Horacio De Marinis, *7,000 años a puñetazos: historia crítica del boxeo* (Buenos Aires: Axioma, 1974); Robert G. Rodriguez, *The Regulation of Boxing: A History and Comparative Analysis of Policies* (Jefferson, NC: McFarland, 2008), ch. 5; Jorge

A. Demárcico, *Historia del boxeo aficionado en la Argentina* (Buenos Aires: Federación Argentina de Box, 1997.

6. Club Atlético Atlanta, *Memoria y Balance General correspondiente al 33° ejercicio administrativo (1° de enero 1937 al 31 de diciembre 1937)* (Buenos Aires: n.p., 1937).

7. Club Atlético Atlanta, *Memoria y Balance* (Buenos Aires: n.p., 1939), 27.

8. *Crítica*, 5 Aug. 1926, 9.

9. On neighborhood identities in Buenos Aires, see Ariel Gravano's books, *Antropología de lo barrial. Estudios sobre la producción simbólica de la vida urbana* (Buenos Aires: Espacio, 2003), and *El barrio en la teoría social* (Buenos Aires: Espacio, 2005).

10. On the history of Independiente, see Club Atlético Independiente, *75° aniversario* (Buenos Aires: n.p., 1980); Comisión Directiva C.A. Independiente, *Historia del C.A.Independiente* (Buenos Aires: n.p., 1968); *Historia de Independiente (una mística copera)* (Buenos Aires: GAM, 1985).

11. Club Atlético Atlanta, *Libro de Actas de Asambleas, 1918–1934.*

12. Stortz, "Historia de Atlanta, fundación y amateurismo."

13. "La marcha Funebrera," *Corazón Funebrero*, 12 Mar. 2012, http://corazonfunebrero.blogspot.co.il/2012/07/la-marcha-funebrera.html. Accessed on May 26, 2014.

14. Francavilla and Lafuente, *Villa Crespo*, 37.

15. Rodrigo Daskal, *Los clubes en la Ciudad de Buenos Aires (1932–1945)* (Buenos Aires: Biblioteca Nacional, 2013), 94–95.

16. Club Atlético Atlanta, *Memoria y Balance General correspondiente al 31° ejercicio administrativo (20 de septiembre 1934 al 31 de diciembre 1935)* (Buenos Aires: n.p., 1936), 28.

17. Ibid., 32.

18. Club Atlético Atlanta, *Memoria y Balance* (Buenos Aires 1940), 25.

19. Club Atlético Atlanta, *Memoria y Balance General correspondiente al 32° ejercicio administrativo (1° de enero 1936 al 31 de diciembre 1936)* (Buenos Aires: n.p., 1937), 16.

20. Ibid., 17.

21. Ibid., 28.

22. Club Atlético Atlanta, *Memoria y Balance* (Buenos Aires: n.p., 1938), esp. 17.

23. On tango in the 1940s, see Maria Susana Azzi, "The Tango, Peronism, and Astor Piazzolla during the 1940s and 50's," in *From Tejano to Tango: Latin American Popular Music*, ed. Walter Aaron Clark (New York: Routledge, 2002), 25–40.

24. Del Pino, *El barrio de Villa Crespo*, 198.

25. Aruj, "Villa Crespo," 60.

26. Gastón Gelblung, " . . . Que tiempos aquellos," http://www.sentimientobohemio.com.ar/produccion_sede2003.htm. Accessed on May 26, 2014.

27. Club Atlético Atlanta, *Memoria y Balance: ejercicio (1° de enero 1941 al 31 de diciembre 1941)* (Buenos Aires: n.p., 1942), 13.

28. Ibid., 19.

29. Gelbung, "Que tiempos aquellos."

30. Club Atlético Atlanta, *Memoria y Balance: ejercicio (1° de enero 1942 al 31 de diciembre 1942)* (Buenos Aires: n.p., 1943), 16.

31. Edgardo Imas, "Un predio con historia," *Sentimiento Bohemio* VII, no. 193 (21 May 2007), http://sentimientobohemio.com.ar/193sede_historia.htm. Accessed on May 26, 2014.

32. Jews played a leading role in Argentine chess. Among Argentine national champions and participants in the Olympic games, we can highlight the names of Miguel Najdorf, Julio Bolbochán, Herman Pilnik, Jacobo Bolbochán, Carlos Bielicki, Bernardo Wexler, Saúl Schweber, and Luis Bronstein.

33. Club Atlético Atlanta, *Memoria y Balance* (Buenos Aires: n.p., 1939), 24.

34. Club Atlético Atlanta, *Memoria y Balance* (Buenos Aires: n.p., 1940), 26.

35. Club Atlético Atlanta, *Memoria y Balance* (Buenos Aires: n.p., 1938), esp. 38.

36. Club Atlético Atlanta, "Fundación," http://wordpress.caatlanta.com.ar/historia. Accessed on Feb. 6, 2013.

37. Del Pino, *Villa Crespo*, 194.

38. Armus, *Ailing City*, 278.

39. On Communist football teams in Buenos Aires, see Hernán Camarero, "Los clubes deportivos comunistas," *Todo es Historia*, no. 448 (Nov. 2004).

40. Fabbri, *El nacimiento de una pasión*, 27.

41. Edgardo Imas, "Buenos Vecinos," *Sentimiento Bohemio* VI, no. 93 (2005), http://sentimientobohemio.com.ar/93_prod_chac1.htm. Accessed on May 26, 2014.

42. Francavilla, *Historia de Villa Crespo*, 63.

43. Imas, "Buenos Vecinos."

44. Club Atlético Atlanta, *Memoria y Balance* (Buenos Aires: n.p., 1938), 18–19.

45. Club Atlético Atlanta, *Memoria y Balance: ejercicio (1° de enero 1941 al 31 de diciembre 1941)*, 43.

46. Korob, "Procesos identitarios e imaginarios locales. Atlanta: bohemios y judíos," 58.

47. *La Nación*, 22 Nov. 1941.

48. Club Atlético Atlanta, *Memoria y Balance: ejercicio (1° de enero 1941 al 31 de diciembre 1941)*, 44.

49. Korob, "Procesos identitarios e imaginarios locales. Atlanta: bohemios y judíos," 58.

50. Fabbri, *El nacimiento de una passion*, 28.

51. Francavilla, *Historia de Villa Crespo*, 64.

52. Imas, "Buenos Vecinos."

53. Korob, "Procesos identitarios e imaginarios locales. Atlanta: bohemios y judíos," 8.

54. Korob, 61.

CHAPTER 5

1. Club Atlético Atlanta, *Memoria y Balance: ejercicio (1° de enero 1942 al 31 de diciembre 1942)* (Buenos Aires: n.p., 1943), 13–14.

2. Ibid., 32.

3. Club Atlético Atlanta, *Memoria y Balance: ejercicio (1° de enero al 31 de diciembre 1944)* (Buenos Aires: n.p., 1945), 38.

4. Club Atlético Atlanta, *Memoria y Balance: ejercicio (1° de enero 1942 al 31 de diciembre 1942)*, 49–51. On the June 1943 coup, see Robert A. Potash, *The Army and*

Politics in Argentina, 1928–1945: Yrigoyen to Peron (Stanford, CA: Stanford University Press, 1969), ch. 7; and Alain Rouquié, *Poder militar y sociedad politico en la Argentina, 1943–1973* (Buenos Aires: Emece Editores, 1983), 2: 13–27.

5. Club Atlético Atlanta, *Memoria y Balance: ejercicio (1° de enero al 31 de diciembre 1944)*, 17.

6. *La Cancha*, 17 Oct. 1945.

7. See the cover story of *El Gráfico*, 7 Dec. 1945.

8. Club Atlético Atlanta, *Memoria y Balance: ejercicio (1° de enero al 31 de diciembre 1944)* (Buenos Aires: n.p., 1945), 40.

9. See Ministerio de Education y Justicia, *Boletín de Comunicaciones* IX, no. 508 (10 Jan. 1958). In March 1953, the Peronist government instituted physical education as a compulsory subject in all the elementary and secondary schools. On the importance attributed to physical education, see *2° Plan Quinquenal* (Buenos Aires: n.p., 1953), IV.E.7, 64–65; and *Manual práctico del 2° Plan Quinquenal* (Buenos Aires: n.p., 1953), 76. On the history of physical education in Argentina before the rise of Peronism, see Angela Aisenstein, *El modelo didáctico en la Education Fisica: entre la escuela y la formación docente* (Buenos Aires: Miño y Dávila, 1995).

10. Juan José Sebreli, *Fútbol y masas* (Buenos Aires: Galerna, 1981), 154. On the Berlin Olympics, see, for example, D. C. Large, *Nazi Games: The Olympics of 1936* (New York: W. W. Norton, 2007); Duff Hart-Davis, *Hitler's Games: The 1936 Olympics* (London: Harper & Row, 1986); and Richard D. Mandell, *The Nazi Olympics*, 2d ed. (Urbana and Chicago: University of Illinois Press, 1987). On sports and politics in Mussolini's Italy, see Victoria de Grazia, *The Culture of Consent: Mass Organization of Leisure in Fascist Italy* (New York: Cambridge University Press, 1981), esp. 169–180; and F. Fabrizio, *Sport e fascismo: La política sportiva del regime, 1928–1936* (Rimini-Florence, Italy: Guaraldi, 1976).

11. Perón, of course, was not the first Argentine president, or the last, to seek popularity by emphasizing sports. On Argentine politicians and their interest in sports, from General Julio A. Roca at the turn of the century up to Carlos Saul Menem (who in this respect, at least, is Peron's faithful follower), see Ariel Scher, *La patria deportista: cien años de política y deporte* (Buenos Aires: Planeta, 1996); and Pablo A. Ramirez, "Los gobernantes y el futbol," *Todo es Historia*, no. 324 (July 1994), 90–93.

12. See Raanan Rein, "El primer deportista": The Political Use and Abuse of Sport in Peronist Argentina, *The International Journal of the History of Sport* 15, no. 2 (1998): 54–76; and Ariel Scher et al., *Deporte nacional: dos siglos de historia* (Buenos Aires: Deportea, 2010), ch. 10.

13. See, for example, *Diario de Sesiones de la Cámara de Diputados* (1948), vol. III: 2150, 2294–95, 2306–7; (1951), vol. III: 2045; and (1955), vol. 1: 188. For petitions by citizens and various provincial organizations to President Peron for financial assistance in founding and developing sports clubs, see Archivo General de la Nación (Buenos Aires), Fondo Asuntos Técnicos, Presidencia de la Nación, Legajos 513 and 681.

14. Raanan Rein, "From Juan Perón to Hugo Chávez and Back: Populism Reconsidered," in *Shifting Frontiers of Citizenship: The Latin American Experience*, ed. Mario Sznajder, Luis Roniger, and Carlos Forment (Boston: Brill, 2013), 289–311.

15. Carlos Aloé, "Cada hombre forja su destino," *Mundo Deportivo* (Buenos Aires) 227 (20 Aug. 1953): 26. This was also reflected in the 1948 drama directed by Leopoldo Torres Ríos, *Pelota de trapo*.

16. See A. Guttmann, *Games and Empires: Modern Sport and Cultural Imperialism* (New York: Columbia University Press, 1994), 3; A. Guttmann, *From Ritual to Record: The Nature of Modern Sports* (New York: Columbia University Press, 1978); Joseph L. Arbena, "Sport and the Study of Latin American Society: An Overview," in *Sport and Society in Latin America*, ed. J. L. Arbena (New York: Greenwood Press, 1988), 2; Juan Domingo Perón, *La gimnasia y los deportes* (Buenos Aires: n.p., 1949).

17. During the years 1947–55 the Argentine Soccer Association had five different presidents, all of them—from Oscar L. Nicolini, the minister of communication, to the syndicalist Cecilio Conditti—committed to the Peronization of Argentine soccer.

18. "Los dividendos del deporte," *Primera Plana*, 6 Sept. 1966, 40.

19. Mariano Ben Plotkin, "La 'ideología' de Perón: Continuidades y rupturas," in *Perón del exilio al poder*, ed. Samuel Amaral and M. B. Plotkin (Buenos Aires: Editorial Cántaro, 1993), 45–67.

20. Juan Perón, *Doctrina Peronista* (Buenos Aires: n.p., 1971), 20.

21. In December 1920, Peron's picture appeared in the sporting weekly *El Grafico*, no. 79, as the sword and saber champion of the Circulo Militar (Military Club).

22. "Fútbol y boxeo," *Primera Plana*, 13 Sept. 1966, 38.

23. In its August 1950 edition, the fan magazine *Racing: una auténtica voz racinguista* thanked Perón, Carlo Aloé, and Ramón Cereijo for their support.

24. See *Democracia* (Buenos Aires), 24 Nov. 1947, 10; Pablo A. Ramírez, "Política y fútbol," *Todo es Historia*, no. 248 (Feb. 1988): 34–43. Opposition members of Congress more than once presented interpellations concerning the transfer of government monies to the sports clubs, the size of these transfers, the criteria that determined them, and the conditions they entailed. See Scher, *La patria deportiva*, 251.

25. Municipalidad de la Ciudad de Buenos Aires, *Autódromo '17 de Octubre'—Inauguración oficial* (Buenos Aires: Municipalidad de la Ciudad, 1952).

26. Santiago Ganduglia, *El nuevo espíritu del deporte argentino* (Buenos Aires: Presidencia de la Nación, Secretaría de Prensa y Difusión, 1954).

27. Quoted in Ganduglia, *El nuevo espíritu*, 8–9.

28. Roberto Di Giano, "Peronismo y fútbol: El triunfo sobre Inglaterra en 1953," *EFDeportes.com, Revista Digital* 17 (Dec. 2013). http://www.efdeportes.com/. Accessed on May 26, 2014.

29. Mark A. Healey, *The Ruins of the New Argentina: Peronism and the Remaking of San Juan after the 1944 Earthquake* (Durham, NC: Duke University Press, 2011).

30. Both Ávalos and then-vice president Perón met with the heads of various football clubs in March 1945 to discuss ways to ensure the success of their operation. See *La Cancha* 878, 21 Mar. 1945.

31. Club Atlético Atlanta, *Memoria y Balance: 42° ejercicio (1° de diciembre 1945 al 30 de noviembre 1946)* (Buenos Aires: n.p., 1946), 13.

32. Ibid., 11.

33. Club Atlético Atlanta, *Memoria y Balance General correspondiente al 43° ejercicio (1° de diciembre 1946 al 30 de noviembre 1947)* (Buenos Aires: n.p., 1947), 12–13.

34. See the relevant chapters in the profuse biographies of Evita. For example, Otelo Borroni and Roberto Vacca, *La vida de Eva Perón: testimonios para su historia* (Buenos Aires: Editorial Galerna, 1971); Marysa Navarro, *Evita* (Buenos Aires: Corregidor, 1981); Alicia Dujovne Ortiz, *Eva Perón: la biografía* (Buenos Aires: Aguilar, 1995).

35. Club Atlético Atlanta, *Memoria y Balance: ejercicio (1° de diciembre 1951 al 30 de noviembre 1952)* (Buenos Aires: n.p., 1952), 4.

36. Ibid., 16.

37. *Democracia*, 24 Nov. 1947, 10.

38. Martin Stawski, "Asistencia social y buenos negocios: política de Fundación Eva Perón (1948–1955)" (MA thesis, Universidad Nacional del General Sarmiento, 2008); Peter Ross, "Policy Formation and Implementation of Social Welfare in Peronist Argentina, 1943–1955" (PhD diss., University of New South Wales, 1988), 280–81.

39. See, for example, "Pequeños futbolistas," *Mundo Infantil* 40 (3 July 1950): 49; "Futuros astros del deporte platense," *Mundo Infantil* 48 (28 Aug. 1950): 37; "Escuela de campeones," *Mundo Peronista* 13 (15 Jan. 1952): 35; "¡Honor al privilegio!, *Mundo Peronista* 18 (1 Apr. 1952): 18–19; "Los campeonatos infantiles Evita apasionan nuevamente," *Mundo Deportivo* 231 (17 Sept. 1953); "Entusiasmo y calidad en los campeonatos infantiles Evita y juveniles Juan Perón," *Mundo Deportivo* 249 (21 Jan. 1954): 18–19.

40. See, for example, *Diario de Sesiones de la Camara de Diputados* (1950), vol. 1: 818, vol. 11: 863, 1099, 1306, vol. V: 3964; (1955), vol. 1: 188, 411.

41. *Mundo Deportivo* 257 (18 Mar. 1954): 4–10, 22–23; *Mundo Deportivo* 307 (3 Mar. 1955): 12–13; *Mundo Deportivo* 308 (10 Mar. 1955): 12–15.

42. Club Atlético Atlanta, *Memoria y Balance: ejercicio (1° de diciembre 1951 al 30 de noviembre 1952)*, 14.

43. Club Atlético Atlanta, *Memoria y Balance: ejercicio (1° de diciembre 1953 al 30 de noviembre 1954)* (Buenos Aires: n.p., 1955), 4.

44. Club Atlético Atlanta, *Memoria y Balance: ejercicio (12 de diciembre 1954 al 30 de noviembre 1955)* (Buenos Aires: n.p., 1956), 6.

45. Rwany Sibaja, "¡Animales! Civility, Modernity, and Constructions of Identity in Argentine Soccer, 1955–1970" (PhD diss., George Mason University, 2013), 120.

46. Ibid., 11.

47. On the efforts to de-Peronize Argentine society, see Robert A. Potash, *The Army and Politics in Argentina, 1945–1962: Perón to Frondizi* (Stanford, CA: Stanford University Press, 1980), ch. 7; Marcos Novaro, *Historia de la Argentina contemporánea: de Perón a Kirchner* (Buenos Aires: Edhasa, 2006). On the history of the AFA, see Ariel Scher and Héctor Palomino, *Fútbol, pasión de multitudes y de elites: un estudio institucional de la Asociación de Fútbol Argentino (1934–1986)* (Buenos Aires: Centro de Investigaciones Sociales sobre el Estado y la Administración, 1988).

48. Raanan Rein, *Argentina, Israel, and the Jews: Perón, the Eichmann Capture and After* (Bethesda: University Press of Maryland, 2003), 139.

49. Raanan Rein, "Un pacto de olvido: peronismo y las divisiones dentro de la colectividad judeo-argentina," *Investigaciones y Ensayos* 58 (2009): 429–68.

50. Edgardo Imas, "Cincuenta años del cajoncito," *Sentimiento Bohemio* X, no. 297 (29 Apr. 2009), http://www.sentimientobohemio.com.ar/289_cajoncito.htm. Accessed on May 26, 2014.

51. Edgardo Imas, "43 años de la Copa Suecia," *Sentimiento Bohemio* IV, no. 1 (6 May 2003), http://www.sentimientobohemio.com.ar/copasuecia43.htm. Accessed on May 26, 2014.

CHAPTER 6

1. On the early history of the Argentine Communist Party, see Hernán Camarero, *A la conquista de la clase obrera: los comunistas y el mundo de trabajo en la Argentina, 1930–1935* (Buenos Aires: Siglo XXI, 2007); Oscar Arévalo, *El Partido Comunista* (Buenos Aires: CEAL, 1983); Isidoro Gilbert, *La FEDE alistandose para la revolución: La Federación Juvenil Comunista, 1921–2005* (Buenos Aires: Sudamericana, 2009).

2. On Frondizi, his electoral campaign, and his presidential term, see Hugo Gambini, *Frondizi, el estadista acorralado* (Barcelona: Vergara, 2006); Nicolás Babini, *Arturo Frondizi y la Argentina moderna* (Barcelona: Gedisa, 2006); Celia Szusterman, *Frondizi and the Politics of Developmentalism in Argentina* (Pittsburgh, PA: University of Pittsburgh Press, 1993).

3. The following biographical information is based on the unpublished manuscript by Kolbowski's late son, Jorge, "La vida de mi padre," as well as a series of interviews with him, held in Buenos Aires, July 2008.

4. On the history of the cooperative movement in Argentina, see Mario Roitter and Inés González Bombal, eds., *Estudios sobre el sector sin fines de lucro en Argentina* (Buenos Aires: CEDES-Johns Hopkins University, 2000).

5. Andrew Graham-Yooll, "Osvaldo Pugliese" (obituary), *Independent* (London), 31 July 1995; María Susana Azzi, "The Golden Age and After: 1920s–1990s," in *Tango!: The Dance, the Song, the Story*, ed. Simon Collier et al. (London: Thames and Hudson, 1995).

6. *Tribuna*, Oct. 1955.

7. Katz specialized in Yiddish-Spanish translation. A close friend of Alberto Gerchunoff, he translated into Yiddish the most famous Jewish Argentine literary work, *Los gauchos judíos*, published originally by Gerchunoff in 1910. On Katz's views, see Pinie Katz, *Páginas selectas* (Buenos Aires: ICUF, 1980).

8. Daskal, "Clubes, deporte y política en el Honorable Concejo Deliberante de la Ciudad de Buenos Aires (1895–1920)," 203–39.

9. *La Cancha*, 22 Sept. 1928, 2.

10. *La Internacional*, 31 Mar. 1928, 6.

11. Bilsky et al., *El movimiento obrero judío en la Argentina*, 61. Jews have played a key role yet to be studied in the PCA. For a pioneering book, see Daniel Kersffeld, *Rusos y rojos: judíos comunistas en los tiempos de la Comintern* (Buenos Aires: Capital Intelectual, 2012).

12. Claudia Bacci, "Las políticas culturales del progresismo judío argentine: la revista Aporte y el ICUF en la década de 1950," *Políticas de la Memoria* 5 (2004–2005): 159–68; Silvia Schenkolwvski-Kroll, "El Partido Comunista en la Argentina ante Moscú," *EIAL* 10, no. 2 (1999): 91–107.

13. Torcuato S. Di Tella, "La Union Obrera Textil, 1930–1945," *Desarrollo Económico* 33, no. 129 (Apr.–June 1993): 121.

14. Hernán Camarero, "El Partido Comunista argentino y sus políticas en favor de una cultura obrera en las decadas de 1920 y 1930," *Pacarina del Sur, Revista de pensamiento critico latinoamericano* 7 (Apr.–June 2011), http://www.pacarinadelsur.com/home/amautas-y-horizontes/236-el-partido-comunista-argentino-y-sus-politicas-en-favor-de-una-cultura-obrera-en-las-decadas-de-1920-y-1930. Accessed on May 26, 2014.

15. Nerina Visacovsky, "Las escuelas obreras judías y el anticomunismo de Matías Sánchez Sorondo" (paper presented at the XIII LAJSA conference, Biblioteca Nacional, Buenos Aires, July 2007).

16. The ad in *Tribuna* (May 1955), said, "León Kolbowski presents: Galería Durero— Exposición y venta de cuadros miniaturas y marcos en todos los estilos. Pergaminos y retratos. Corrientes 5590."

17. Jorge Kolbowski, "La vida de mi padre."

18. See, for example, "Kolbowski: Atlanta crece," *La Razón*, 5 Jan. 1965.

19. Bard had an impressive political career in the Unión Cívica Radical, loyally accompanying Hipólito Yrigoyen from an early stage. Bard served as a deputy in the national Congress, becoming president of the Radical bloc in Congress between the years 1922–30. Following the September 1930 military coup he was detained and tortured. Still, he is hardly mentioned in either Argentine political historiography or in the literature on Jewish experiences in Argentina. See Bard's autobiography, *Estampas de una vida*.

20. Club Atlético Atlanta, *Memoria Año 1963* (Buenos Aires: n.p., 1963).

21. On Miller, see David Winner, *Brilliant Orange: The Neurotic Genius of Dutch Football* (London: Bloomsbury Publishing, 2010), ch. 15; Kuper, *Ajax, the Dutch, the War*, passim. On Mogilevsky, see Ezequiel Costa, "Adolfo Mogilevsky, el adiós de un pionero," *Área 18* (blog), 29 Aug. 2012 (11:23 a.m.), http://area18deportes.blogspot.co.il/2012/08/adolfo-mogilevsky-el-adios-de-un-pionero.html; Edgardo Imas, "Aquellas pretemporadas con Mogilevsky," *Sentimiento Bohemio*, 23 Dec. 2012, http://sentimientobohemio.info/?p=13018; Edgardo Imas, "Recordando a Mogilevsky," *Sentimiento Bohemio*, 28 Aug. 2012, http://sentimientobohemio.info/?p=8956. Accessed on May 26, 2014.

22. Archetti, "Death and Violence in Argentinian Football."

23. Edgardo Imas, "El estadio, pasado y presente," *Sentimiento Bohemio* VI, no. 88 (8 Mar. 2005), http://www.sentimientobohemio.com.ar/88_encruestadio.htm. Accessed on May 26, 2014.

24. Club Atlético Atlanta, *Memoria Año 1959* (Buenos Aires: n.p., 1959).

25. Club Atlético Atlanta, *Memoria Año 1960* (Buenos Aires: n.p., 1960).

26. "Kolbowski: Atlanta crece," *La Razón*, 5 Jan. 1965.

27. Club Atlético Atlanta, *Memoria Año 1960*.

28. Club Atlético Atlanta, *Memoria Año 1962* (Buenos Aires: n.p., 1962).

29. Club Atlético Atlanta, *Memoria Año 1963*.

30. "Kolbowski: Atlanta crece," *La Razón*, 5 Jan. 1965.

31. Club Atlético Atlanta, *Memoria Año 1967* (Buenos Aires: n.p., 1967).

32. Club Atlético Atlanta, *Memoria Año 1958* (Buenos Aires: n.p., 1958).

33. Club Atlético Atlanta, *Memoria Año 1961* (Buenos Aires: n.p., 1961).

34. Sibaja, "¡Animales!" 181. See also Héctor Onésimo, "Atlanta y el 'catenaccio' porteño," *El Gráfico*, 16 Sept. 1964, 72–73; Piri García, "Atlanta se comió otro 'grande'," *El Gráfico*, 23 Sept. 1964, 8–9.

35. Adolfo Mogilevsky, "Algunas líneas sobre León Kolbovsky," unpublished article; author's interview with Mogilevski, Tel Aviv, Oct. 2007.

36. Author's interview with Jorge Kolbowski, Buenos Aires, July 2008.

37. *Ma'ariv* (Tel Aviv), 16 Apr. 1963; Edgardo Imas, "Atlanta de gira por Israel," *Sentimiento Bohemio*, n.d., http://www.sentimientobohemio.com.ar/produccion_giraisrael .htm, accessed on May 26, 2014; Avraham Ben Shalom, "The Boys of the National Team Enter the 'South American Era,'" [Hebrew] *Yediot Ahronot/ Yediot Sport*, 4 Apr. 1963, 14; Ieshayahu Porat, "Atlanta Against the Israeli Team," [Hebrew] *Ma'ariv Lesportaim*, 10 Apr. 1963, 6.

38. Avraham Ben Shalom, "The Visit to Israel Gave the Atlanta Management a Big Deficit [Hebrew]," *Yediot Ahronot/ Yediot Sport*, 16 Apr. 1963, 10; Avraham Tabac, "Atlanta Leaves Goals and Complaints," [Hebrew] *Ma'ariv Lesportaim*, 17 Apr. 1963, 6.

39. This Youth Championship was held in Japan. Argentina, with Diego Armando Maradona, defeated the Soviet Union in the final. It was only one year after Argentina won the World Cup (Mundial) held in Argentina, and the military regime was using these sports achievements for political purposes.

40. The Trelew massacre was a retaliatory government killing of sixteen Peronist and left-wing militants held as political prisoners in the Rawson penitentiary.

41. Edgardo Imas, "Hogar, dulce hogar," *Sentimiento Bohemio* VII, no. 149 (19 June 2006), http://www.sentimientobohemio.com.ar/149_estadio46aniv.htm. Accessed on May 26, 2014.

42. Club Atlético Atlanta, *Memoria Año 1965* (Buenos Aires: n.p., 1965).

43. *El Gráfico*, 14 Sept. 1965.

44. Club Atlético Atlanta, *Memoria Año 1965*.

45. *Crónica*, 29 Sept. 1965

46. Ibid.

47. *El Gráfico*, 14 Sept. 1965.

48. *Crónica*, 4 Feb. 1966.

49. Ibid., 26 Dec. 1968.

50. Undated clipping from *Clarín*, private archive of Jorge Kolbowski.

51. Ibid.

52. *La Razón*, 17 Nov. 1968.

53. Author's interview with Julio Winiky, Buenos Aires, Oct. 2010; "Dichos y hechos," *La Nación*, 6 May 1968.

54. Author's interview with Jorge Kolbowski, Buenos Aires, July 2008.

CHAPTER 7

1. On the turbulent 1970s, see Luis Alberto Romero, *A History of Argentina in the Twentieth Century* (University Park: Pennsylvania State University Press, 2002), chs. 6–7; Paul H. Lewis, *Guerrillas and Generals: The "Dirty War" in Argentina* (Westport, CT: Praeger, 2002); Marcos Novaro and Vicente Palermo, *La dictadura militar, 1976–1983: del golpe de estado a la restauración democrática* (Buenos Aires: Paidós, 2003).

2. Domínguez, *La historia de Atlanta*, 123–24.

3. Club Atlético Atlanta Sociedad Civil, *Memoria y Balance General, ejercicio 76°* (Buenos Aires: n.p., 1979–80).

4. "¿Sabe usted donde está su hijo en este momento?" became one of the most infamous slogans of the repressive military dictatorship. See "Carta abierta a los padres argentinos," *Gente*, 16 Dec. 1976. On the military control of the mass media, see Eduardo Blaustein and Martín Zubieta, *Decíamos ayer: la prensa argentina bajo el proceso* (Buenos Aires: Colihue, 1998).

5. Club Atlético Atlanta Sociedad Civil, *Memoria y Balance General, ejercicio 71°–1975* (Buenos Aires: n.p., 1976).

6. Club Atlético Atlanta Sociedad Civil, *Memoria y Balance General, ejercicio 78°* (Buenos Aires: n.p., 1981–82). On the Falklands/Malvinas war, see Vicente Palermo, *Sal en las heridas: las Malvinas en la cultura argentina contemporánea* (Buenos Aires: Sudamericana, 2007).

7. Club Atlético Atlanta Sociedad Civil, *Memoria y Balance General, ejercicio 78°*.

8. Ibid.

9. Club Atlético Atlanta Sociedad Civil, *Memoria y Balance General, ejercicio 76°* (Buenos Aires: n.p., 1979–80).

10. Club Atlético Atlanta Sociedad Civil, *Memoria y Balance General, ejercicio 71°–1975*; and *Memoria y Balance General, ejercicio 76°*.

11. Club Atlético Atlanta Sociedad Civil, *Memoria y Balance General, ejercicio 78°*.

12. Guido Di Tella, *Argentina under Perón, 1973–76: The Nation's Experience with a Labour-Based Government* (New York: St. Martin's Press, 1983).

13. Club Atlético Atlanta Sociedad Civil, *Memoria y Balance General, ejercicio 71°–1975*.

14. Ibid. However, in the early 1980s the club did start publishing a magazine, *Entre Nosotros*; see, for example, the issue celebrating the club's seventy-seventh anniversary: Club Atlético Atlanta, *Entre Nosotros* 1, no. 6 (Aug.–Sept. 1981). The cover of this issue was devoted to a visit by the city's mayor, Osvaldo A. Cacciatore.

15. Club Atlético Atlanta Sociedad Civil, *Memoria y Balance General, ejercicio 76°*, and *Memoria y Balance General, ejercicio 78°*.

16. Club Atlético Atlanta Sociedad Civil, *Memoria y Balance General, ejercicio 71°–1975*.

17. Edgardo Imas, "Un predio con historia," *Sentimiento Bohemio* VII, no. 193 (21 May 2007), http://www.sentimientobohemio.com.ar/193sede_historia.htm. Accessed on May 26, 2014.

18. See "Cuando la pelota se manchó de sangre," in the anthology compiled by Laura Santos, Ulises Muschietti, and Andrés Mazzeo, *1976/Investigaciones/Testimonios/Cronologías* (Buenos Aires: T.E.A. y Deportea, 2006), 18–23.

19. On the junta's use of the World Cup for propagandistic purposes, see Mabel Veneziani, "El Mundial," *Todo es Historia*, no. 229 (1986): 30–54; Tony Mason, *Passion of the People?: Football in South America* (London: Verso, 1995), 71–75; Simon Kuper, *Soccer Against the Enemy* (New York: Nation Books, 2006), ch. 16.

20. Edgardo Imas, "Atlanta y la dictadura," *Sentimiento Bohemio* VII, no. 187 (10 Apr. 2007), http://www.sentimientobohemio.com.ar/187_militares.htm. Accessed on May 26, 2014.

21. "Decreto del Poder Ejecutivo Nacional," N° 555/81, 24 Mar. 1981.

22. Edgardo Imas, "Atlanta y el terrorismo de Estado," *Sentimiento Bohemio* VII, no. 139 (3 Apr. 2006), http://www.sentimientobohemio.com.ar/139_30anios.htm. Accessed on May 26, 2014.

23. Author's interview with Eliezer Nowodworski, Ramat Gan, May 2001.

24. Domínguez, *La historia de Atlanta*, 180–203.

25. James Brooke, "For Argentina, Inflation and Rage Rise in Tandem," *The New York Times*, 4 June 1989.

26. Club Atlético Atlanta, *Memoria y Balance: 1986/1987*.

27. Gustavo Veiga, "Amor por el club," *Página/12*, 7 Nov. 2008, http://www.pagina12.com.ar/diario/deportes/8-114617-2008-11-07.html, accessed on May 26, 2014. On Defensa y Justicia, see Fabbri, *El nacimiento de una pasión*, 61–62.

28. "La historia siempre terminó mal," *Clarín*, 10 Mar. 2000, http://edant.clarin.com/diario/2000/03/10/r-05401d.htm. Accessed on May 26, 2014.

29. Gaston Gelblung, "Mi pasado me condena," *Sentimiento Bohemio* VII, no. 172 (11 Nov. 2006), http://www.sentimientobohemio.com.ar/172_pasadopresente.htm. Accessed on May 26, 2014.

30. Gelblung, " . . . que tiempos aquellos," *Sentimiento Bohemio*, http://www.sentimientobohemio.com.ar/produccion_sede2003.htm. Accessed on May 26, 2014.

31. See the 1999 Resolution of the Ministry of Interior: Ministerio del Interior, Resolución N° 1576/99. For recent studies of violent behavior among Argentine fans, see José Garriga Zucal, *"Haciendo amigos a las piñas": violencia y redes sociales de una hinchada del fútbol* (Buenos Aires: Prometeo, 2007); José Garriga Zucal, *"Nosotros nos peleamos: violencia e identidad de una hinchada de fútbol* (Buenos Aires: Prometeo, 2010).

32. Secretaria de Gobierno de la Ciudad de Buenos Aires. Decreto N° 1012/2000.

33. Jorge Rubinska, Letter to the Comité de Seguridad en el Fútbol (Secretaría de Seguridad Interior), 7 Oct. 2000.

34. Daniel L. Wann et al., *Sport Fans: The Psychology and Social Impact of Spectators* (New York: Routledge, 2001); Matt Hills, *Fan Cultures* (London: Routledge, 2002);

Richard Giulianotti, "Supporters, Followers, Fans, and Flaneurs: A Taxonomy of Spectator Identities in Football," *Journal of Sport & Social Issues* 26, no. 1 (2002): 25–46.

35. See, for example, *La Cancha* 266, 1 July 1933.

36. See, for example, the November 1933 protest of Atlanta fans against the club authorities who sold only a limited number of cheap tickets in order to increase revenue: *La Cancha* 286, 18 Nov. 1933.

37. Mike Cronin and Avid Mayall, "Sport and Ethnicity: Some Introductory Remarks," in *Sporting Nationalisms: Identity, Ethnicity, Immigration and Assimilation*, ed. Mike Cronin and Avid Mayall (London: Frank Cass, 1998), 1–13.

38. Grant Jarvie, ed., *Sport, Racism and Ethnicity* (London: Falmer, 1991); Richard Giulianotti et al., eds., *Football, Violence and Social Identity* (London: Routledge, 1994); Yves Pallade et al., *Antisemitism and Racism in European Soccer* (Berlin: AJC, 2007). On violence in Argentine stadiums, see, for example, Amílcar G. Romero, *Deporte, violencia y política* (Buenos Aires: Centro Editor de América Latina, 1985); Eduardo P. Archetti, "Argentinian Football: A Ritual of Violence?," *The International Journal of the History of Sport* 9, no. 2 (1992): 209–35; E. P. Archetti, "Death and Violence in Argentinian Football," in *Football, Violence and Social Identity*, ed. R. Giulianotti et al., 37–72.

39. Ben Carrington and Ian McDonald, eds., *"Race," Sport and British Society* (London: Routledge, 2001), 2.

40. Lelia Gándara, "Las Ciudades y el Fútbol," *Efdeportes* 7, no. 43 (Dec. 2001), http://www.efdeportes.com/efd43/voces.htm. Accessed on May 26, 2014.

41. See *Siglo Bohemio*, dir. Aníbal Garisto, Mónica Nizzardo, and Javier Orradre (Buenos Aires, 2004), DVD; and *Te llevo en la sangre*, dir. Pablo G. Pérez (Buenos Aires: Instituto Nacional de Cine y Artes Audiovisuales, 2004), DVD.

42. Mikita Hoy, "Joyful Mayhem: Bakhtin, Football Songs, and the Carnivalesque," *Text and Performance Quarterly* 14 (1994): 289–304.

43. Christopher Thomas Gaffney, *Temples of the Earthbound Gods: Stadiums in the Cultural Landscapes of Rio de Janeiro and Buenos Aires* (Austin: University of Texas Press, 2008), ch. 1.

44. Several authors claim that in Latin America masculinity is retained so long as one is the penetrator and not the receiver, whether the partner is male or female. See, for example, Charles T. Parrish and John Nauright, "Fútbol cantitos: Negotiating Masculinity in Argentina," *Soccer & Society* 14, no. 1 (2013): 1–19.

45. See the documentary *Nos otros*, dir. Daniel Raichijk (Argentina, 2010), DVD.

46. Quoted in Franklin Foer, *How Soccer Explains the World* (New York: Harper Perennial, 2004), 79.

47. On the 1994 AMIA bombing, see Sergio Kiernan, *A Cover-Up Exposed: The 1994 AMIA Bombing Case Hits the Wall* (New York: American Jewish Committee, 2004); Federico Pablo Feldstein and Carolina Acosta-Alzuru, "Argentinean Jews as Scapegoat: A Textual Analysis of the Bombing," *Journal of Communication Inquiry* 27 (2003): 152–70; Michelle Amy Cohen, "Delving into the Ruins: The AMIA Bombing, the Struggle for Justice, and the Negotiation of Jewish Belonging in Argentina" (PhD diss., University of

North Carolina at Chapel Hill, 2009); Natasha Zaretsky, "Citizens of the Plaza: Memory, Violence, and Belonging in Jewish Buenos Aires" (PhD diss., Princeton University, 2008).

48. Mauricio Dimant, "Antisemitismo y cultura popular en Argentina: 1995–2004. Una aproximación preliminar," *Índice—Revista de Ciencias Sociales* 24 (2007): 255.

49. "El INADI quiere la intervención de la AFA a causa del racismo," *Página/12*, 4 Mar. 2000, http://www.pagina12.com.ar/2000/00-03/00-03-04/pag24.htm. Accessed on May 26, 2014.

50. Miguel Bossio, "Decir que no," *Clarín*, 26 Oct. 2002.

51. "El racismo en el tablón," *Diario Río Negro*, 8 July 2001, http://www1.rionegro .com.ar/arch200107/c08s02.html. Accessed on May 26, 2014.

52. Gustavo Veiga, "La discriminación se va agudizando con los problemas socio económicos," *Página/12*, 17 Sept. 2000, http://www.pagina12.com.ar/2000/00-09/00 -09-17/pag26.htm. Accessed on May 26, 2014.

53. Dimant, "Antisemitismo y cultura popular en Argentina: 1995–2004," esp. 265.

54. Ibid.

55. Among the names of Jewish footballers in Argentina, the first two that come to mind are León Goldbaum and Luis Ernesto Abramovich.

56. Unlike in Chile or Brazil, ethnic soccer clubs in Buenos Aires—such as Sportivo Italiano, Deportivo Armenio, Deportivo Español, and Deportivo Paraguayo—were formed in a later period, from the 1950s onward.

57. Pablo Alabarces, *Hinchadas* (Buenos Aires: Prometeo, 2005); Pablo Alabarces, ed., *Futbologías: fútbol, identidad y violencia en América Latina* (Buenos Aires: CLACSO, 2003); Eduardo Archetti, "Argentine Football: A Ritual of Violence?" *International Journal of the History of Sport* 9, no. 2 (1992): 209–35; Vic Duke and Liz Crolley, "Football Spectator Behaviour in Argentina: A Case of Separate Evolution," *Sociological Review* 44, no. 2 (1996): 93–116; Amilcar Romero, *Las barras bravas y la contrasociedad deportiva* (Buenos Aires: Nueva América, 1994).

58. Parrish and Nauright, "Fútbol cantitos," 3.

59. Foer, *How Soccer Explains the World*, 79–80.

60. Enrique Gastañag, "Racismo por Internet," *Clarín*, 16 Mar. 2000, http://old.clarin .com.ar/diario/2000/03/16/r-01101d.htm, accessed on May 26, 2014; Gustavo Veiga, interview with Jorge Rubinska (president of Atlanta, 1999–2002), *Página/12*, 17 Sept. 2000, http://www.pagina12.com.ar/2000/00-09/00-09-17/pag26.htm. Accessed on May 26, 2014.

61. Lelia Gándara, "Diálogos en la pared," *Graffiti* (Buenos Aires: EUDEBA, 2003), 76–83.

62. Philip Roth, *Reading Myself and Others* (New York: Penguin, 1985), 181.

63. Author's interview with Alejandro Melincovsky, Buenos Aires, Oct. 2012.

64. Bernardo Lichtensztajn, response to author's questionnaire, 2007.

65. Nick Hornby, *Fever Pitch* (New York: Penguin Books, 2005).

66. Daniel L. Wan et al., eds., *Sport Fans* (New York: Routledge, 2001); Matt Hills, *Fan Culture* (London: Routledge, 1989); Richard Giulianotti, "Supporters, Followers, Fans and Flaneurs," *Journal of Sport and Social Issues* 26, no. 1 (2002): 25–46.

67. Guillermo Estiz and Clody Plotinky, responses to author's questionnaires, 2008.

68. Andrés Darío Goldberg, response to author's questionnaire, 2008.

69. Víctor Zamenfeld, response to author's questionnaire, 2007.

70. J. Schafer, "'As Obsessed As the Men': Argentine Women's Participation During the 1978 World Cup" (paper presented at the American Historical Association Conference, New Orleans, Jan. 2013).

71. Raanan Rein, "Football, Politics and Protests: The International Campaign Against the 1978 World Cup in Argentina", in *The Relevance and Impact of FIFA World Cups, 1930–2010*, ed. S. Rinke and K. Schiller (Goettingen, Germany: Wallstein, 2014).

72. Julio Bichman, response to author's questionnaire, 2008.

73. Cecilio Barak, response to author's questionnaire, 2007.

74. Author's interview with Esther Rollansky, Tel Aviv, July 2010.

75. Manuela Fingueret, *Blues de la calle Leiva* (Buenos Aires: Planeta, 2006); Edgardo Imas, "Falleció la escritora Manuela Fingueret," *Sentimiento Bohemio*, 12 Mar. 2013, http://sentimientobohemio.info/?p=15365. Accessed on May 26, 2014.

76. Alejandro Meter, "Jewishness and Sports: The Case for Latin American Fiction," in *Muscling in on New Worlds: Jews, Sport, and the Making of the Americas*, ed. David Sheinin and Raanan Rein (Boston: Brill, 2014).

77. Guido Martín Nejamkis, response to author's questionnaire, 2007.

78. On the importance of Yiddish in twentieth-century Jewish Argentine culture, see Eliahú Toker, *El ídish es también Latinoamérica* (Buenos Aires: Instituto Movilizador de Fondos Cooperativos, 2003); Perla Sneh, ed., *Buenos Aires idish* (Buenos Aires: CPPHC, 2006); Perla Sneh, "Ídish al sur, una rama en sombras," in *Pertenencia y alteridad. Judíos en/de America Latina: Cuarenta años de cambios*, ed. Haim Avni et al. (Madrid: Iberoamericana, 2011), 657–76.

79. Benjamín Fryd and Jaime Mandelman, responses to author's questionnaire, 2008.

80. Guido Martín Nejamkis, response to author's questionnaire, 2007.

81. Mario Nizzardo and Gastón Gelblung, "El gol más esperado," *Sentimiento Bohemio* IV, no. 31 (9 Dec. 2003), http://www.sentimientobohemio.com.ar/4del12.htm. Accessed on May 26, 2014.

82. On the active Israeli branch of Atlanta, see "Histórico encuentro en Israel," *Sentimiento Bohemio* IV, no. 20 (23 Sept. 2003), http://www.sentimientobohemio.com. ar/mundo_reunion_israel.htm, accessed on May 26, 2014; Gaston Gelbung, "Concretamente fanáticos," *Sentimiento Bohemio* VII, no. 212 (1 Oct. 2007), http://www.sen timientobohemio.com.ar/213_israel.htm; "Mociulski en Israel," *Sentimiento Bohemio* XI, no. 376 (23 Jan. 2011), http://www.sentimientobohemio.com.ar/277_mocoiulsly.htm. Accessed on May 26, 2014.

83. Federico Kotlar and Ezequiel San Martín, "Atlanta volvió a gozar en su cancha," *Clarín*, 29 Mar. 2009, http://edant.clarin.com/diario/2009/03/29/um/m-01887196.htm. Accessed on May 26, 2014.

EPILOGUE

1. See *O ano em que meus pais saíram de férias* [The year my parents went on vacation], dir. Cao Hamburger (Brazil, 2006), DVD.

2. See Carolina Rocha, "Jewish Cinematic Self-Representations in Contemporary Argentine and Brazilian Films," *Journal of Modern Jewish Studies* 9, no. 1 (Mar. 2010): 37–48.

3. See their Internet sites: Club Deportivo Palestino, official website, http://www .palestino.cl/; Los Baisanos—Intifada (Foro de la Barra del Club Deportivo Palestino), http://losbaisanos.foroactivo.com/; Club Palestino http://www.clubpalestino.cl/.

4. See Tim Sturtridge, "South America Football Connections: Chile and Palestine," *Soccerphile*, http://www.soccerphile.com/soccerphile/south-america/chile-palestine. html, accessed on May 26, 2014; and the documentary by the Chilean Marcelo Piña, *Tiro Libre* (Chile/ USA /Egypt /Kuwait, 2007).

5. On the Palestinians in Chile, see Lorenzo Agar Corbinos and Antonia Rebolledo, "La inmigración árabe en Chile: los caminos de la integración," in *El Mundo árabe y América Latina*, ed. Raymundo Kabchi (Madrid: Ediciones Libertarias/Prodhufi/ Unesco, 1997), 283–309; Cecilia Baeza, "Les Palestiniens du Chili: de la conscience diasporique à la mobilisation transnationale," *Revue d'études palestiniennes* 95 (spring 2005):51–87; Cecilia Baeza, "Les Palestiniens d'Amérique Latine et la cause palestinienne (Chili, Brésil, Honduras. 1920–2010)" (PhD diss., Institut d'Etudes Politiques de Paris, 2010); and Isaac Caro, *Islam y judaísmo contemporáneo en América Latina* (Santiago, Chile: Ril Editores, 2010).

6. See Brenda Elsey, *Citizens and Sportsmen: Fútbol and Politics in Twentieth-Century Chile* (Austin: University of Texas Press, 2011), esp. 149–64. Audax Italia and Unión Española of Santiago are two additional examples of ethnic soccer clubs in Chile.

7. Obviously, not all Chileans of Arab descent have been fans of Deportivo Palestino. Many Chileans of Syrian descent *are* considered fans of Colo-Colo.

8. Much of my scholarly work on this subject was written jointly with Jeffrey Lesser. See, for example, Jeffrey Lesser and Raanan Rein, "Challenging Particularity: Jews as a Lens for Ethnicity in Latin America," *Latin American and Caribbean Ethnic Studies* 1, no. 2 (2006): 249–63; and Jeffrey Lesser and Raanan Rein, *Rethinking Jewish-Latin Americans* (Albuquerque: University of New Mexico Press, 2008).

9. See also Raanan Rein, ed., *Arabes y judíos en Iberoamérica: similitudes, diferencias y tensiones sobre el trasfondo de las tres culturas* (Madrid: Fundación Tres Culturas, 2008); Raanan Rein, ed., *Más allá del Medio Oriente: Las diásporas judía y árabe en América Latina* (Granada, Spain: Editorial de la Universidad de Granada, 2012); Ignacio Klich, *Árabes y judíos en América Latina: historia, representaciones y desafíos* (Buenos Aires: Siglo XXI, 2006); Ignacio Klich and Jeffrey Lesser, eds., *Arab and Jewish Immigrants in Latin America: Images and Realities* (London: Routledge, 1998), 125–45.

10. Claudio Cerda, "Soccer—Chile's Palestino Tapping Roots to Go Public," *Reuters. com*, 17 Aug. 2009, http://uk.reuters.com/article/idUKLH07455520090817. Accessed on May 26, 2014.

11. See "Tarjeta roja para los cantos antisemitas de Chacarita Juniors," *Radio Jai*, http://www.radiojai.com.ar/online/notiDetalle.asp?id_Noticia=59056; Julio Carvajal, "Informe AFA: Sancionaron a Chacarita," *Todo Ascenso* (blog), 19 Apr. 2012 (8:10 p.m.), http://blog.todoascensoweb.com.ar/2012/04/19/informe-afa-sancionaron-a-chacarita/, accessed on May 26, 2014; and "Wiesenthal Center to Argentine Football Association: 'Show Red Flag to Chacarita Juniors Soccer Club Anti-Semitic Hate Chants,'" *The Simon Wiesenthal Center*, 12 Mar. 2012, http://www.wiesenthal.com/site/apps/nlnet/content2 .aspx?c=lsKWLbPJLnF&b=4441467&ct=11661353#.URjQLh285Mi. Accessed on May 26, 2014.

12. *Los Graduados*, official website, http://losgraduados.telefe.com/; Guido Burdman, "'Graduados' también triunfa en Israel," *La Opinión Judía*, 18 Oct. 2012, http://laopinion judia.com/2012/10/18/graduados-tambien-triunfa-en-israel/. Accessed on May 26, 2014.

13. "La Resurrección," *La Taberna del Siome*, 8 Apr. 2012, http://latabernadelsiome .blogspot.co.il/2012/04/la-resurreccion.html, accessed on May 26, 2014; Bajurtov, "Club de segunda division, identificado con la comunidad judía, derrota a River Plate en Argentina," *Patria Judía*, 9 Apr. 2012, http://bajurtov.wordpress.com/2012/04/09/club -de-segunda-divisionidentificado-con-la-comunidad-judiaderrota-a-river-plate-en -argentina/, accessed on May 26, 2014; "La venganza de Atlanta siguió con los afiches de cargadas a River," *Clarín*, 9 Apr. 2012, http://eldiario.tristangrimaux.com/id/415662. Accessed on May 26, 2014.

14. Anthony Clavane, *Does Your Rabbi Know You're Here?: The Story of English Football's Forgotten Tribe* (London: Quercus, 2012).

15. Ricardo Feierstein, *Mestizo* (Albuquerque: University of New Mexico Press, 2000), 309, 314.

BIBLIOGRAPHY

PRIMARY SOURCES

ARCHIVES

Archivo de la Asociación del Fútbol Argentino, Buenos Aires
Archivo del Club Atlético Atlanta, Buenos Aires
Archivo General de la Nación, Buenos Aires
Archivo Personal de Jorge Kolbowski, Buenos Aires

PRINTED DOCUMENTS AND OFFICIAL PUBLICATIONS

Club Atlético Atlanta. *Libro de Actas de Asambleas, 1918–1934.*
———. *Memoria y Balance (20 de septiembre al 20 de noviembre)*, Buenos Aires, 1934.
———. *Memoria y Balance General correspondiente al 31° ejercicio administrativo (20 de septiembre 1934 al 31 de diciembre 1935)*, Buenos Aires, 1936.
———. *Memoria y Balance General correspondiente al 32° ejercicio administrativo (1° de enero 1936 al 31 de diciembre 1936)*, Buenos Aires, 1937.
———. *Memoria y Balance General correspondiente al 33° ejercicio administrativo (1° de enero 1937 al 31 de diciembre 1937)*, Buenos Aires, 1937.
———. *Memoria y Balance*, Buenos Aires, 1938.
———. *Memoria y Balance*, Buenos Aires, 1939.
———. *Memoria y Balance*, Buenos Aires, 1940.
———. *Memoria y Balance: ejercicio (1° de enero 1941 al 31 de diciembre 1941)*, Buenos Aires, 1942.
———. *Memoria y Balance: ejercicio (1° de enero 1942 al 31 de diciembre 1942)*, Buenos Aires, 1943.
———. *Memoria y Balance: correspondiente al 40° ejercicio (1° de enero 1944 al 31 de diciembre 1944)*, Buenos Aires, 1945.
———. *Memoria y Balance: correspondiente al 41° ejercicio (1° de enero 1945 al 30 de noviembre 1945)*, Buenos Aires, 1946.
———. *Memoria y Balance General correspondiente al 43° ejercicio (1° de diciembre 1946 al 30 de noviembre 1947)*, Buenos Aires, 1947.

———. *Memoria y Balance: correspondiente al 48° ejercicio (1° de diciembre 1951 al 30 de noviembre 1952)*, Buenos Aires, 1952.

———. *Memoria y Balance General del 51° ejercicio anual (1° de diciembre 1954 al 30 de noviembre 1955)*, Buenos Aires, 1955.

Club Atlético Atlanta Sociedad Civil. *Memoria y Balance General, ejercicio 71°-1975*, Buenos Aires, 1976.

———. *Memoria y Balance General, ejercicio 76°*, Buenos Aires, 1979–80.

———. *Memoria y Balance General, ejercicio 78°*, Buenos Aires, 1981–82.

Club Atlético Independiente, *75° aniversario*, Buenos Aires, 1980.

Comisión Directiva C.A. Independiente. *Historia del C.A. Independiente*, Buenos Aires, 1968.

Ganduglia, Santiago. *El nuevo espíritu del deporte argentino*. Buenos Aires: Presidencia de la Nación, Secretaría de Prensa y Difusión, 1954.

Municipalidad de la Ciudad de Buenos Aires. *Autódromo '17 de Octubre'—Inauguración oficial*. Buenos Aires: Municipalidad de la Ciudad, 1952.

Perón, Juan Domingo. *Doctrina Peronista*. Buenos Aires, 1971.

———. *La gimnasia y los deportes*, 1949.

República Argentina, Cámara de Diputados de la Nación. *Diario de Sesiones*, 1948–55.

República Argentina, Presidencia de la Nación. Decreto del Poder Ejecutivo Nacional, no. 555/81, 24 Mar. 1981.

———. *Manual práctico del 2° Plan Quinquenal*. Buenos Aires, 1953.

República Argentina, Ministerio de Educación y Justicia. *Boletín de Comunicaciones* IX, 508 (10 Jan. 1958).

República Argentina, Ministerio del Interior. Resolución N° 1576/99.

———. Subsecretaría de Informaciones. *2° Plan Quinquenal*. Buenos Aires, 1953.

República Argentina, Secretaría de Gobierno de la Ciudad de Buenos Aires. Decree N° 1012/2000.

Tissoni, Juan Carlos. *Los 75 años de Atlanta* (revista del 75 aniversario del club). Buenos Aires, 1979.

CONTEMPORARY SOURCES AND ACCOUNTS OF PROTAGONISTS

Alberdi, Juan Bautista. *Bases y puntos de partida para la organización de la República Argentina*. Buenos Aires: Centro Editor de América Latina, 1979.

Alemandri, Próspero. *Moral y deporte*. Buenos Aires: Librería del Colegio, 1937.

Aráoz, Ernesto M. *La inmigración en la Argentina y sus vinculaciones con la cuestión social*. Salta, Argentina: Imprenta de las Llanas, 1919.

Arlt, Roberto. *Obras*. Buenos Aires: Losada, 1998.

Bard, Leopoldo. *Estampas de una vida. La fe puesta en un ideal. "Llegar a ser algo."* Buenos Aires: Juan Perrotti, 1957.

Bavio, Ernesto Escobar. *El football en el Río de la Plata (desde 1893)*. Buenos Aires: Editorial Sports, 1923.

Cadícamo, Enrique D. "Salón Peracca." In *Poemas del bajo fondo—Viento que lleva y trae*. Buenos Aires: Editorial Fermata, 1945.

Cortázar, Julio. "Adán Buenosayres, de Leopoldo Marechal." *Realidad. Revista de Ideas* [Buenos Aires] V, no. 14 (Mar.–Apr. 1949): 232–38.

Gerchunoff, Alberto. *Los Gauchos judíos*. La Plata, Argentina: Talleres Gráficos Joaquín Sesé, 1910.

——. *The Jewish Gauchos of the Pampa*. Trans. Prudencio de Pereda. Albuquerque: University of New Mexico Press, 1998.

Glusberg, Samuel. "Mate Amargo." In *La levita gris: cuentos judíos de ambiente porteño*. Buenos Aires: Editorial Babel, 1924.

Katz, Pinie. *Páginas selectas*. Buenos Aires: ICUF, 1980.

Kolbowski, Jorge. "La vida de mi padre." Unpublished manuscript.

Marechal, Leopoldo. *Adán Buenosayres*. 14th ed. Buenos Aires: Sudamericana, 1992.

——. *Historia de la calle Corrientes*. Buenos Aires: Municipalidad de la Ciudad, 1937.

Mogilevsky, Adolfo. "Algunas líneas sobre León Kolbovsky." Unpublished article.

Moorne, Dr. *Las industrias fabriles en Buenos Aires*. Buenos Aires: Librairie Française, 1893.

Rubinska, Jorge. Letter to the Comité de Seguridad en el fútbol (Secretaría de Seguridad Interior). 7 Oct. 2000.

Sarmiento, Domingo Faustino. *Obras completas*. Buenos Aires: Luz del Día, 1956.

Scardin, Francesco. *La Argentina y el trabajo*. Buenos Aires: Peuser, 1906.

Straimel, Nestor. "Los judeoargentinos del deporte." *Piedra Libre*, 12 Jan. 2010.

Torello, Florentino N. "La industria del calzado en la República Argentina." *Revista de Ciencias Económicas*, 3 May 1928.

Vaccarezza, Alberto. *El barrio de los judíos: sainete en un acto y tres cuadros y en verso*. Buenos Aires: El Teatro Nacional, 1919.

——. *El Conventillo de La Paloma*. Buenos Aires: Ediciones del Carro de Tespis, 1965.

Wilde, Eduardo. *Obras Completas*. Buenos Aires: Talleres Peuser, 1917.

Zimerman de Faingold, Raquel. *Memorias*. Buenos Aires: n.p, 1987.

NEWSPAPERS AND PERIODICALS

Clarín, Crítica, Crónica, Democracia, Diario Río Negro, El Argentino, El Día, El Gráfico, Gente, La Cancha, La Internacional, La Nación, La Razón, Maáriv, Mundo Deportivo, Mundo Infantil, Mundo Peronista, Página12, Primera Plana, Tribuna

PERSONAL INTERVIEWS

Manuela Fingueret, Buenos Aires, 2009, 2010, 2012
Edgardo Imas, Buenos Aires, 2008, 2009, 2010

Mario Katzman, Buenos Aires, September–October 2010
Jorge Kolbowski, Buenos Aires, 2008, 2009
Adolfo Mogilevsky, Tel Aviv, October 2007
Esther Rollansky, Tel Aviv, July 2010
Julio Winiky, Buenos Aires, October 2010

QUESTIONNAIRES ANSWERED BY THE FOLLOWING ATLANTA FANS:

Bichman, Julio
Bronstein, Ariel
Cecilio, Barak
Cyrulnik, Eduardo
Dejtiar, Alejandro
Estiz, Guillermo
Fingueret, Manuela
Fleker, Marcelo
Fryd, Benjamin
Fryd, Raul
Giezes, Adolfo
Goldberg, Andrés Darío
Golstein, Roberto
Graschinsky, Carlos
Halfon, Samuel
Imas, Edgardo Mario
Jablkowsky, Andres
Julio, Winiky
Jungman, Esteban
Kaminker, Alberto Jaime
Katzman, Mario
Kolbowski, Jorge

Kotlar, Joel
Kuravsky, Dario Javier
Kwaterka, Isaac
Leibovich, Felipe
Lichtensztajn, Bernardo
Mandelman, Jaime
Mellincovsky, Silvio
Merwaiss, Ricardo
Mogilevsky, Adolfo
Nejamkis, Guido Martin
Plotnitky, Clody
Rucki, Carlos
Rucki, David
Steizel, Sebastian
Stortz, Carlos
Szmulewicz, Edgardo
Szpigiel, Issac Carlos
Szwarcberg, Nestor
Taraciuk, Leandro
Taraciuk, Luciano
Veitz, Tomás
Waisberg, Pablo

SECONDARY SOURCES

Aisenstein, Angela. *El modelo didáctico en la Educación Física: entre la escuela y la formación docente.* Buenos Aires: Miño y Dávila, 1995.
———, and Pablo Scharagrodsky. *Tras las huellas de la educación física escolar argentina: cuerpo, género y pedagogía.* Buenos Aires: Prometeo, 2006.
Alabarces, Pablo. *Fútbol y patria: el fútbol y las narrativas de la nación en la Argentina.* Buenos Aires: Prometeo, 2002.
———, ed. *Futbologías: fútbol, identidad y violencia en América Latina.* Buenos Aires: CLACSO, 2003.
———, et al. *Hinchadas.* Buenos Aires: Prometeo, 2006.

————, ed. *Peligro de gol: estudios sobre deporte y sociedad en América Latina.* Buenos Aires: Clacso, 2000.

Aloé, Carlos. "Cada hombre forja su destino." *Mundo Deportivo* (Buenos Aires) 227 (8 Aug. 1953).

Andrade De Melo, Victor, and Maurício Drumond. "Esporte, cinema e política na Argentina de Juan Perón (1946–1955)." *Estudos Ibero-Americanos* 35, no. 1 (2009): 56–72.

Araújo, José Renato de Campos. *Imigração e futebol. O caso Palestra Itália.* São Paulo: Editora Sumaré, 2000.

Arbena, Joseph L., ed. *Sport and Society in Latin America: Diffusion, Dependency, and the Rise of Mass Culture.* New York: Greenwood Press, 1988.

Archetti, Eduardo P. "Argentinian Football: A Ritual of Violence?" *The International Journal of the History of Sport* 9, no. 2 (1992): 209–35.

————. "Death and Violence in Argentinian Football." In *Football, Violence and Social Identity,* ed. Richard Giulianotti et al., 37–72. London: Routledge, 1994.

————. "Estilos y virtudes masculinos en El Gráfico: La creación del imaginario del fútbol argentine." *Desarrollo Económico* 35, no. 139 (1995).

————. *Masculinities: Football, Polo and Tango in Argentina.* Oxford: Berg, 1999.

————. "Masculinity and Football: The Formation of National Identity in Argentina." In *Games Without Frontiers: Football, Identity and Modernity,* ed. Richard Giulianotti and John Williams, 225–43. Aldershot, UK: Arena, 1994.

————. *El potrero, la pista y el ring: las patrias del deporte argentino.* Buenos Aires: Fondo de Cultura Económic, 2001.

Arévalo, Oscar. *El Partido Comunista.* Buenos Aires: CEAL, 1983.

Armus, Diego. *The Ailing City: Health, Tuberculosis, and Culture in Buenos Aires, 1870–1950.* Durham, NC: Duke University Press, 2011.

Aruj, Eduardo. *Villa Crespo: Historia de Villa Crespo.* Buenos Aires: Ediciones Argentinas, 1978.

Avni, Haim. "Antisemitism in Argentina: The Dimensions of Danger." In *Approaches to Antisemitism: Context and Curriculum,* ed. Michael Brown, 57–77. New York: American Jewish Committee, 1994.

————. *Argentina and the Jews: A History of Jewish Immigration.* Tuscaloosa: University of Alabama Press, 1991.

————. *Argentine Jewry: Social Status and Organizational Profile* [Hebrew]. Jerusalem: Minister of Education and Culture, 1972.

————. *Argentina, "The Promised Land": Baron de Hirsch's Colonization Project in the Argentine Republic* [Hebrew]. Jerusalem: Magnes, 1973.

————. *Clients, Prostitutes and White Slavers in Argentina and Israel* [Hebrew]. Tel Aviv: Yedioth Ahronoth, 2009.

————, and Leonardo Senkman, eds. *Del campo al campo: colonos de Argentina en Israel.* Buenos Aires: Milá-AMIA, 1993.

Azzi, Maria Susana. "*The Golden Age and After*" *in Tango*. London: Thames and Hudson, 1995.

———. "The Tango, Peronism, and Astor Piazzolla during the 1940s and 50's." In *From Tejano to Tango: Latin American Popular Music*, ed. Walter Aaron Clark, 25–40. New York: Routledge, 2002.

Babini, Nicolás. *Arturo Frondizi y la Argentina moderna*. Barcelona: Gedisa, 2006.

Bacci, Claudia. "Las políticas culturales del progresismo judío argentino: la revista Aporte y el ICUF en la década de 1950." *Políticas de la Memoria* 5 (2004–5): 159–68.

Baeza, Cecilia. "Les Palestiniens du Chili: de la conscience diasporique á la mobilisation transnationale." *Revue d'études palestiniennes* 95 (spring 2005): 51-87.

———. "Les Palestiniens d'Amérique Latine et la cause palestinienne (Chili, Brésil, Honduras. 1920–2010)." PhD diss., Institut d'Etudes Politiques de Paris, 2010.

Baily, Samuel. *Immigrants in the Land of Promise: Italians in Buenos Aires and New York City, 1870–1914*. Ithaca, NY: Cornell University Press, 1999.

Bargman, Daniel Fernando. "Un ámbito para las relaciones interétnicas: las colonias agrícolas judías en Argentina." *Revista de Antropología* 11 (1992): 50–58.

Bejarano, Margalit. "The Sephardic Communities of Latin America." In *Contemporary Sephardic Identity in the Americas: An Interdisciplinary Approach*, ed. Margalit Bejarano and Edna Aizenberg, 3–30. Syracuse, NY: Syracuse University Press, 2012.

Ben-Dror, Graciela. *The Catholic Church and the Jews: Argentina, 1933–1945*. Lincoln: University of Nebraska Press, 2009.

Bergel, Martín, and Pablo Palomino, "La revista El Gráfico en sus inicios: una pedagogía deportiva para la ciudad moderna." *EFDeportes.com, Revista Digital* (Buenos Aires), no. 17 (1999). http://www.efdeportes.com/.

Bilsky, Edgardo. *La semana trágica*. Buenos Aires: Centro Editor de América Latina, 1984.

———, Gabriel Trajtenberg, and Ana Epelbaun Weinstein. *El movimiento obrero judío en la Argentina*. Buenos Aires: Centro de Documentación e Información sobre Judaismo Argentino Marc Turkow, 1987.

Blaustein, Eduardo, and Martín Zubieta. *Decíamos ayer: la prensa argentina bajo el proceso*. Buenos Aires: Colihue, 1998.

Bocketti, Gregg P. "Italian Immigrants, Brazilian Football, and the Dilemma of National Identity." *Journal of Latin American Studies* 40 (2008): 275–302.

Borroni, Otelo, and Roberto Vacca. *La vida de Eva Perón: Testimonios para su historia*. Buenos Aires: Editorial Galerna, 1971.

Brauner, Susana. "Syrian Jews in Buenos Aires." In *Contemporary Sephardic Identity in the Americas: An Interdisciplinary Approach*, ed. Margalit Bejarano and Edna Aizenberg, 88–105. Syracuse, NY: Syracuse University Press, 2012.

Brenner, Michael, and Gideon Reuveni, eds. *Emancipation Through Muscles: Jews and Sports in Europe*. Lincoln: University of Nebraska Press, 2006.

Bristow, E. J. *Prostitution and Prejudice: The Jewish Fight Against White Slavery, 1870–1939.* New York: Schocken Books, 1983.

Brodsky, Adriana Mariel. "Re-configurando comunidades: judíos sefardíes/árabes en Argentina, 1900-1950." In *Árabes y judíos en Iberoamerica,* ed. Raanan Rein, 117–34. Seville, Spain: Fundación Tres Culturas, 2008.

———, and Raanan Rein, eds. *The New Jewish Argentina: Facets of Jewish Experiences in the Southern Cone.* Boston: Brill, 2013.

Buonocore, Domingo. *Libreros, editores e impresores de Buenos Aires.* Buenos Aires: Bowker, 1974.

Camarero, Hernán. *A la conquista de la clase obrera: los comunistas y el mundo de trabajo en la Argentina, 1930-1935.* Buenos Aires: Siglo XXI, 2007.

———. "El Partido Comunista argentino y sus políticas en favor de una cultura obrera en las décadas de 1920 y 1930." *Pacarina del Sur, Revista de pensamiento crítico latinoamericano* (Apr. 2011).

———. "Los clubes deportivos comunistas." *Todo es Historia,* no. 448 (Nov. 2004).

Caro, Isaac. *Islam y judaísmo contemporáneos en América Latina.* Santiago, Chile: Ril Editores, 2010.

Cherjovsky, Iván. "La faz ideológica del conflicto colonos/JCA: el discurso del ideal agrario en las memorias de Colonia Mauricio." In *Marginados y consagrados: nuevos estudios sobre la vida judía en la Argentina,* ed. Emmanuel Kahan et al., 47–66. Buenos Aires: Luniere, 2011.

Clavane, Anthony. *Does Your Rabbi Know You're Here? The Story of English Football's Forgotten Tribe.* London: Quercus, 2012.

Claxton, Robert H. *From Parsifal to Perón: Early Radio in Argentina, 1920-1944.* Gainesville: University Press of Florida, 2007.

Cohen, Michelle Amy. "Delving into the Ruins: The AMIA Bombing, the Struggle for Justice, and the Negotiation of Jewish Belonging in Argentina." PhD diss., University of North Carolina at Chapel Hill, 2009.

Collier, Simon. *The Life, Music and Times of Carlos Gardel.* Pittsburgh, PA: University of Pittsburgh Press, 1986.

———. "The Popular Roots of the Argentine Tango." *History Workshop Journal* 34 (1992): 92–100.

———, with Maria Susana Azzi. *Le Grand Tango: The Life and Music of Astor Piazzola.* New York: Oxford University Press, 2000.

Corbinos, Lorenzo Agar, and Antonia Rebolledo. "La inmigración árabe en Chile: los caminos de la integración." In *El Mundo árabe y América Latina,* ed. Raymundo Kabchi, 283–309. Madrid: Ediciones Libertarias/Prodhufi/Unesco, 1997.

Cronin, Mike, and Avid Mayall, eds. *Sporting Nationalisms: Identity, Ethnicity, Immigration and Assimilation.* London: Routledge, 1998.

Cutolo, Vicente Osvaldo. *Historia de los barrios de Buenos Aires*. Buenos Aires: Elche, 1998.

Daskal, Rodrigo. "Clubes, deporte y política en el Honorable Concejo Deliberante de la Ciudad de Buenos Aires (1895-1920)." In *Fútbol, historia y política*, ed. Julio Frydenberg and Rodrigo Daskal, 203–39. Buenos Aires: Aurelialibros, 2010.

———. Leopoldo Bard y la vida como compromiso." *EFDeportes.com, Revista Digital* (Buenos Aires), no. 108 (May 2007), http://www.efdeportes.com/.

———. *Los clubes de la Ciudad de Buenos Aires (1932–1945)*. *Revista La Cancha: sociabilidad, política y Estado*. Buenos Aires: Biblioteca Nacional, 2013."

———, and Mariano Gruschetsky. "Clubes de fútbol: su dimensión social. El Club Atlético River Plate a comienzos del siglo XX." *EFDeportes.com, Revista Digital* (Buenos Aires), no. 176 (Jan. 2013). http://www.efdeportes.com/.

De Grazia, Victoria. *The Culture of Consent: Mass Organization of Leisure in Fascist Italy*. New York: Cambridge University Press, 1981.

De Marinis, Horacio. *7,000 años a puñetazos. Historia crítica del boxeo*. Buenos Aires: Axioma, 1974.

De Privitellio, Luciano, and Luis Alberto Romero. "Organizaciones de la sociedad civil, tradiciones cívicas y cultura política democrática: el caso de Buenos Aires, 1912–1976." *Revista de Historia* 1 (2005).

Del Pino, Diego A. *El barrio de Villa Crespo*. Buenos Aires: Municipalidad de la Ciudad de Buenos Aires, 1974.

———. *Los cafés de Villa Crespo*. Buenos Aires: InterJuntas, 1992.

———. *Villa Crespo: sencilla historia*. Buenos Aires: Librerías Turísticas, 1997.

Delgado, Verónica, and Fabio Espósito. "La emergencia del editor moderno." In *Editores y políticas editoriales en Argentina, 1880-2000*, ed. José Luis de Diego, 59–88. Buenos Aires: Fondo e Cultura Económica, 2006.

DellaPergola, Sergio. "Jewish Autonomy and Dependency: Latin America in Global Perspective." In *Identities in an Era of Globalization and Multiculturalism: Latin America in the Jewish World*, ed. Judit Bokser Liweran, Eliezer Ben-Rafael, Yossi Gorny, and Raanan Rein, 47–80. Boston: Leiden and Brill, 2008.

Demárcico, Jorge A. *Historia del boxeo aficionado en la Argentina*. Buenos Aires: Federación Argentina de Box, 1997.

Di Tella, Guido. *Argentina Under Perón, 1973-76: The Nation's Experience with a Labour-Based Government*. New York: St. Martin's Press, 1983.

Di Tella, Torcuato S. "La Unión Obrera Textil, 1930–1945." *Desarrollo Económico* 33, no. 129 (Apr.–June 1993).

Dimant, Mauricio. "Antisemitismo y cultura popular en Argentina: 1995–2004. Una aproximación preliminar." *Índice—Revista de Ciencias Sociales* 37, no. 24 (2007): 246–73.

Dimenstein, Marcelo. "En busca de un pogrom perdido: memoria en torno de la Semana Trágica de 1919." In *Marginados y consagrados: nuevos estudios sobre la vida judía en la Argentina*, ed. Emmanuel Kahan et al., 121–41. Buenos Aires: Luniere, 2011.

Dizgun, John. "Immigrants of a Different Religion: Jewish Argentines and the Boundaries of Argentinidad, 1919–2009." PhD diss., Rutgers University, 2010.

Domínguez, Alejandro. *La historia de Atlanta*. Buenos Aires: Bemase Artes Gráficas, 1998.

Drumond, Maurício. "Vargas, Perón e o esporte: propaganda política e a imagem da nação." *Estudos históricos* (Rio de Janeiro) 22, no. 44 (2009): 398–421.

Dujovne Ortiz, Alicia. *Eva Perón: la biografía*. Buenos Aires: Aguilar, 1995.

Duke, Vic, and Liz Crolley. "Football Spectator Behavior in Argentina: A Case of Separate Evolution." *Sociological Review* 44, no. 2 (1996): 93–116.

Efron, John. "When Is a Yid Not a Jew? The Strange Case of Supporter Identity at Tottenham Hotspur." In *Emancipation Through Muscles: Jews and Sports in Europe*, ed. Michael Brenner and Gideon Reuvani, 235–56. London: University of Nebraska Press, 2006.

Eisen, George. "Jewish Sport History and the Ideology of Modern Sport: Approaches and Interpretations." *Journal of Sport History* 25 (1998): 482–531.

Elsey, Brenda. *Citizens and Sportsmen: Fútbol and Politics in Twentieth-century Chile*. Austin: University of Texas Press, 2011.

Erdei, Ezequiel. "Demografía e identidad: a propósito del estudio de la población judía en Buenos Aires." In *Pertenencia y alteridad. Judíos en/de América Latina: cuarenta años de cambios*, ed. Haim Avni et al., 235–56. Madrid: Iberoamericana, 2011.

Fabbri, Alejandro. *El nacimiento de una pasión: historia de los clubes de fútbol*. Buenos Aires: Capital Intelectual, 2006.

Fabrizio, Felice. *Sport e fascismo: La politica sportiva del regime, 1928–1936*. Rimini-Florence: Guaraldi, 1976.

Feierstein, Ricardo. *Historia de los judíos argentinos*. Buenos Aires: Planeta, 1993.

——, ed. *Los mejores relatos con gauchos judíos*. Buenos Aires: Ameghino Editora, 1998.

——. *Vida cotidiana de los judíos argentinos: del gueto al country*. Buenos Aires: Editorial Sudamericana, 2007.

Feldstein, Federico Pablo, and Carolina Acosta-Alzuru. "Argentinean Jews as Scapegoat: A Textual Analysis of the Bombing." *Journal of Communication Inquiry* 27 (2003): 152–70.

Finchelstein, Federico. "The Anti-Freudian Politics of Argentine Fascism: Antisemitism, Catholicism and the Internal Enemy, 1932–1945." *Hispanic American Historical Review* 87, no. 1 (2007): 77–110.

———. *La Argentina fascista: los orígenes de la dictadura.* Buenos Aires: Sudamericana, 2008.

Fiszerman, Ezequiel. "Ese nacionalismo incómodo. La izquierda internacionalista argentina y el Estado de Israel, 1946–1956." MA thesis, Universidad Torcuato Di Tella, 2012.

Foer, Franklin. *How Soccer Explains the World.* New York: Harper Perennial, 2004.

Francavilla, Cayetano. *Historia de Villa Crespo.* Buenos Aires: Ediciones Argentinas, 1978.

———, and Miguel Ángel Lafuente. *Villa Crespo.* Buenos Aires: Fundación Banco de Boston, 1993.

Frasso, Hugo. *Argentinos Juniors: historia de un sentimiento.* Buenos Aires: Aguafuertes Libros, 2003.

Freidenberg, Judith Noemi. *The Invention of the Jewish Gaucho: Villa Clara and the Construction of Argentine Identity.* Austin: University of Texas Press, 2009.

Frydenberg, Julio. *Historia social del fútbol: del amateurismo a la profesionalización.* Buenos Aires: Siglo XXI, 2011.

———. "Los clubes de fútbol de Buenos Aires en los años veinte." In *Fútbol, historia y política,* ed. Julio Frydenberg and Rodrigo Daskal, 23–81. Buenos Aires: Aurelia Libros, 2010.

———. "Los nombres de los clubes de fútbol, Buenos Aires, 1880–1930." *EFDeportes. com, Revista Digital* (Buenos Aires), no. 2 (Sept. 1996). http://www.efdeportes.com/.

———, and Rodrigo Daskal, eds. *Fútbol, historia y política.* Buenos Aires: Aurelia Rivera, 2010.

Gaffney, Christopher Thomas. *Temples of the Earthbound Gods: Stadiums in the Cultural Landscape of Rio de Janeiro and Buenos Aires.* Austin: University of Texas Press, 2008.

Galeano, Eduardo. *El fútbol a sol y sombra.* 7th ed. Mexico City: Siglo XXI Editores, 2006.

Gambini, Hugo. *Frondizi, el estadista acorralado.* Barcelona: Vergara, 2006.

Gándara, Lelia. *Graffiti.* Buenos Aires: EUDEBA, 2003.

———. "Las voces del fútbol en la ciudad." *Efdeportes.com,* seventh year, no. 43 (Dec. 2001). http://www.efdeportes.com/efd43/voces.htm.

Garriga Zucal, José. *"Haciendo amigos a las piñas": violencia y redes sociales de una hinchada del fútbol.* Buenos Aires: Prometeo, 2007.

———. *Nosotros nos peleamos: violencia e identidad de una hinchada de fútbol.* Buenos Aires: Prometeo, 2010.

Gilbert, Isidoro. *La FEDE alistandose para la revolución: La Federación Juvenil Comunista, 1921–2005.* Buenos Aires: Sudamericana, 2009.

Giulianotti, Richard. "Supporters, Followers, Fans, and Flaneurs: A Taxonomy of Spectator Identities in Football." *Journal of Sport & Social Issues* 26, no. 1 (2002): 25–46.

———, et al., eds. *Football, Violence and Social Identity*. London: Routledge, 1994.

———, and John Williams, eds. *Game Without Frontiers: Football, Identity and Modernity*. Aldershot, UK: Arena, 1994.

Godio, Julio. *La semana trágica de enero de 1919*. Buenos Aires: Granica, 1985.

Goldhurst, John. *Playing for Keeps: Sport, the Media and Society*. Melbourne: Longman Cheshire, 1987.

Goñi, Uki. *The Real Odessa: How Perón Brought the Nazi War Criminals to Argentina*. London: Granta, 2002.

Gorelik, Adrián. *La grilla y el parque: espacio público y cultura urbana en Buenos Aires, 1887–1936*. Buenos Aires: Universidad Nacional de Quilmes, 2010.

Graham-Yooll, Andrew. "Osvaldo Pugliese" (obituary). *Independent* (London), 31 July 1995.

Gravano, Ariel. *Antropología de lo barrial. Estudios sobre la producción simbólica de la vida urbana*. Buenos Aires: Espacio, 2003.

———. *El barrio en la teoría social*. Buenos Aires: Espacio, 2005.

Gruschetsky, Valeria. "'El espíritu de la calle Corrientes no cambiará con el ensanche': la transformación de la calle Corrientes en avenida. Debates y representaciones. Buenos Aires 1927–1936." MA thesis, Universidad de Buenos Aires 2008.

Gutiérrez, Leandro, and Luis Alberto Romero. *Sectores populares, cultura y política. Buenos Aires en la entreguerra*. Buenos Aires: Sudamericana, 1995.

Gutkowski, Helene. *Rescate de la herencia cultural. Vidas . . . en las colonias*. Buenos Aires: Editorial Contexto, 1991.

Guttmann, Allen. *From Ritual to Record: The Nature of Modern Sports*. New York: Columbia University Press, 1978.

———. *Games and Empires: Modern Sports and Cultural Imperialism*. New York: Columbia University Press, 1994.

Hart-Davis, Duff. *Hitler's Games—The 1936 Olympics*. London: Harper & Row, 1986.

Healey, Mark A. *The Ruins of the New Argentina: Peronism and the Remaking of San Juan After the 1944 Earthquake*. Durham, NC: Duke University Press, 2011.

Hills, Matt. *Fan Cultures*. London: Routledge, 2002.

Historia de Independiente (Una mística copera). Buenos Aires: GAM, 1985.

Historia de los cinco grandes del fútbol argentino. Buenos Aires: Castroman Hnos., n.d.

Hourani, Albert, and Nadim Shehadi, eds. *The Lebanese in the World: A Century of Emigration*. London: I. B. Tauris, 1992.

Hoy, Mikita. "Joyful Mayhem: Bakhtin, Football Songs, and the Carnivalesque." *Text and Performance Quarterly* 14 (1994): 289–304.

Horvath, Ricardo. *Esos malditos tangos: apuntes para la otra historia*. Buenos Aires: Biblos, 2006.

Iwanczuk, Jorge. *Historia del fútbol amateur en la Argentina*. Buenos Aires: n.p., 1992.

Jarvie, Grant, ed. *Sport, Racism and Ethnicity*. London: Falmer Press, 1991.

Jmelnizky, Adrián, and Ezequiel Erdei. *La población judía de Buenos Aires: estudio so-ciodemográfico*. Buenos Aires: AMIA, Centro de Documentación e Información sobre Judaismo Argentino Marc Turkow, 2005.

Judkovsky, José. *El Tango: una historia con judíos*. Buenos Aires: IWO, 1998.

Kabchi, Raymundo, ed. *El mundo árabe y América Latina*. Madrid: UNESCO, Prodhufi, 1997.

Kahan, Emmanuel, et al., eds. *Marginados y consagrados: nuevos estudios sobre la vida judía en la Argentina*. Buenos Aires: Luniere, 2011.

Karush, Matthew B. *Culture of Class: Radio and Cinema in the Making of a Divided Argentina, 1920–1946*. Durham, NC: Duke University Press, 2012.

——. "National Identity in the Sports Pages: Football and the Mass Media in 1920s Buenos Aires." *The Americas* 60, no. 1 (July 2003): 11–32.

Kaufman, Haim. "Jewish Sports in the Diaspora, Yishuv, and Israel: Between Nationalism and Politics." *Israel Studies* 10, no. 2 (2005): 147–67.

Kersffeld, Daniel. *Rusos y rojos: judíos comunistas en los tiempos de la Comintern*. Buenos Aires: Capital Intelectual, 2012.

Kiernan, Sergio. *A Cover-up Exposed: The 1994 AMIA Bombing Case Hits the Wall*. New York: American Jewish Committee, 2004.

Klich, Ignacio. *Árabes y judíos en América Latina: historia, representaciones y desafíos*. Buenos Aires: Siglo XXI, 2006.

——, and Jeffrey Lesser, eds. *Arab and Jewish Immigrants in Latin America: Images and Realities*. London: Routledge, 1998.

Korob, Ariel. "Procesos identitarios e imaginarios locales. Atlanta: bohemios y judíos." MA thesis, Universidad de Buenos Aires, 1998.

Kuper, Simon. *Ajax, the Dutch, the War: Football in Europe During the Second World War*. London: Orion, 2003.

——. *Soccer Against the Enemy*. New York: Nation Books, 2006.

Large, David Clay. *Nazi Games: The Olympics of 1936*. New York: W. W. Norton, 2007.

Laskier, Michael M. *The Jews of Egypt, 1920–1970: In the Midst of Zionism, Anti-Semitism, and the Middle East Conflict*. New York: New York University Press, 1992.

Lesser, Jeffrey, and Raanan Rein. "Challenging Particularity: Jews as a Lens for Ethnicity in Latin America." *Latin American and Caribbean Ethnic Studies* 1, no. 2 (2006): 249–63.

——. *Rethinking Jewish-Latin Americans*. Albuquerque: University of New Mexico Press, 2008.

Levine, Peter. *Ellis Island to Ebbets Field: Sport and the American Jewish Experience*. New York: Oxford University Press, 1992.

Lewis, Paul H. *Guerrillas and Generals: The "Dirty War" in Argentina*. Westport, CT: Praeger, 2002.

Literat-Golombek, Lea. *Moisés Ville: crónica de un shtetl argentino*. Jerusalem: La Semana Publicaciones, 1982.

Lupano, María Marta. "Villa Crespo: una villa obrera entre el modelo higienista y el paternalismo obrero." *Anales del Instituto de Arte Americano e Investigaciones Estéticas Mario J. Buschiazzo*, no. 27-28 (1989-91).

Lvovich, Daniel. *Nacionalismo y antisemitismo en la Argentina*. Buenos Aires: Vergara, 2003.

MacClancy, Jeremy, ed. *Sport, Identity and Ethnicity*. Oxford: Berg, 1996.

Mandell, Richard D. *The Nazi Olympics*. Urbana and Chicago: University of Illinois Press, 1987.

Mason, Tony. *Passion of the People? Football in South America*. London: Verso, 1995.

Maturo, Graciela. *Marechal, el camino de la belleza*. Buenos Aires: Biblos, 1999.

Miller, Rory M., and Liz Crolley, eds. *Football in the Americas: Fútbol, Futebol, Soccer*. London: Institute for the Study of the Americas, 2007.

Millones, Luis, Aldo Panfichi, and Víctor Vich, eds. *En el corazón del pueblo: pasión y gloria de Alianza Lima, 1901-2001*. Lima: Fondo Editorial del Congreso del Peru, 2002.

Minaberrigaray, Sara Gabriela, and Silvia Ester Oviedo. "Club Social y Deportivo Villa Malcolm." *Todo es Historia*, no. 448 (Nov. 2004).

Mirelman, Victor A. *Jewish Buenos Aires, 1890-1930: In Search of an Identity*. Detroit: Wayne State University Press, 1990.

———. "Sephardim in Latin America after Independence." In *Sephardim in the Americas*, ed. Martin A. Cohen and Abraham J. Peck, 235-65. Tuscaloosa: American Jewish Archives, 1993.

Moya, José. *Cousins and Strangers: Spanish Immigrants in Buenos Aires, 1850-1930*. Berkeley: University of California Press, 1998

———. "The Jewish Experience in Argentina in a Diasporic Comparative Perspective." In *The New Jewish Argentina: Facets of Jewish Experiences in the Southern Cone*, ed. Adriana Brodsky and Raanan Rein, 7-29. Boston: Brill, 2013.

Nadel, Joshua H. *Fútbol: Why Soccer Matters in Latin America*. Gainesville: University Press of Florida, 2014.

Navarro, Marysa. *Evita*. Buenos Aires: Corregidor, 1981.

Newton, Ronald C. *The "Nazi Menace" in Argentina, 1931-1947*. Stanford, CA: Stanford University Press, 1992.

Nouwen, Mollie Lewis. *"Oy, My Buenos Aires": Jewish Immigrants and the Creation of Argentine National Identity, 1905-1930*. New Mexico: University of New Mexico Press, 2013.

Novaro, Marcos. *Historia de la Argentina contemporánea: de Perón a Kirchner*. Buenos Aires: Edhasa, 2006.

———, and Vicente Palermo. *La dictadura militar, 1976-1983: del golpe de estado a la restauración democrática*. Buenos Aires: Paidós, 2003.

Palermo, Vicente. *Sal en las heridas: las Malvinas en la cultura argentina contemporánea*. Buenos Aires: Sudamericana, 2007.

Pallade, Yves, et al. *Antisemitism and Racism in European Soccer*. Berlin: AJC, 2007.

Parrish, Charles T., and John Nauright. "Fútbol cantitos: Negotiating Masculinity in Argentina." *Soccer & Society* 14, no. 1 (2013): 1–19.

Plotkin, Mariano Ben. "La 'ideología' de Perón: Continuidades y rupturas." In *Perón del exilio al poder*, ed. Samuel Amaral and M. B. Plotkin, 45–67, Buenos Aires: Cántaro, 1993.

———. *Mañana es San Perón: A Cultural History of Perón's Argentina*. Wilmington, DE: Scholarly Resources, 2003.

Potash, Robert A. *The Army and Politics in Argentina, 1928–1945: Yrigoyen to Perón*. Stanford, CA: Stanford University Press, 1969.

———. *The Army and Politics in Argentina, 1945–1962: Perón to Frondizi*. Stanford, CA: Stanford University Press, 1980.

Raffo, Víctor. *El origen británico del deporte argentino*. Buenos Aires: Prendergast, 2004.

Ramírez, Pablo A. "Los gobernantes y el futbol." *Todo es Historia*, no. 324 (July 1994): 90–93.

———. "Política y fútbol." *Todo es Historia*, no. 248 (Feb. 1988).

Rapoport, Mario, et al. *Historia económica, política y social de la Argentina*. Buenos Aires: Editores Macchi, 2000.

Rein, Raanan. *Argentina, Israel, and the Jews: Perón, the Eichmann Capture and After*. Bethesda: University Press of Maryland, 2003.

———. "Deporte y etnicidad: Club Deportivo Palestino (Chile) y Club Atlético Atlanta (Argentina)." In *Más allá del Medio Oriente: las diásporas judía y árabe en América Latina*, ed. Raanan Rein, 117–40. Granada, Spain: Editorial de la Universidad de Granada, 2012.

———. "Diplomacy, Propaganda, and Humanitarian Gestures: Francoist Spain and Egyptian Jews, 1956–1968." *Iberoamericana* 23 (2006): 21–33.

———. *The Franco-Perón Alliance: Relations between Spain & Argentina, 1946–1955*. Pittsburgh, PA: University of Pittsburgh Press, 1993.

———. "From Juan Perón to Hugo Chávez and Back: Populism Reconsidered." In *Shifting Frontiers of Citizenship: The Latin American Experience*, ed. Mario Sznajder, Luis Roniger, and Carlos Forment, 289–311. Boston: Brill, 2013.

———. *¿Judíos-argentinos o argentinos-judíos? Identidad, etnicidad y diáspora*. Buenos Aires: Lumiere, 2011.

———. *Peronismo, populismo y política: Argentina 1943–1955*. Buenos Aires: Editorial de Belgrano, 1998.

———. "Politically Incorrect: César Tiempo and the Editorial Staff of the Cultural Supplement of La Prensa." In *The New Jewish Argentina: Facets of Jewish Experiences in the Southern Cone*, ed. Adriana Brodsky and Raanan Rein, 213–33. Boston: Brill, 2013.

———. "'El primer deportista': The Political Use and Abuse of Sport in Peronist Argentina." *The International Journal of the History of Sport* 15, no. 2 (1998).

———. "Un pacto de olvido: peronismo y las divisiones dentro de la colectividad judeo-argentina." *Investigaciones y Ensayos* 58 (2009): 429–68.

———, ed. *Árabes y judíos en Iberoamérica: similitudes, diferencias y tensiones*. Sevilla, Spain: Fundación Tres Culturas, 2008.

———, ed. *Más allá del Medio Oriente: las diásporas judía y árabe en América Latina*. Granada, Spain: Editorial de la Universidad de Granada, 2012.

Richey, Jeffrey William. "Playing at Nation: Soccer Institutions, Racial Ideology, and National Integration in Argentina, 1912–1931." PhD diss., University of North Carolina at Chapel Hill, 2013.

Rocchi, Fernando. *Chimneys in the Desert: Argentina During the Export Boom Years, 1870–1930*. Stanford, CA: Stanford University Press, 2006.

Rocha, Carolina. "Jewish Cinematic Self-Representations in Contemporary Argentine and Brazilian Films." *Journal of Modern Jewish Studies* 9, no. 1 (Mar. 2010): 37–48.

Rock, David. *Politics in Argentina, 1890–1930: The Rise and Fall of Radicalism*. London: Cambridge University Press, 1975.

Rodriguez, Robert G. *The Regulation of Boxing: A History and Comparative Analysis of Policies*. Jefferson, NC: McFarland, 2008.

Roitter, Mario, and Inés González Bombal, eds. *Estudios sobre el sector sin fines de lucro en Argentina*. Buenos Aires: CEDES-Johns Hopkins University, 2000.

Romero, Amílcar G. *Las barras bravas y la contrasociedad deportiva*. Buenos Aires: Nueva América, 1994.

———. *Deporte, violencia y política*. Buenos Aires: Centro Editor de América Latina, 1985.

Romero, Luis Alberto. *A History of Argentina in the Twentieth Century*. University Park: Pennsylvania State University Press, 2002.

Rosenswaike, Ira. "The Jewish Population of Argentina: Census and Estimate, 1887–1947." *Jewish Social Studies* XXII, no. 4 (Oct. 1960): 195–214.

Ross, Peter. «Policy Formation and Implementation of Social Welfare in Peronist Argentina, 1943–1955." PhD diss., University of New South Wales, 1988.

Rouquié, Alain. *Poder militar y sociedad política en la Argentina, 1943–1973*. Vol. 2. Buenos Aires: Emece Editores, 1983.

Rubel, Yaacov. *La población judía de la Ciudad de Buenos Aires. Perfil sociodemográfico*. Buenos Aires: Agencia Judía, 2005.

———. *Los judíos de Villa Crespo y Almagro: perfil socio-demográfico*. Buenos Aires: AMIA, 1989.

Sábato, Hilda. Luis Alberto Romero and José Luis Moreno. *De las cofardías a las organizaciones de la sociedad civil: historia de la iniciativa asociativa en la Argentina, 1776–1990*. Buenos Aires: Gadis, 2002.

Saítta, Sylvia. "Fútbol y prensa en los años veinte: Natalio Botana, presidente de la Asociación Argentina de Fútbol." *EFDeportes.com, Revista Digital* (Buenos Aires), no. 50 (July 2002). http://www.efdeportes.com/.

———. *Regueros de tinta. El diario Crítica en la década de 1920*. Buenos Aires: Sudamericana, 1998

Santos, Laura, Ulises Muschietti, and Andrés Mazzeo. *1976/ Investigaciones/ Testimonios/ Cronologías*. Buenos Aires: T.E.A. y Deportea, 2006.

Sánz, Tomás, and Roberto Fontanarrosa. *El fútbol argentino: pequeño diccionario ilustrado*. Buenos Aires: Clarín/Aguilar U.T.E., 1994.

Sassone, Susane M. "Migraciones ilegales y amnistías en la República Argentina." *Estudios Migratorios Latinoamericanos* 6–7 (1987): 249–89.

Schafer, J. "'As Obsessed as the Men': Argentine Women's Participation During the 1978 World Cup." Paper presented at the American Historical Association Conference, New Orleans, Jan. 2013.

Schenkolewski-Kroll, Silvia. "El Partido Comunista en la Argentina ante Moscú." *Estudios interdisciplinarios de América latina y el Caribe* 10, no. 2 (1999): 91–107.

Scher, Ariel, et al. *Deporte nacional: dos siglos de historia*. Buenos Aires: Deportea, 2010.

———. *La patria deportista: cien años de política y deporte*. Buenos Aires: Planeta, 1996.

———, and Héctor Palomino. *Fútbol, pasión de multitudes y de elites: un estudio institucional de la Asociación de Fútbol Argentino (1934–1986)*. Buenos Aires: Centro de Investigaciones Sociales sobre el Estado y la Administración, 1988.

Scobie, James R. *Argentina: A City and a Nation*. New York: Oxford University Press, 1971.

———. *Buenos Aires: Plaza to Suburb, 1870–1910*. New York: Oxford University Press, 1974.

Senkman, Leonardo. *Argentina, la Segunda Guerra Mundial y los refugiados indeseables, 1933–1945*. Buenos Aires: Grupo Editor Latinoamericano, 1991.

———. "Etnicidad e inmigración durante el primer peronismo." *Estudios interdisciplinarios de América latina y el Caribe* 3, no. 2 (1992): 5–38.

———. *La identidad judía en la literatura argentina*. Buenos Aires: Pardes, 1983.

———, ed. *El antisemitismo en la Argentina*. 2d ed. Buenos Aires: CEAL, 1989.

Sibaja, Rwany. "¡Animales! Civility, Modernity, and Constructions of Identity in Argentine Soccer, 1955–1970." PhD diss., George Mason University, 2013.

Sirvent, María Teresa. *Cultura popular y participación social: una investigación en el barrio de Mataderos*. Buenos Aires: Miño y Dávila, 1999.

Sneh, Perla, ed. *Buenos Aires ídish*. Buenos Aires: CPPHC, 2006.

———. "Ídish al sur, una rama en sombras." In *Pertenencia y alteridad. Judíos en / de America Latina*, ed. Haim Avni et al., 657–76. Madrid: Iberoamericana, 2011.

Sofer, Eugene F. *From Pale to Pampa: A Social History of the Jews of Buenos Aires*. New York: Holmes & Meier, 1982.

Solberg, Carl. *Immigration and Nationalism: Argentina and Chile, 1890–1914*. Austin: University of Texas Press, 1970.

Stawski, Martin. "Asistencia social y buenos negocios: política de Fundación Eva Perón (1948–1955)." MA thesis, Universidad Nacional del General Sarmiento, 2008.

Szusterman, Celiz. *Frondizi and the Politics of Developmentalism in Argentina*. Pittsburgh, PA: University of Pittsburgh Press, 1993.

Tal, Tzvi. "The Other Becomes Mainstream: Jews in Contemporary Argentine Cinema." In *The New Jewish Argentina: Facets of Jewish Experiences in the Southern Cone*, ed. Adriana Brodsky and Raanan Rein, 365–91. Boston: Brill, 2013.

Taylor, Jullie M. "Tango: Themes of Class and Nation." *Ethnomusicology* 20, no. 2 (1976): 273–91.

Ulanovsky, Carlos Marta Merkin, and Juan José Panno. *Días de radio: 1920–1959*. Buenos Aires: Emecé, 2004.

Van Onselen, Charles. *The Fox and the Flies: The Secret Life of a Grotesque Master Criminal*. New York: Walker Publishing Company, 2007.

Veneziani, Mabel. "El Mundial." *Todo es Historia*, no. 229 (1986): 30–54.

Visacovsky, Nerina. "Las escuelas obreras judías y el anticomunismo de Matías Sánchez Sorondo." Paper presented at the XIII LAJSA conference, Biblioteca Nacional, Buenos Aires, July 2007.

———. "Los judíos textiles de Villa Lynch y el I. L. Peretz." Paper presented at the seminar "Democracia, Estado y Sociedad en la Argentina contemporánea," University of Buenos Aires, 2005.

Waisman, Carlos. "La ideología del nacionalismo de derecha en Argentina: el capitalismo, el socialismo y los judíos." In *El antisemitismo en la Argentina*, 2d ed., ed. Leonardo Senkman, ch. 3. Buenos Aires: CEAL, 1989.

Walter, Richard. *Politics and Urban Growth in Buenos Aires, 1910–1942*. New York: Cambridge University Press, 1993.

Wann, Daniel L., et al. *Sports Fans: The Psychology and Social Impact of Spectators*. New York: Routledge, 2001.

Weisbrot, Robert. *The Jews of Argentina: From Inquisition to Perón*. Philadelphia, PA: Jewish Publication Society of America, 1979.

Winner, David. *Brilliant Orange: The Neurotic Genius of Dutch Football*. London: Bloomsbury Publishing, 2010.

Toker, Eliahú, ed. *Buenos Aires esquina Sábado. Antología de César Tiempo*. Buenos Aires: Archivo General de la Nación, 1997.

———. *El ídish es también Latinoamérica*. Buenos Aires: Instituto Movilizador de Fondos Cooperativos, 2003.

Yarfitz, Mir. "Uprooting the Seeds of Evil." In *The New Jewish Argentina: Facets of Jewish Experiences in the Southern Cone*, ed. Adriana Brodsky and Raanan Rein, 55–79. Boston: Brill, 2013.

Zadoff, Efraim. *A Century of Argentinean Jewry: In Search of a New Model of National Identity*. Jerusalem: Institute of the World Jewish Congress, 2000.

———. *Historia de la educación judía en Buenos Aires (1935–1957)*. Buenos Aires: Milá, 1994.

Zaretsky, Natasha. "Citizens of the Plaza: Memory, Violence, and Belonging in Jewish Buenos Aires." PhD diss., Princeton University, 2008.

INTERNET SITES

Atlanta Pasión: http://www.atlantapasion.com.ar
Argentine Football Association 1906: http://futsandokan76.blogspot.co.il/2012/01/argentine-association-football-league.html
Asociación Atlética Argentinos Juniors: http://www.argentinosjuniors.com.ar/
"Atlanta: Alma de Bohemios": http://galeon.com/villacrespo/deportes/atlanta.html
Club Atlético Atlanta: http://www.caatlanta.com.ar; http://wordpress.caatlanta.com.ar/historia
Club Deportivo Palestino: http://www.palestino.cl/
Club Palestino: http://www.clubpalestino.cl/
Corazon funebrero: http://corazonfunebrero.blogspot.co.il/
Dictionary of American Naval Fighting Ships, Index to Ships Histories: http://www.history.navy.mil/danfs/a13/atlanta-ii.htm
EFDeportes.com, Revista Digital, Buenos Aires: http://www.efdeportes.com
La Gloriosa Tricolor-Atlético Chacarita Juniors: http://www.lagloriosatricolor.com.ar/p/historia.html
La Opinión Judía: http://laopinionjudia.com
La Taberna del Siome: http://latabernadelsiome.blogspot.co.il
Los Baisanos—Intifada (Foro de la Barra del Club Deportivo Palestino): http://losbaisanos.foroactivo.com/
Los Graduados: http://losgraduados.telefe.com/
Patria Judiá: http://bajurtov.wordpress.com/
Planeta Bohemio: www.planetabohemio.com.ar
Sentimiento Bohemio: www.sentimientobohemio.com.ar
Soccerphile: http://www.soccerphile.com/
The Simon Wiesenthal Center: http://www.wiesenthal.com
Todo Ascenso: http://blog.todoascensoweb.com.ar/

FILMS

Escuela de campeones (dir. Ralph Pappier), Argentina, 1950.
Los tres berretines (dir. Enrique Telémaco Susini), Argentina, 1933.
Luna de Avellaneda (dir. Juan José Campanella), Argentina, 2004.
Nos otros (dir. Daniel Raichijk), Argentina, 2010.
O ano em que meus pais saíram de férias [The Year My Parents Went on Vacation] (dir: Cao Hamburger), Brazil, 2006.
Pelota de trapo (dir. Leopoldo Torres Ríos), Argentina, 1948.

Siglo Bohemio (dir. Aníbal Garisto, Mónica Nizzardo, and Javier Orradre), Argentina, 2004.

Te llevo en la sangre (dir. Pablo G. Pérez), Argentina, 2004.

Tiro Libre (dir: Marcelo Piña), Chile/ USA/ Egypt/ Kuwait, 2007.

NOVELS

Fingueret, Manuela. *Blues de la calle Leiva*. Buenos Aires: n.p., 2006.

Martín, Enrique. *Bohemios*. Buenos Aires: n.p., 1999.

INDEX

ABC Café, 41

Abramovich, Luis Ernesto, 190n55

Academia Porteña del Lunfardo, 39

Acassuso, 70

Adelante Atlanta (magazine), 126

AFA. *See* Argentine Football Association

African descent, 1, 8

Agrupación Juvenil y Democrática Alerta, 82

Ajax (Dutch football club), 11, 119

Alabarces, Pablo, 3–4

Alberdi, Juan Bautista, 16

Aldao, Ricardo C., 58

Alemandri, Próspero: *Moral y deporte*, 73

Alende, Oscar, 129

Alfonsín, Raúl, 141

Alianza Lima, 13

Allaria, Ángel, 58

All Boys, 12, 74, 145, 146, 152

Almagro, 74; stadium, 60, 61

Almagro neighborhood, 30, 74, 91–92

Aloé, Carlos, 108, 182n23

Alonso, Alfredo, 107

Altamura, Amadeo, 132, 134, 140

Alt, Roberto: "Canning and Rivera," 32

Alumni (magazine), 64

Álvarez Pereyra, Manuel, 11, 101, 108

Amalfitani, José, 125

Ameal, Jorge, 141

AMIA. *See* Asociación Mutual Israelita Argentina

anarchists, 85, 116

Angelis, Alfredo de, 81

anti-Semitism, 1, 25, 143–44; and Catholicism, 109–10, 171n23; regarding Jewish immigrants, 17, 20–21; pogroms,

10, 15, 19, 22, 36, 37, 114; in slogans of rival fans, 2, 12, 144, 145–49, 150, 151, 161–62

Arab immigrants, 19, 20–21, 33. *See also* Club Deportivo Palestino

Arana, Adolfo, 100

Arata, Selma Filomena de, 92

Arbeter Shuln, 117

Archetti, Eduardo, 3, 143, 150

Argentina: collective identity (*argentinidad*), 3, 6–7, 20, 35, 38, 63, 97, 98, 163; coup of 1930, 24, 185n19; currency devaluations, 137; economic conditions, 16, 32–33, 35, 137, 138, 140–41; hyperinflation in, 140–41; immigration policies, 15–17, 19, 20–21, 23, 24–25, 170n10; Jewish population, 17–18, 21–22, 24, 142; Malvinas (Falklands) War, 137; Ministry of Education and Justice, 94–95; Ministry of Health, 137; Ministry of Social Action, 137; national football team, 7, 70, 99, 121, 127, 139, 155; nationalism in, 10, 16–17, 20, 21, 24, 29, 109, 171n23; relations with Great Britain, 20, 137; vs. United States, 7, 22, 24; Videla dictatorship/National Reorganization Process, 35, 134, 137, 138–40, 148, 155, 186nn39,40, 187n4; xenophobia in, 12, 16–17, 20, 21, 24. *See also* Buenos Aires; Perón, Eva; Perón, Juan; Peronism; social integration

Argentina, La (newspaper), 53

Argentine Basketball Association, 110

Argentine Boxing Federation, 83, 110

Argentine Football Association (AFA), 48, 53, 58, 94, 122, 133; and Atlanta-Argentinos Juniors merger, 10–11, 64–65;